Wer—
Try out some of these foods.

Jerry & Mary Behrens

June 03

8,000 Miles of Dirt

A backroad travel guide to Wyoming

Dan Lewis

8,000 MILES OF DIRT: A Backroad Travel Guide to Wyoming.

First Edition printing November, 1988.
Second Edition printing April, 1992.

Published by the Wyoming Naturalist, Box 863, Douglas, Wyoming 82633.

Printed by Endeavor Books, 7307 6WN Road, Casper, Wyoming 82604.

Typesetting, layout and cover design by Creative Communications, Drawer 1380, Douglas, Wyoming 82633.

ISBN: 0-941875-16-4

Other products by Dan Lewis:

The Floater's Guide to Wyoming Rivers: Paddle and Portage. Guide to twenty-seven Wyoming Rivers containing flow data, float times, classifications, maps and trip descriptions.

Stock Photo Software. The Photographer's Database Management System. For IBM AT/XT/PS2 compatible computers.

The How To Build Your Own Photographic Equipment Book. Details on over 60 photographic projects, 108 pages and 130 photos.

NOTICE

LET THE TRAVELER BEWARE

This book is not a permit to trespass. Considerable time and effort has been expended in an attempt to describe only public access road. However, due to the breadth and depth of this guide, the possibility of error exists. Furthermore, back country roads are in a state of change: new roads are being made and older roads are being discontinued. Therefore, the author assumes no responsibility regarding the public accessibility of the roads described in this guide. When in doubt, ask for permission.

In addition, some of the roads described in this guide travel through hazardous areas: mine sites, oil field areas, creek crossings, sharp curves, steep hills. Furthermore, the conditions of the roads described in this guide are in a state of flux: precipitation may render the roads hazardous or untravelable, snow fields may cover some roads until mid-summer, and road surfaces may contain large rocks, ruts, and holes. Therefore, the author assumes no responsibility regarding the conditions or travelability of the roads described in this guide. Check local conditions before traveling.

Furthermore, the author assumes no responsibility regarding: becoming lost, vehicle damage, personal damage or discomfort, loss of time or monies. You travel the roads described in this guide at your own risk.

PREFACE

This guide was written in the spirit of living, the excitement of adventure, and awe of wonderment. Although I had wandered through Wyoming's back country for many years previous to this venture, I had not done so with the intensity and passion that consumed me during this endeavor. The feelings, awareness, emotion, and love of this state resulting from this journey are inside of me. You will not find them in the words on the pages of the text. That is personal for me. What I sensed is hard to share.

What you will find in this guide and what I can share with you are the routes I followed. My intent is simple and honest: To present an alternate path through Wyoming with the vision of imparting a greater appreciation and respect for what lies within her boundaries.

From my heart, I sincerely hope that you will take time to sense the raw beauty of the land you travel across. Truly look at the life that is here and put some of it inside. Kindle a love of understanding, humility, awareness, respect, and compassion. Let your passage along these routes be special. Let your passage along these routes change you and not the land.

Below are some passages from my diary to present my mood:

Tue. 5-10 camped at Fort LaClede

. . . just finished supper and brushing Smeagle. It sure is strange here at the fort. Pitch black with zillions of stars. Quiet! So quiet that your ears have to make noise just for something to do. It's unbelievable what I see every minute of every day. My body is continually being hammered by the outside world and the living that I do there. I wonder how much more I can take and I'm terribly scared that I'll wake up and find that it has only been some kind of fairy-tale dream. My private world is so choked full of amazement and awe that I can barely stand it: wild horses running across alkali flats and leaving a dusty trail behind, muskrats flipping in the murky water at Bean Springs, a Ferruginous Hawk flashing its white tail, and the pink/white highlights and deep shadows in the eroded hill sides of Delaney Rim at sunset. My head is spinning from the countless events that force their way into my brain. I'm happy. I now prepare to snuggle in my lair for the night.

Wed. 6-28 camped at Oregon Buttes

. . . later in the day I crossed a desolate depression at Chain Lake Flat. One particular spot, near a rusty well, held power. I remember seeing it from a long way off and the two-track road passed within a quarter mile of it. As I walked over I felt that there was something here. I heard the crunch that my boots made with each step I took. I looked down and saw my soles break through the dried layer of dirt on top and sink into the parched earth below. That crunch told a story about this place. It was a dry and brittle land. What little living that took place here was hard. The dwarf greasewood and saltbush that waited to drink were spaced evenly apart from each other. A space just large enough to latch on to what little water fell from the sky and steal from the desiccated earth. Smeagle saw a cottontail and began to chase it. There were holes in the immediate area for the rabbit to duck into, but it chose not to. It ran in circles, 30 feet across, and then stopped under some weathered wood to catch its breath and feel the excitement. It would then dart out and the chase would continue. After this happened three times, a feeling came over me. It was as though this rabbit was thriving on the game. It was as though it had not encountered another living creature in such a long time that it was long past due for some interaction.

No date

    . . . it's 11 pm and it's dark and raining and I'm lost. The Barrel Springs/ Willow Creek Rim area is giving me fits. Today I followed a beautiful rim and went past domes, gullies, rimrock, buttes, and mud slides. At the end of one of the two-track roads is a BLM wild horse corral and loading ramp. Nearby, I found a Prairie Falcon nest. The Indian Paintbrush is just out down here and it's more fantastic than I remember (deep rich colors). It started raining as I crossed a big draw (the road was washed out) and it has been raining ever since. The road was so bad with clay-mud that I just jumped a ditch to park for the night (or week). It sure is snug in the back of Black Irene tonight. (Smeagle is up front, wet and covered with mud!)

Fri. 7-1 a note on the Powder River Road

    . . . and I see two antelope lying on a nearby hill side. How often do I see such a similar thing with no affect. This time is different. This time I see. This time I feel. My eyes mist over and my heart rises to my throat and I stop and look and stare. I see a creature. To name it "antelope" is to label it and dismiss it. To see it as a creature is to live with that impression for the rest of my life. Why has it taken me so long to get here and where will I go next?

Mon. 7-11 cold peach break near the Outlaw Cave Trail

    . . . it was warm with my damp clothes sticking to me and the sun was heating everything around me like a toaster oven. I say it was warm and not hot or insufferable because it wasn't. It was warm enough to make me uncomfortable. That degree of unpleasantness was enough to make me feel alive. To feel the sticky sweat, the wrap and cling of material around my body, the heaviness of my boots, the tightness of the skin around my squinting eyes, the pestering sound Smeagle makes as he pants in the heat, and the cotton spit in my mouth as I think about cool water waiting for me back at Black Irene. (I can see why people go crazy during sensory deprivation.) I do not believe this to be some type of masochistic behavior that I exhibit. I think of it as finding the experience of living to be so great.

This book is dedicated to:

    SMEAGLE - MY COMPANION AND THE LUCKIEST DOG IN THE WORLD
    BLACK IRENE - MY TRUSTWORTHY TRUCK

and in memory of:

    GRANDMA MANNING
    PAPPY
    GRANDMA DURBIN
    POP

    I thank my family for their support. They kept my spirit high, the belly full, and helped with the financing to complete this book. I also thank my good friends. They sheltered me from storms, provided me a place to rest, and encouraged me on. Thanks also to Rick Darnell for his valuable help and great improvements in the redesigning of the general layout.

TABLE OF CONTENTS

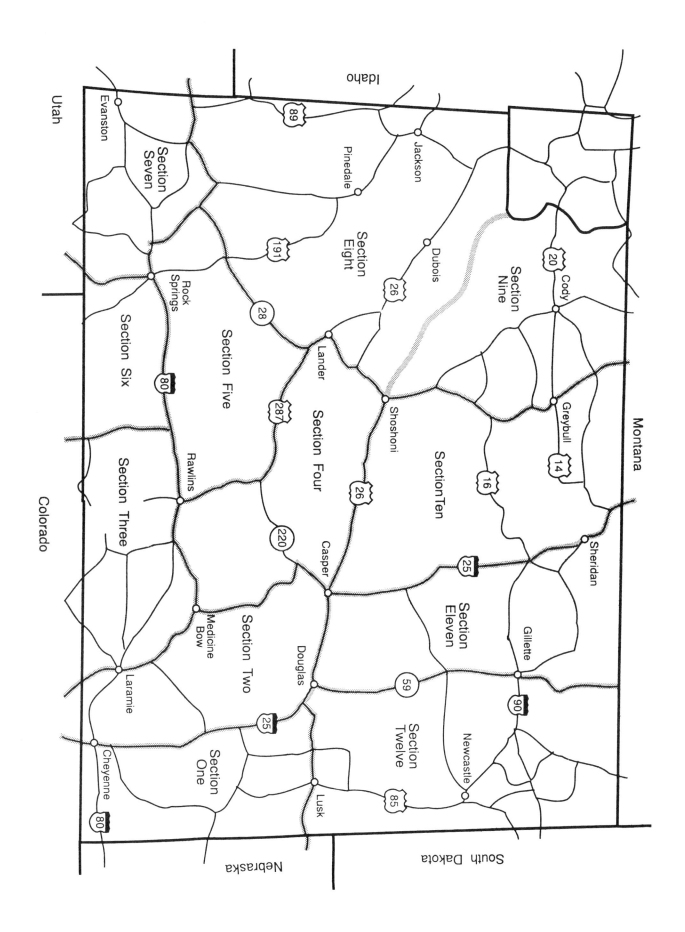

INTRODUCTION

The materials and methods

I drove all of the main roads that are described in this guide at least twice, once in 1988 and again in 1992. In addition, I drove the majority of the side roads outlined in the text (and numerous others that are not mentioned). During the course of these travels, I covered over 40,000 miles. The vehicle I used was Black Irene (small sized, two-wheel drive pickup) and my co-pilot was Smeagle #3 (male golden retriever). I logged the routes as I went along and after returning from short excursions (lasting from five to ten days), I wrote the trips up before leaving for new places. During the rewrite stages, I checked the trips for accuracy by retracing them on my maps. Approximately 7,000 miles of dirt road trips are detailed in this guide. In addition, an estimated 1,000 miles of side roads are outlined and another 1,000 miles of Wyoming secondary highways are described.

The maps I used were purchased from the Bureau of Land Management (BLM) and the Department of Agriculture (National Forest Service, NF). In addition, supplemental county maps were purchased (or were donated) from county seats across the state. These maps were used during the preliminary planning stages (in house) and during the actual travels.

Identification of landmarks (buttes, creeks, mountains, etc.) were determined from compass bearings, adjacent landmarks, and the help of locals along the way. The names of these landmarks were taken from the BLM maps (Wyoming Quadrangles, topographic 1:100,000 series, produced by the U. S. Geological Survey, 1974-82). In addition, NF maps (forest visitor type) and local information was used.

The criteria I used to select routes varied according to the situation. Primary consideration was given to public accessibility and road surface type (eg. automobile versus four-wheel drive). Other pertinent considerations included: scenic country, opportunity for optional routes, water courses (rivers and streams), less confusing junctions, and networking with other highways and towns.

The guidelines

I do not intend to scare someone off, nor do I wish to lead someone on. The trips described in this guide travel through some of Wyoming's fantastic country. They also travel through some of Wyoming's treacherous country. This is the "Yin and Yang" of it.

I am not a bridge builder, road engineer, designer of automobiles, or forecaster of events to come. I do not know the road clearance of your vehicle, the driving skills that you have, nor do I know the amount of common sense that you possess. I have written this guide to describe some of what you might see along the way. It is you who must judge and make the decision to travel a route or turn back.

A considerable amount of Wyoming's land falls under Public Domain. A considerable amount does not! This guide is not a permit to trespass. I have made an honest attempt to describe only public access roads. The possibility of error is real. Do not assume too much and when in doubt—Ask First!

The following is my list of minimum essentials:

full tank of gas	good spare tire	a jack that works
blanket	water and food	assortment of tools
first aid kit	flashlight	extra quart of oil

A preplanned trip and descriptions read ahead of time.
A check of local conditions before leaving.
A reliable vehicle and someone who knows where you're going.
A good deal of common sense and personal responsibility.
A respect and appreciation for people and property.

The following is my list of supplements for additional safety, comfort, and fun:

field guides	CB radio	compass
field glasses	shovel	tow rope
jumper cables	camera/film	more film
thermos	cooler	sunglasses
hat/rain gear	extra clothing	hiking boots
notebook/diary	swim suit	additional tools
bug repellent	sun screen	camping gear
day pack	more film	more food and water
tolerance	joy of living	time to stop
curiosity	passion	time to play

The nuts and bolts

The guide is organized so that you can use it several different ways. First you can look at the state map on page 9. I have divided Wyoming into 12 sections that are bordered by highways. (Section eight and nine are separated by an imaginary divide line and section six and seven by the Green River.) Therefore, most trips will begin and end from towns or commonly traveled highways. You need to find the section of the state that you are interested in exploring and locate the corresponding section map in the text.

The section map(s) will show the trips that are described in the text (as well as other small side roads). You then pick a particular trip (identified by trip number) and turn to the text pages describing the particular route.

For example, you want to travel through the area south of I-80, between Wamsutter and Rock Springs. Look at the maps for section six. Trip Eight looks good, so you turn to page 96 and read the description for the Fort LaClede Road. You then drive to the appropriate starting point and you're off. (It is a bit more difficult to follow the trip in reverse but I have tried to write it the best way for both directions.)

A second method is to pick a town in the state and look it up in the index. The index will indicate what pages in the text reference that particular town. You can then skim through the written descriptions to find various ways that you can enter or exit the town.

For example, you are at Wamsutter and wish to know what roads are available from this town. Look Wamsutter up in the index and you find that it is referenced on several different pages. The next step is to skim these pages and find a trip that satisfies your needs (eg. time, direction, or interest).

A third method is to combine or arrange the various routes according to your individual needs. At each major junction, the text identifies alternate roads and refers you to the appropriate section and trip number.

For example, you are traveling the Great Basin Road (Section Five, Trip Three) and you come to the junction just past Chalk Butte. Instead of continuing west to Rock Springs on Trip Three, the text refers you to the Oregon Buttes Road (Section Five, Trip Five). On this route, you can go north to South Pass (W-28) or south to Table Rock (I-80).

The jargon

I have tried to keep the text clean and simple: What you see at a particular spot or stretch of road, how far to the next landmark or junction, and starting/ending points. There are a few points I would like to clarify.

Landmarks (streams, buttes, etc.) are used for interest as well as providing direction of travel information. If the text says you should have crossed Sage Creek in two miles and you've traveled five miles without crossing the creek—STOP. Check things out and backtrack if necessary to properly locate where you are.

There are numerous roads that are not described or mentioned in the text. I have generally mentioned only major roads or roads that may provide possible points for a wrong turn. (Pay close attention to where you are going when traveling through oil field areas.)

There are numerous small "towns" that are named in the guide. Some of them do not exist as towns, but are rather locations where there may be a community mail box or a stop along a railroad. I would not plan on finding comfort in one of these places.

The following is a list of some definitions:

4WD - a four wheel drive vehicle is recommended,

2-track - this is a seldom used road that has grass growing between the two tire ruts, they may or may not be suitable for cars,

OFR - an oil field road,

crossing - may have a bridge or you may have to ford the creek,

off to the "south" - if you look to the "south" you can see a landmark ("just off to the south" is similar to "to the south a bit"),

mile #14 - the point falls within a half mile of mile marker #14, look for it from #13 to #15,

hit - the road you are on joins another road at a junction, usually the "trip" road you are on ends and you come to a highway,

W-# - Wyoming highway system,

US-# - United States highway system,

I-# - Interstate highway system,

X-# - a county road system (S-1 for Sweetwater County #1 or C-1 for Carbon County #1), they may also be designated by "Rd-#" or a name (there is considerable variation in the state)

NF-# - a US National Forest road system, may also be designated by a name,

BLM-# - a US Bureau of Land Management road system, may also be designated by a name,

direction - the directions or compass bearings (north, south, southwest, etc.) are used as a general guide. Although I used a compass during my travels, I incorporated a general "lay of the land" into the descriptions.

H2S - this means that somewhere along the trip there is a warning sign posted that you are entering an area with possible exposure to poison gas (H2S, hydrogen sulfide). Take heed of the warning. (Note: I have put these in where I have seen the warnings; be on the lookout for ones that I might have missed.)

Finally, on a few roads I have indicated that the route may not be suitable for car travel and that a high clearance vehicle is recommended. This was a difficult choice for me to make and its presence OR absence should be used only as a guide—check for local conditions.

**0.0
Let the trips begin!**

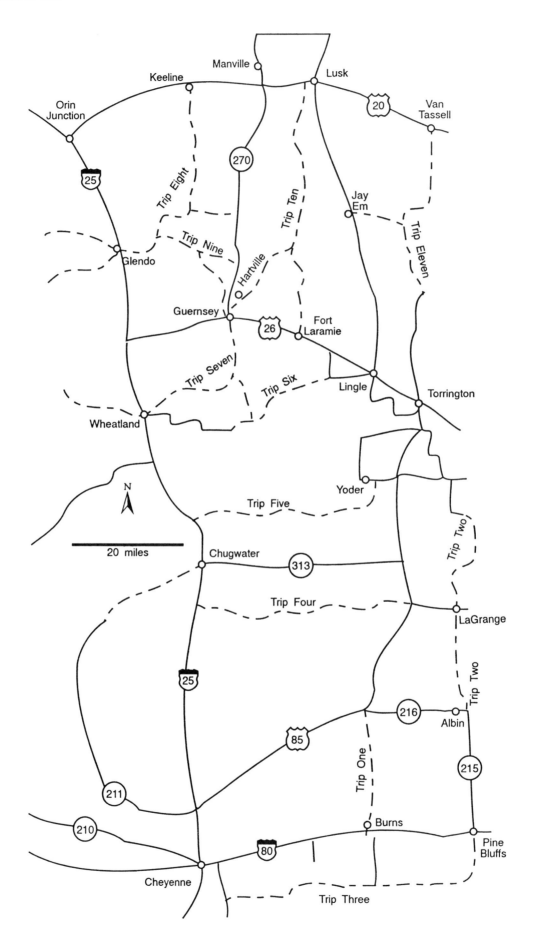

Trip One

The Burns Cutoff Road from I-80 north to US-85

This trip begins by taking I-80 exit #386. Here you can turn south on W-214 to Carpenter and the State Line Road (see page 19). For the cutoff to US-85, take W-213 west one mile and then north across North Fork Muddy Creek to Burns at mile #2. After going through Burns, the road crosses the tracks to the east. The road then turns back to the north and up a hill.

After about two miles, the road crosses Lodgepole Creek and you can see the Laramie Mountains to the west. As you continue north, the road crosses Spring Creek (two miles) and Antelope Draw (two more miles). About four miles further, you cross Chivington Draw and in five more miles, you hit W-216. Here you can turn east to Albin (12 miles), go west to US-85 at mile #43 (three miles), or you can continue north to US-85 at mile #47 (two miles).

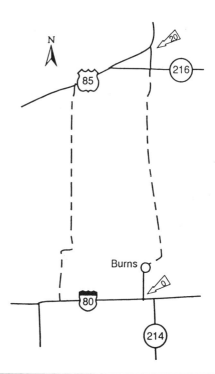

If you get out and knock about for a bit, you're likely to see one of these little Earless Lizards basking in the sun or scampering between small rocks, cactus, and yucca plants.

Trip Two

The State Line Road from Pine Bluffs north to Torrington

This is one of the more common types of silos found in the area. The military keeps their produce underground.

This trip begins by taking I-80 exit #401 into Pine Bluffs. Just after the exit, you head west on W-215 and then north out of town. At mile #1 the road crosses Lodgepole Creek and begins to climb up a bit. The road then travels north along the top of a pancake (wheat fields and flat). At mile #15 the road makes an unprecedented jog to the west and then north again to a junction at mile #17. Here you can turn west on W-216 to Albin.

Continue north on Rd-162. After four miles the road swings northwest and drops over a rim. Along here you can see Steamboat Rock in the foreground to the west and above it is Flattop and Round Top. To the northwest is Bear Mountain and to the north is Sixtysix Mountain. This is a nice area along here and the trees are ponderosa pine and cedar.

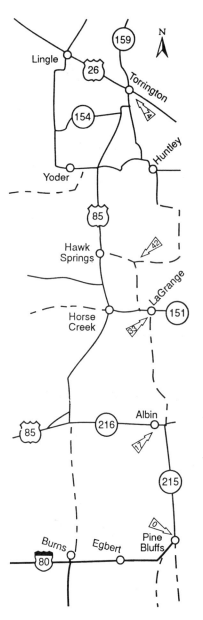

As you drop down the rim, Bushnell Creek is on the west and Stinking Creek is on the east. When the road crosses Stinking Creek at the bottom, you see a large sand dune off to the west. After about three miles, you pass Nine-mile Hill off to the east and the Horse Creek drainage is off to the west. Three miles further you can see Nine-mile Rock to the east. After five more miles you hit W-151 at mile #6 east of LaGrange.

Turn west on W-151 (toward Bear Mountain) and at mile #4 you enter La-Grange. Here you can continue west on W-151 to US-85. To continue on the State Line Road to Torrington, turn north before crossing Horse Creek. After passing by the school, you turn west for one block and then north out of town to a paved road.

After three miles the pavement ends and Hawk Springs Reservoir is to the west. As the road passes by the cliffs of Sixtysix Mountain, you can see Needle Rock and Goshen Hole Rim to the far west. A bit further north is

a junction. Here you can turn west for six miles and hit US-85 at mile #70 south of Hawk Springs. You can also turn northwest for seven miles on this road to Hawk Springs.

Turn east and after two miles you pass Three Tubs. As you pass Double Hump (four more miles), the road turns north along the state line. (Do not turn east again in 100 yards.) Here you can see Laramie Peak to the far northwest and to the near northeast is Eagle Nest. You are now actually in Nebraska, but the scenery is not that much different than in Wyoming—20 feet to the west.

As you travel north, the road crosses Robb Draw after one mile, and in two more miles you pass by a road going west to Hawk Springs and US-85. Continue north across the Laramie Canal (two miles) and two miles further you hit W-158 at mile #8.

Turn west on W-158 for three miles and then north past Togy Mound and Table Mountain. Just after crossing Horse Creek is the junction with W-92. The road east goes to Lyman, Nebraska.

Turn west on W-92 and after making a couple of zig-zags, you come to a junction at Huntley. Wyoming #161 goes seven miles west to US-85 (mile #82) at Silver Tip. Stay on W-92 past Huntley and in eight miles you hit US-85 at mile #91, just south of Torrington.

Trip Three

The State Line Road from Cheyenne east to Pine Bluffs

This trip begins by taking I-80 exit #362 and going south on US-85 toward Greeley, Colorado. After passing by W-223 (going west), you turn east at mile #3 on to the Chalk Bluffs Road. You follow along above Porter Draw (on the north) and go past wheat fields and across the rolling prairie for eight miles. Here the pavement ends and the road turns north across the draw for one mile, and then back to the east again. This is "straight as an arrow" country and you see a lot of Lark Buntings, Horned Larks, and Meadowlarks. There are also big thunderheads in the late afternoon.

The Hognose Snake is a cute and harmless little snake and is erroneously called a "sand viper" by some of the locals. This snake is found in the sandy soils of this area.

After traveling east on the dirt for four miles, you hit pavement at a junction. Here Rd-138 goes north four miles to Campstool. Stay east on Rd-203 for three miles and the road makes a jog to the southeast at another junction. Here you can take Rd-141 north one mile, west one mile, and then north again on W-217 to I-80 at exit #377.

Continue east on Rd-203 and after about two miles the road drops over a rim. Five miles further you cross Crow Creek and come to a junction. Here W-214 goes north from Carpenter to I-80 at exit #386.

Continue east on Rd-203 for two miles to where the pavement turns south toward Colorado. Here you continue east on Rd-203 (dirt) toward the Pine Bluffs. After about three miles, Rd-154 goes north to I-80 (exit #391) near Egbert.

Continue east for seven more miles and Rd-203 ends at the base of Pine Bluffs. You now turn north on Rd-161 (paved) for three miles to Rd-206. At this point you have two exciting options for going to Pine Bluffs (city)—one is a creek crossing and the other is a climb over something high.

If you continue north on Rd-161, the road crosses Muddy Creek and after four miles it turns east along I-80. Three miles further you hit US-30 in Pine Bluffs. There you can turn south on Parson Street to I-80 exit #401.

For the more challenging route, turn east on Rd-206 and head toward a cut in the Pine Bluffs (two miles). The road follows along the top for one mile where Rd-206 ends. Here you turn north on the paved Rd-164 and continue along the top for another five miles. The road then drops down to Pine Bluffs (city). There you can continue north on Beech Street to US-30 and west to Parson Street and I-80.

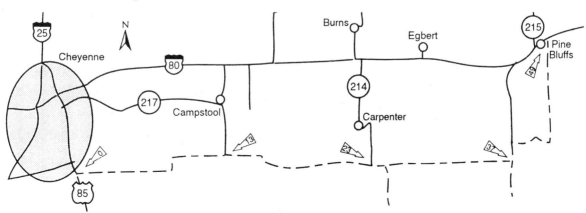

Trip Four

The Bear Creek Road from I-25 to LaGrange

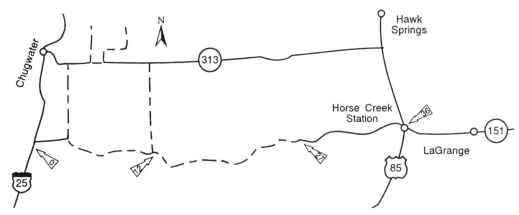

This trip begins by turning off I-25 at exit #47 and going east on the Bear Creek Road. After three miles the Windmill Road turns north for six miles to W-313. Turn south and then east where the dirt road drops down along the creek. This is now the Marsh Road #245 in Laramie County. After about four miles the road climbs up a bit and five miles further is a junction. Here you can see Laramie Peak to the northwest. At this junction you can take the County Line Road north seven miles to W-313 at mile #109.

Continue east and the road once again drops down along the creek and begins traveling through a shallow canyon. The trees in this area are boxelder, cottonwood, and peachleaf willow. On this stretch of road is the Griffin-Gardener House National Historic Site. After seven miles you pass by a road going north and the canyon begins to narrow. (Pretty drive through here.)

After crossing the creek a couple of times, the pavement begins and the valley begins to widen. A few miles further you can see Keseler Gap to the north (between Castle Rocks on the left and Bear Mountain on the right). As the road swings by the base of Bear Mountain, you can see Pine Bluff to the far east. Nine miles from the beginning of the pavement is the Horse Creek Station on US-85 at mile #63. Here you can now see Sixtysix Mountain to the northeast.

The Griffin-Gardener House National Historic Site is about half way between I-25 and US-85 on the Bear Creek Road.

Trip Five

Silver Tip west to Slater on the Mers Hill Road

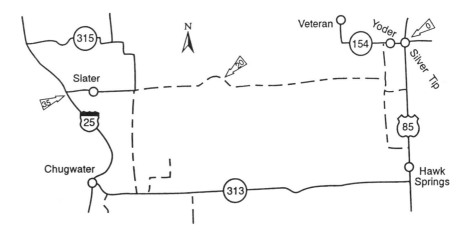

This trip begins by turning off US-85 (mile #82) at Silver Tip. As you head west toward Goshen Hole Rim on W-152, you can see Laramie Peak to the northwest and Sixtysix Mountain off to the southeast. After one mile you pass Yoder and come to a junction at mile #2. Here W-154 continues west and then north to Veteran.

Turn south on W-152 and at mile #3 the road swings west across the railroad tracks. After crossing the tracks, the road turns south one mile to another junction. Here W-153 goes east one mile where the pavement ends. There you can go through the Springer Wildlife Unit to US-85.

Turn west on W-152 and you can see Keseler Gap to the south (between Bear Mountain on the west and Castle Rocks on the east). At mile #10 the pavement ends and you continue west on a gravel road. After about seven miles, you pass Glomill Lake off to the north. Two miles further the road crosses Eider Creek and you can see Needle Rock along the rim to the southeast.

Here the road swings around to the northwest and climbs up Mers Hill. On top you have a good view of Goshen Hole to the east and the Laramie Mountains to the west. The road travels west across Slater Flats and joins W-314 (five miles). Two miles further is a junction. Here W-315 turns northwest on the Bordeaux Road to I-25 at exit #70. Along this route you can also take the South Gap Road north to Wheatland (see page 22).

Also at this junction, you can turn south on the Pioneer Road. Along this route, the road travels across the Chugwater Flats for nine miles to W-313. There you can turn east to Chugwater and I-25 at exit #54.

If you continue west on W-314, you drop down the rim, pass by the South Gap Road going north to Wheatland, and cross Chugwater Creek. The road then crosses the tracks at Slater where you can see Chimney Rock to the south. After two miles you cross Richeau Creek and hit I-25 at exit #65.

The short trip to the top of Mers Hill offers a good view of Goshen Hole to the north and around to the east.

Trip Six

The Antelope Gap-Deer Creek Road from Wheatland to Lingle

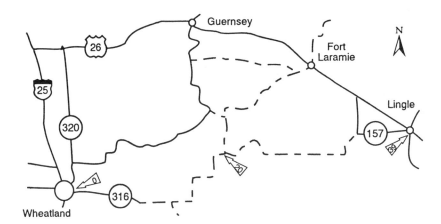

This trip begins by taking I-25 exit #78 into Wheatland. Turn north on 16th Street and then east on South Street. After seven blocks the road swings north on 9th Street to a stop light. Turn east on Gilchrist and take W-316 across the tracks out of town.

Paul and Tim, Wyoming natives from Cheyenne, check out the Oregon Trail Ruts near Guernsey.

The Antelope Gap Road (W-316) goes past the airport and crosses Chugwater Creek. The road then makes a long climb up a hill and goes past some bluffs to a junction at mile #8. Here the South Gap Road turns south to Slater (see page 21).

Continue up the hill on W-316. After passing through Antelope Gap you come to a junction at mile #12. Here the Dickinson Hill Road turns southeast to Yoder and Veteran.

Turn north on the Deer Creek Road and you pass by the head of Eagle Nest Canyon off to the west. Here you can see Laramie Peak to the northwest and to the far west is Collins Peak and Britania Mountain. The road does a bit of zig-zagging for the next few miles to a junction. Here you can take the Guernsey Road north toward the Haystack Range for four miles to pavement again. There you can either head back to Wheatland on the Grayrocks Road, or continue north to Guernsey or Fort Laramie (see page 23).

Continue east for one mile and the road swings northeast where the pavement ends. The road travels above the Deer Creek Breaks for two miles and then drops down to the creek (nice area). The road climbs back up again and passes by some chalk buttes. You then travel east across Harmony Heights to pavement.

The road does some more zig-zagging and drops down a bit to W-157 on the London Flats. If you turn north here, the road crosses the North Platte River and then hits US-26 at mile #33, between Fort Laramie and Lingle. If you turn east on W-157, the road crosses the North Platte River and then hits W-156 in Lingle at the junction of US-85 and US-26.

Trip Seven

The Grayrocks Road from Guernsey to Wheatland

One of the interesting stops along this route is the Register Cliffs Historical Site.

This trip begins by turning off US-26 in Guernsey. You go south on Wyoming Avenue and just after crossing the North Platte River, you pass by a road going west to the Oregon Trail Ruts (nice little stop).

Continue east along the river for two miles to the turnoff to Register Cliffs (another nice little stop). Here the road swings south. After one mile you pass by the Tank Farm Road (going east to Fort Laramie) and you begin traveling across the Bettelyoun Flats. Five miles further, you drop down to the Laramie River and the road begins to climb up again.

Two miles from the river crossing, you pass by the Fort Laramie Road going east. One mile further is another junction. Here you can continue south to the Deer Creek Road. There you can either go east to Lingle or west to Wheatland (see page 22).

Turn west toward Laramie Peak on the Grayrocks Road and you drop down along the reservoir for about seven miles. The road then follows along the Laramie River for three miles to Chugwater Creek. Here the road swings around the power plant and hits the North Wheatland Highway (six miles). Turn south for two miles to Wheatland.

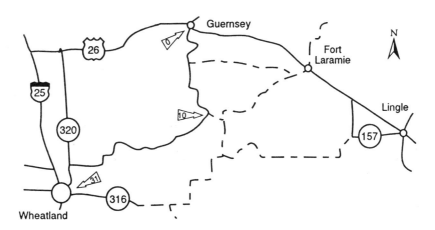

Trip Eight

Glendo to Keeline on the Spanish Diggings Road

Cedar Top and Pin Top near the junction of the Spanish Diggings/Meadowdale Road.

This trip begins by taking the Glendo Park Road east from Glendo. After passing by the marina and Two Moons Campground, the road crosses the dam (five miles from town) and turns north. Six miles from the dam is the turnoff to Sandy Beach and a junction with the Patton Creek Road going southeast to Guernsey (see page 25). Here you can see

(see page 25)

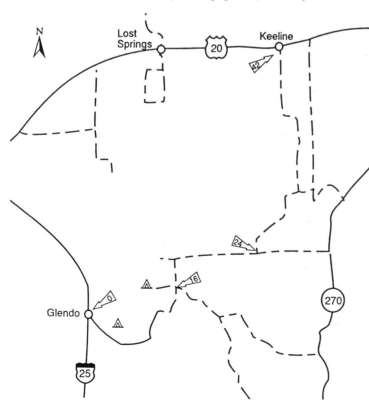

Laramie Peak to the west, Sheep Mountain to the east, and just north of Sheep Mountain is Cedar Top.

Continuing north, the road crosses Cotton-wood Creek to a junction with the Meadowdale Road. Here a side road turns west to the state park. Turn east on the Meadowdale Road and, after climbing a small hill, you can see Pin Top behind Cedar Top. The pointed butte just off to the south is called Horsetooth.

At the base of Cedar Top is another junction. Here you can continue east (past the Hogback on the north) for five miles to W-270 at mile #518 at Meadowdale.

Turn north on the Cedar Top Road. Five miles down the road is a junction with the Flat Top Road. Here you can turn east for four miles to a junction with the Jireh Road. There you can either continue east two miles to W-270, or you can turn north for 11 miles to US-20 east of Keeline.

Stay north on the Spanish Diggings Road and you cross Muddy Creek after five miles. Two miles further the pavement begins and after one more mile is another small junction. Here a dirt road turns northwest for 10 miles to Lost Springs and US-20 at mile #15. Turn east for two miles and then north for four miles to US-20 at mile #22, just west of Keeline.

Trip Nine

Guernsey to Glendo on the Patton Creek Road (with an option on the Emigrant Hill Road)

This trip begins by turning off US-26 just east of Guernsey and taking W-270 north. The road climbs up past ponderosa pines and cedar trees. At mile #498 is a junction with the Whalen Canyon Road going northeast (see page 26). At mile #500 W-318 turns off to Hartville and Sunrise and one mile further is the Lakeside Drive road going to Guernsey State Park (see option below).

Stay north on W-270 and the road continues to climb up through Webb Canyon to the top of the Hartville Uplift. After traveling across the top for a bit, you come to a junction at mile #510. Here W-270 continues north to US-20 at Manville.

Turn northwest on the Patton Creek Road and you travel through open parks and pine woods and then across the open top. (Nice drive!) Eight miles from the highway, the road passes by the base of Sheep Mountain where you have a good view of Laramie Peak to the west. One mile further is the junction with the Emigrant Hill Road.

Continue west for five miles to a junction with the Glendo Park Road (at the Sandy Beach turnoff). Here you can turn north for two miles to the Meadowdale Road. On that road you can turn east to Cedar Top and then go either east to W-270 or north to US-20 (see page 24).

Turn south on the Glendo Lake Road. After six miles the road drops down a bit as you enter the state park. After crossing the dam, you pass by the marina boat ramp and four more miles further is Glendo (I-25 at exit #111).

Emigrant Hill Option

The Emigrant Hill Road is not often maintained by the county and it could be closed sometime in the future. A six mile section of the trip has some poor bridges and the road may require a high clearance vehicle. There are two scenic routes you can take to get to Emigrant Hill. **Trip one begins** by turning off US-26 at mile #17 east of Guernsey. You go north on W-270 for about five miles (just past W-318 going to Sunrise) and turn west at mile #501. The road then climbs up to Rocky Pass and down one mile to the dirt road going up Emigrant Hill.

Trip two begins by turning north on to W-317 from US-26 at mile #15 just west of Guernsey. After about one mile the road forks. The road northwest goes to Sandy Beach and several access points on the west side of the lake. Take the pavement north and across the dam. The road follows along the shore (with several access roads to the lake) for about six miles to Long Canyon. Here a dirt road continues along the shore to the north, but take the pavement east for about two miles to the dirt road going over Emigrant Hill.

Now that both routes have joined, you climb up a couple of switchbacks to the top of Emigrant Hill. From the summit you have a terrific view of Laramie Peak and the Laramie Range to the southwest. After traveling northwest for a few miles, the road passes through private property and the Wyoming National Guard Artillery Firing Range. (Do not take any side roads, turns, or drives of any kind. Stay on the main road to the northwest!)

After traveling through the artillery range for four miles, the Emigrant Hill Road turns into a two-track at the top of a hill (where a slightly better road goes east). After about six miles, you cross Boxelder Creek and get a great view of the Sheep Mountain buttress to the east. Just after crossing the creek is the junction with the Patton Creek Road.

Trip Ten

The Rawhide Buttes Road from Lusk south to Guernsey or Fort Laramie

This trip begins by turning off US-20 at mile #39 on the west side of Lusk. As you head south toward Rawhide Buttes, you can see the Wanker Hills off to the west. Five miles from the highway, you begin passing by small buttes and stands of ponderosa pine. The road then climbs up a bit to a small divide and overlook (four miles). Here you can see Rawhide Buttes to the southeast, the Haystack Range to the south, and the Wild Cat Hills to the southwest. About five miles from this overlook you cross Rawhide Creek. (Nice drive through this area.)

Two and a half miles from the creek crossing is the first main junction. The road east crosses the creek to another junction in one mile. There, choice one takes the road going east through an auto-gate. That road then follows along Rawhide Creek for eight miles and crosses J M Creek to US-85 at mile #129. Choice two takes the road going northeast and around the base of Rawhide Butte for four miles. You then turn north for three miles and hit US-85 at mile #139.

Back at the first main junction, turn west for about 200 yards and the road begins making a series of turns to the southwest toward the Haystack Range. After about five miles you cross Muskrat Creek. Three miles further is the second main junction (option to Fort Laramie).

If you turn east for five miles (and go past a small road going south), the road crosses Muskrat Creek again to another junction. There, choice one takes the road continuing east along the creek for six miles to Jay Em and US-85 at mile #127. Choice two takes the lane south for four miles to a junction where a side road goes east to US-85 at mile #124. If you continue south for two and a half miles, you come to another junction. There you can take the pavement south for 12 miles to US-26 at Fort Laramie. (You can also take the pavement west for three miles and then turn northwest around Round Top to rejoin the road going to Guernsey.)

Back at the second main junction and going toward Guernsey, you continue south and west on the main road for two miles to a small road heading west toward the Whalen Range. Stay southwest for three more miles to the old Rawhide Stage Station and a junction with the road from Fort Laramie (via Round Top). Turn west here and after about three miles you pass through the Hell Gap area and travel south through a small canyon. After eight miles you hit W-270 at mile #498. Here you can go north to Manville. Turn south on W-270 for three miles and you hit US-26 at mile #1, just east of Guernsey.

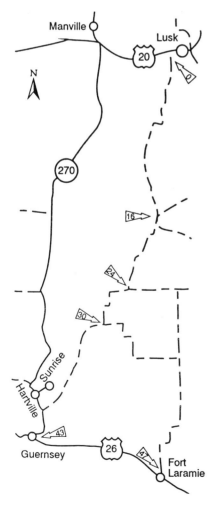

The old Rawhide Stage Station is just south of the option to Fort Laramie.

Trip Eleven

Van Tassell south past Prairie Center to Torrington

This trip begins by turning south off US-20 at mile #61 at Van Tassell. The road crosses the Niobrara River and climbs to the top of a small bench. Here you can see Rawhide Butte to the west. You continue traveling south (past a few side roads going east/west) to a junction 11 miles from the highway. Here you can turn west under the tracks and travel to Prairie Center (five miles). From there you can go west to US-85 at mile #133 or #127, or you can go north back to US-20 on the McMaster Road.

Continue south and you cross over the tracks in a couple of miles. The road then turns west for three miles to pavement. From this area you can see Laramie Peak to the west, Pine Ridge to the southwest, and Spoon Butte to the southeast.

After traveling three miles south on the pavement you come to another junction. Here you can turn west to US-85 (mile #127) at Jay Em (11 miles). Also on this road, you can turn north to Prairie Center (seven miles).

Continue south for seven miles and you pass by Spoon Butte off to the east. About six miles further, the road drops down through some small breaks and the state maintenance begins on W-159. Along this stretch you can see Tea Kettle Rock off to the west.

Eleven miles further south, you enter the outskirts of Torrington and roads begin turning off to residential areas. Stay on W-159 (West C Drive) and after passing the hospital and college, you hit US-26 (Valley Road).

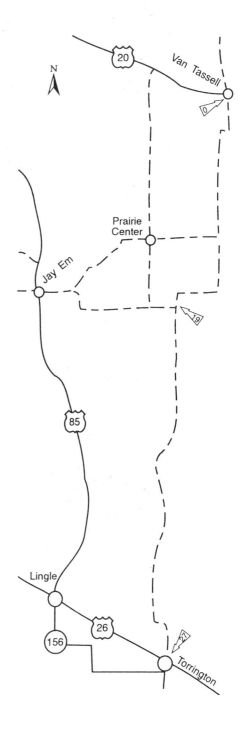

Old snapping turtles like this one are common in some of the ponds and mud holes in the Torrington and Lusk area.

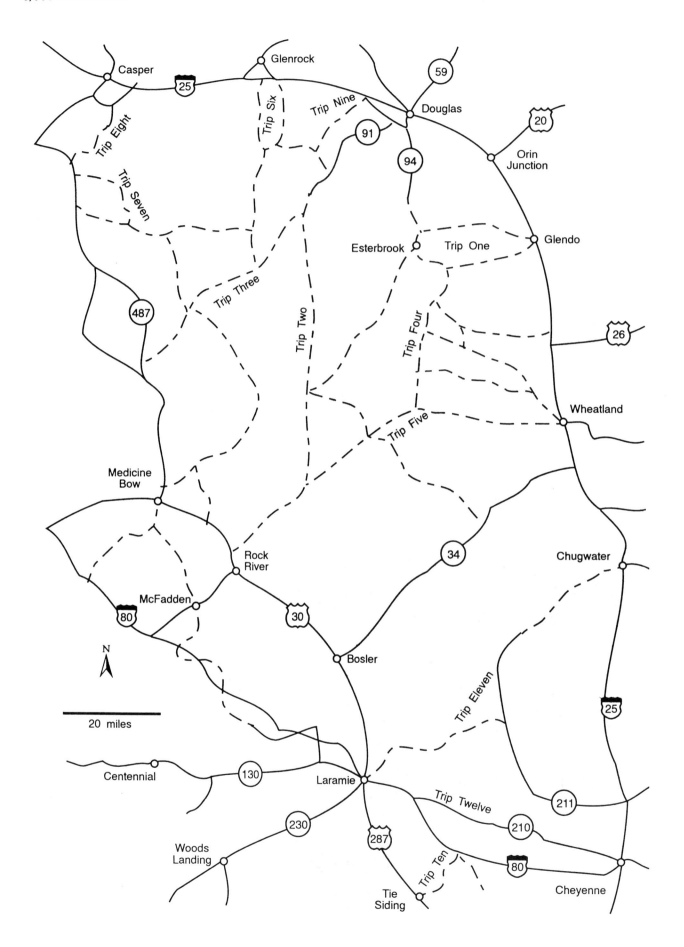

Trip One

The Esterbrook Loop from Glendo and back

This trip begins by taking I-25 exit #111 to Glendo and turning west on the Ridge Road toward Esterbrook. As the road heads west, you can see Laramie Peak to the southwest a bit. On the north side of the peak is Eagle Peak and Windy Peak, and on the south side is Albany Peak and Bear Head Mountain.

After about 12 miles, you begin following Elkhorn Creek and you can see Sawtooth Mountain to the far west. As you enter Converse County (and begin traveling on C-6), you cross Spring Creek and Coyote Creek. The road then climbs a ridge past Sunset Hill (just off to the south).

The road swings south across a small saddle and you begin traveling past ponderosa pine trees. You then come to a junction on Prairie Dog Hill. Here you can take C-5 north to Douglas (see page 34).

Turn south on C-5 and after one mile you come to a junction in Ullman Park. Here you can see Windy Peak to the southwest. Squaw Peak is in the foreground between Laramie Peak and Eagle Peak. At this junction you can take C-5 west toward Sawtooth Mountain and hit C-7 (three miles). There you can turn north to Douglas on the Brae Road, or you can go south to Friend Park and the Fetterman Road near Garrett (see page 30).

Turn south toward Rock Mountain and as you enter Esterbrook the road turns east. You then travel past lodgepole pine for three miles to the Esterbrook Campground. After leaving the campground, the road drops down some switchbacks to another junction at Three Cripples Creek. Here you can turn south toward Harris and Cottonwood Park (see page 34).

Continue east and you begin following along Horseshoe Creek. After crossing several draws, the road goes by the base of Reeder Hill (three miles). Three miles further you hit pavement and cross Horseshoe Creek. You follow along the creek for another seven miles and, after crossing the creek a second time, the road goes under I-25 to the South Glendo Highway, one mile south of Glendo.

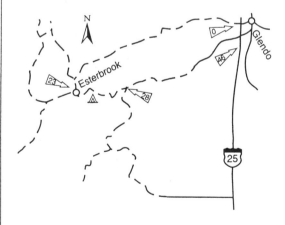

The "boot" was once a common sight along Wyoming secondary highways. However, due to Highway Department safety standards, it is now only rarely seen along county roads.

Trip Two

The Fetterman Road from Rock River north to Douglas

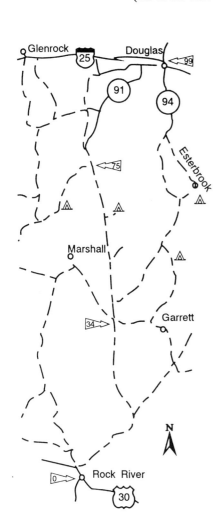

This trip begins by turning off US-30 at mile #287, just north of Rock River. As you head east on the Fetterman Road (A-61), Laramie Peak is to the northeast, the Snowy Range is south, and to the southwest is Elk Mountain. After two miles, the road swings northeast and follows along Rock Creek. Four miles after crossing the creek, a small road turns northwest toward the Freezeout and Shirley Mountains, but continue northeast across the Laramie Plains.

You pass Rock Lake after about four miles and four miles further is a junction at Wheatland Reservoir #3. Here the Palmer Canyon Road (A-721) goes northeast to Cottonwood Park (34 miles). Along this road you can go to Sybille Canyon (W-34), Wheatland, Glendo, or Douglas (see pages 34 and 36).

Turn north on A-61 and after three miles you cross Spring Creek and pass by Red Hill (off to the east a bit). The road continues north across Seven-mile Creek (three miles) and across the plains to a small lake at Twenty-mile Draw (nine more miles). North of the lake is a junction at Twentytwo-mile Draw. Here the Mule Creek Road (A-64) turns northwest for 16 miles to a junction with the Marshall Road (A-610). There you can travel to Rock River, Medicine Bow, Casper, or Douglas (see pages 34 and 38).

Continue north on A-61 for one mile to another junction. Here the Garrett Road (A-713) turns east toward Cow Creek Mountain. Along this road you can hit the Palmer Canyon Road by turning south at Garrett, or you can go through Friend Park to Esterbrook (and then over to Douglas, Glendo, or Wheatland).

Stay to the north for three more miles and you come to another junction. Here the Esterbrook/Eagle Peak Road (A-710) turns east toward Cow Creek Mountain. On this road you can join the road going through Friend Park at the base of Eagle Peak (15 miles). From there you can travel to Esterbrook.

Stay on A-61 to the north. The road passes by Toltec Reservoir (two miles) and then by the Hay Creek Road (A-76, dead end to the east). About two miles north of A-76, you go by a small lake and pass between Smith Mountain on the west and Bar-M Mountain on the east. Two miles north of the lake, you get a quick glimpse of Bell Butte and Bell Mountain, by looking northeast up the North Laramie River Drainage. Also here, the road to Toltec turns east and dead ends.

Just past this view, the road goes by Soldier Creek Reservoir. Here Mule Creek Mountain is just off to the west. About three miles north of the reservoir, you pass between Forty-mile Peak (to the west) and Flattop Mountain (to the east). Along here you can see Blacktail Peak to the northeast. To the northwest is Brumley Mountain and behind it is the taller Camelback Mountain.

After a few miles, you begin following LaBonte Creek past willow, spruce, pine, aspen, and a few cedar trees. The road crosses the creek several times during the next four miles down to the LaBonte Canyon Road. This is a beautiful drive and return road to the Curtis Gulch Campground.

The road then climbs a bit, away from the creek, and you can see Camelback Mountain (and why it got the name) to the west. Behind Brumley Mountain to the south is Forty-mile Peak. To the southeast is Flattop Mountain.

Two miles after crossing Indian Creek, A-61 changes to C-16 at the county line and you begin traveling through Downy Park. Here you can see Warbonnet Peak to the west. As the road crosses Gould Creek, you can see a cut in the mountains to the east where West Fork LaBonte Canyon drops over the other side. Packsaddle Mountain is now to the southeast.

As you continue north, you pass by School Section Mountain (small hump to the west) and you can see Squaw Mountain (pointed) and Buffalo Peak (domed) to the far west. The road follows along a ridge and, as you drop down to the junction below, you can see Baldy Point off to the east.

At the junction with the Cold Springs Road, you can take C-24 southwest along La-Prele Creek to the North Fork Little Medicine Bow River and the Shirley Basin. From there you can travel to Rock River, Medicine Bow, or Casper (see page 32).

Turn north on C-24 and the road drops down Virden Hill and crosses Little LaPrele Creek. Two miles further, C-24 ends and you join W-91 at mile #23. Here C-11 goes north to the Windy Ridge Road.

As you follow LaPrele Creek to the northwest on W-91, you pass by Moss Agate Hill and at mile #17 is a junction where C-15 turns west to join C-11. One mile further on W-91, the Windy Ridge Road (C-14) turns west and hits the Boxelder Road (about ten miles, see page 37).

Continuing north on W-91, you pass by LaPrele Reservoir and at mile #11 you go through Hazenville Pass. As the road begins to drop down Nine-mile Hill, Sheep Mountain is to the south.

At mile #7 the Bedtick Road (C-8) turns southeast to W-94, and at mile #6 you pass by the Chalk Buttes Road (C-9) also going east to W-94. Stay on W-91 and the road climbs a small hill to a junction at mile #3. Here W-96 goes west to I-25 at exit #151. Turn east for three miles to I-25 at Douglas.

I once had a girl friend who said she thought the Laramie plains looked like the moon. I think the fact that she meant this in a derogatory way had something to do with why she is now an old girl friend.

Trip Three

Douglas south to Medicine Bow on the Cold Springs Road

This trip begins by taking W-91/94 south from Douglas (I-25, exit #140) and going under I-25 to a junction. Here you can take W-94 south to Esterbrook (see page 34).

Turn west on W-91. At mile #3 is another junction. Here W-96 continues west to the Spring Canyon Road and I-25. Turn south on W-91 and the road climbs up to the next junction at mile #6. Here the Chalk Buttes Road (C-9) turns east back to W-94 and Douglas.

Stay on W-91 and the road goes up the hill and passes by the Bed Tick Road (C-8, going southeast to Sheep Mountain and back to W-94). The road climbs to the top of Nine-mile Hill and at mile #11 you go through Hazenville Pass. The road then drops down to LaPrele Reservoir and you begin following LaPrele Creek toward the Laramie Mountains.

At mile #16 the Windy Ridge Road (C-14) turns west. On this road you can take the Spring Canyon Road (C-11) south to Natural Bridge and I-25 (exit #151), or you can continue west to the Boxelder Road (C-17) north of Glenrock (see pages 37 and 40).

Continue south on W-91 (passing by C-15 going west to the Spring Canyon Road) and you travel through the valley for about six miles to the end of the pavement. Here the Spring Canyon Road turns back to the north.

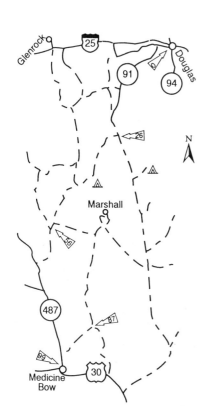

Continue south on the Cold Springs Road (C-24) and you cross Little LaPrele Creek in one mile. The road then climbs Virden Hill to the next junction. Here you can take the Fetterman Road (C-16), south through Downy Park, to Rock River (see page 30). At this junction, the pointed Squaw Mountain and the doomed Buffalo Peak are off to the southwest.

Turn southwest on C-24 and after crossing Blue Nose Creek, the road travels along the open top for about three miles. You then drop down to the Rabbit Creek crossing. The road climbs up past the base of Bear Rock to a small saddle. The road then drops down across La-Prele Creek and crosses Meadow Creek (one more mile). Along here you begin passing by limber pine, ponderosa pine, spruce and aspen trees.

You continue following LaPrele Creek up the valley and after crossing Woodchopper Creek you begin seeing lodgepole pine and fir trees. One mile further, you pass by Cold Springs and come to the Campbell Creek Campground. The road leaves the creek after one mile and then travels through the forest for two miles to open country again.

Three miles after leaving the forest, you come to the next junction. Here you can take the road to the northwest and hit the Deer Creek and Boxelder Creek Roads (see page 37). At this junction you can see Twin Peaks and Squaw Mountain to the north and Warbonnet Peak to the east.

Continue southwest on the Little Medicine Road (A-62) and across the North Fork Little Medicine Bow River. The road travels along the top for four miles to the edge of the rim. Here you can see the Snowy Range Mountains and Elk Mountain to the south; to the southwest are the Shirley Mountains and to the west is Chalk Mountain.

The road drops down the rim to the South Fork Little Medicine Bow River (six miles) in the Shirley Basin. Three miles further you come to a main junction. Here you can continue southwest on A-62, across the Little Medicine Bow River (seven miles), and hit W-487 at mile #18 north of Medicine Bow. Also on this route, you can turn north on C-97 (two miles from here) and hit the Bates Hole Reservoir Road (10 miles, see page 38).

Turn southeast on the Holiday Road (A-619) and you follow along the Laramie Range for nine miles to the next junction. Here you can continue southeast on A-619 for one and a half miles to the Marshall Road (A-610). There you can go east for two miles and hit the Mule Creek Road (A-64) going south to the Fetterman Road (see page 30).

Turn southwest on the Marshall Road (A-610). After one mile you pass by the other end of this three-corner junction. As you continue southwest, the road passes by the Boot Heel (four miles) where you begin traveling across the Johnson Flats toward Elk Mountain.

Seven miles from the Boot Heel, you cross Sheep Creek. Here you can see Laramie Peak to the east and to the west are the Freezeout Mountains. The road follows along Sheep Creek to the southwest for about four miles and then turns south for six miles to a junction at Greasewood Creek. Here you can take the Marshall Road west and then south for six miles to Rock Creek. After crossing Rock Creek, that road then climbs up Como Ridge and hits US-30 at mile #283 north of Rock River.

Turn west toward Medicine Bow and you follow along Greasewood Creek for about three miles. The road then swings southwest through the Greasewood Flats where you can see Como Ridge to the south. Ten miles from the junction on Greasewood Creek, you hit W-487 one mile north of Medicine Bow.

Squaw Rock (also known as Bare Rock) is rumored to have gotten the name because a young indian princess turned to stone waiting for her brave to come home. She is pictured here with a blanket wrapped around her and grinding corn in a large bowel. (Neither of these conditions would probably exist in the world today.)

Trip Four

Douglas southeast to Wheatland on the Esterbrook Road

This trip begins by taking W-94 from Douglas (I-25 exit #140) and going south under I-25 to a junction. Here W-91 goes west to the Cold Springs Road (see page 32). Turn south on W-94 and at mile #1 you pass by the Chalk Buttes Road (C-9) going west back to W-91 and Douglas.

As the road follows along the North Platte River, you pass by C-2 going back to Douglas. Here you can see the top of Laramie Peak to the south and to the west is Sheep Mountain. At mile #4 the Bed Tick Road (C-8) turns west toward Sheep Mountain and at mile #7 the Wagonhound Road (C-3) turns west. (If you take this road it will connect with the Poison Lake Road and then rejoin W-94 at mile #10.)

The road now climbs Warm Springs Hill and leaves the river. After crossing Wagonhound Creek (mile #9) and passing the Poison Lake Road, you can see Eagle Peak to the west of Laramie Peak. At mile #15 you cross West Fork LaBonte Creek and at mile #17 the pavement ends at a junction. Here you can take the Brae Road (C-7) to the southwest. On this road you can loop back over to Esterbrook, or you can continue south past Eagle Peak to Garrett and Rock River (see pages 30 and 36).

Turn southeast on the Esterbrook Road (C-5). The road crosses LaBonte Creek and then climbs up for the next two miles. You then drop down a bit to Mill Creek and the Bruner Cutoff Road (going west to the Brae Road). Here you can see Slick Rock to the southwest (exposed granite on the side on the mountain) and Baldy Peak on top.

As you continue south, the road crosses Mill Creek and passes below Elk Mountain. Here you see willow, cottonwood, boxelder, pine, and a few aspen trees. The road crosses the creek a couple of times and then climbs up Mill Hill to a junction on top of Prairie Dog Hill. Here the Glendo Road (C-6) goes east to Glendo and I-25 at exit #111 (see page 29).

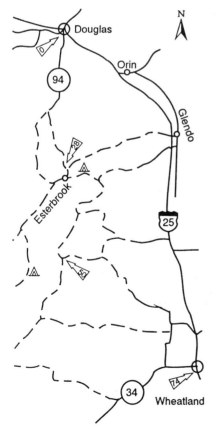

Continue south for two more miles to the next junction at Ullman Park. Here you can see Windy Peak to the southwest, Squaw Peak is in the foreground between Eagle Peak and Laramie Peak, and Rock Mountain is to the south. At this junction, C-5 turns west toward Sawtooth Mountain. On this road you can hit the Brae Road going back to Douglas, or you can continue southwest past Laramie Peak to Rock River.

Stay to the south and as you drop down the hill to Esterbrook, the road turns to the east. The road then passes through a stand of lodgepole pine and goes by the Esterbrook Campground (three miles). Here you leave the forest and drop down a few switchbacks to a junction at Three Cripples Creek. At this junction you can go east along Horseshoe Creek to Glendo (see page 29).

Turn south across the creek and you begin following Horseshoe Creek (nice drive here). After about two miles, the road crosses the creek and climbs up some steep switchbacks to Memorial Overlook. The road then passes below Rock Mountain and crosses Soldier Creek to Harris Park (three miles). After traveling through the park for one mile, you come to a junction. Here you can see Harmon Height to the southeast, Elliot Point to the south, and Black Mountain to the southwest a bit. At this junction, you can take the Harris Park Road east to I-25 (exit #94), between Glendo and Wheatland.

Stay south toward Cottonwood Park (10 miles). After crossing Fall Creek (one mile), you begin following Cottonwood Creek to the crossing at Hubbard's Cupboard. The road then follows the creek between Albany Peak (on the east) and the Haystack Peaks (on the west, below Laramie Peak).

After crossing the creek again, the road travels through Cottonwood Park to a junction. Here you can see the Haystacks to the north and behind them is Black Mountain. To the west is Bear Head Mountain, northwest is Laramie Peak, and to the south is Britania Mountain. At this junction, the Cottonwood Park Road (A-71) continues south where you can hit the Palmer Canyon Road going to Wheatland or Rock River (see page 36).

Turn east on the Fletcher Park Road (A-716). The road gradually climbs up through the forest for about three miles and then drops down a bit to Fletcher Park. You continue to drop down through the forest for three more miles and then down through the open country. Six miles from Fletcher Park, you come to another junction. Here you can take the Fish Creek Road northeast for five miles to another junction. There you can either loop back to Harris Park, or you can turn east to I-25 at exit #94.

Continue southeast on the Fletcher Park Road and you pass between Sheep Mountain on the southwest and Johnson Mountain on the northeast. The road continues southeast around Sheep Mountain and travels through a small basin. You then follow along a sandy wash and cross the North Laramie River.

Two miles after crossing the river you hit pavement. The road then crosses the Dry Laramie River and follows it for a few miles to the Laramie River. After crossing the Laramie River, the road climbs up a small bench and you join W-311 (Hightower Road). Continue south on W-311 for three miles to a junction with W-310. Turn east for four miles to 16th Street in Wheatland. Here you can turn north for one mile to I-25 at exit #80, or you can turn south for one mile to exit #78.

One of the things the Laramie Range is noted for is its stark contrast between the earth and sky.

Trip Five

The Palmer Canyon Road from Wheatland west to Rock River

This trip begins by taking W-312 west from Wheatland (I-25, exit #78). After one mile, the road turns south to a junction on top of a hill. Here you can continue south to W-34. Turn west on the Palmer Canyon Road. As the road heads west past several side roads, you can see Laramie Peak to the northwest, Collins Peak and Britania Mountain to the west, and Squaw Mountain to the southwest.

Two miles after passing Hightower Road, the road crosses Sybille Creek and you can see the Cooney Hills to the near south. After four more miles, you cross the Laramie River and begin following Luman Creek toward Green Mountain. The road then crosses Luman Creek and you begin climbing above Palmer Canyon and traveling past ponderosa pine trees.

The pavement ends as you enter Albany County (A-721) and you continue to climb above the canyon for two more miles. You then drop down into a small canyon that travels between Collins Peak (The Notch) and Britania. Along here you see a few cottonwood and aspen trees. The road climbs again for about two miles and you can see Split Rock and Reese Mountain to the south.

The road drops down a bit to Ashley Creek and then climbs up again. Here you begin traveling along the open country on top where you have a great view of Collins Peak and the cut where Ashley Creek passes between Split Rock and Reese Mountain. After three miles you come to a junction. Here you can take the Cottonwood Park Road (A-71) north toward Laramie Peak. On this road, you drop down into a beautiful canyon along Sturgeon Creek and follow it to the North Laramie River. That road then cross the river and climbs up a bit to Cottonwood Park. There you can either go east to Wheatland or continue north to Esterbrook and Douglas (see page 34).

Continue southwest toward Rock River on A-721. The road travels nine miles across the Davidson Flats and part of the Laramie Peak Big Game Winter Range to another junction. Here you can take the Garrett Road (A-713) north to the Bear Creek Road going through Friend Park, the Fetterman Road going to either Douglas or Rock River, or the Medicine Bow Road going to either Douglas or Medicine Bow (see pages 30 and 32). The small 2-track going south at this junction connects with the Tunnel Road.

Continue southwest toward Rock River on A-721 to the next junction (two miles). Here you can take the Tunnel Road (A-727) east across Dodge Creek (four miles). After four more miles, that road then drops down past Elmers Rock to the Laramie River. After crossing the river, it travels southeast for about 12 miles to W-34 at mile #36.

Continue southwest on A-721. After about two miles the road drops over a small divide where you can see Wheatland #3 ahead of you. The road heads toward the Snowy Range Mountains and Elk Mountain for nine miles to another junction where A-721 ends. Here you can take the Fetterman Road A-61 north through Downy Park to Douglas (see page 30). Along this route, you can also take the Garrett Road toward Wheatland, or the Mule Creek Road to Marshall and then to Rock River, Medicine Bow, or Douglas.

Turn southwest on the Fetterman Road (A-61) and after four miles, you pass Rock Lake off to the north. After about four more miles, you pass a small road turning northwest toward the Freezeout and Shirley Mountains.

Stay to the southwest and the road begins following along Rock Creek and then crosses it in four miles. You continue to follow the creek for about two miles and the road swings to the west. Here you can see the Snowy Range to the south, Elk Mountain to the southwest, and Laramie Peak to the northeast. After two more miles, you hit US-30 at mile #287 north of Rock River.

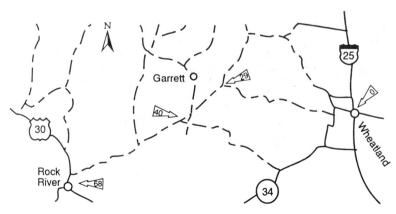

Trip Six

The Mormon Canyon-Boxelder Canyon Loop from Glenrock

This trip begins by taking the Mormon Canyon Road (C-18) south from Glenrock (US-20 at mile #165, accessed from I-25 exit #160). The road heads south along Deer Creek and then goes under I-25 after two miles. Here the pavement turns west to a park, but continue south on C-18 toward the Laramie Mountains. After about four miles, you begin following Dry Creek through Mormon Canyon. The creek here is lined with aspen, chokecherry, boxelder, and cottonwood trees and the hillsides are covered with ponderosa pine.

The road comes out on top after three miles and you have a good view of the Laramie Range. During the next four miles to the Willow Creek crossing, you can see Davis and Lookout Peak to the southwest Prostsman Knob is below them and a bit to the west and Buck Peak to the south. After crossing Willow Creek, the road climbs a hill and swings east away from the knob. Three miles further is the junction with the Boxelder Road (C-17). Here you can go south toward Little Medicine Creek and Deer Creek. (This is a 4WD road after about six miles; see option below.)

To continue the loop back to Glenrock, turn northeast on C-17 and follow Boxelder Creek downstream past Lacy Mountain. Two miles after crossing the creek, you come to a junction. Here you can take the Windy Ridge Road (C-14) east to the Spring Canyon Road. There you can go north to the Natural Bridge Road or east to the Cold Springs Road.

Continue north on C-17 and over a small saddle. The road drops down a bit and then crosses Boxelder Creek at the head of the canyon. The road now leaves the creek and travels past aspen trees and a few lodgepole pine for about one mile. Here you hit pavement and drop down a steep hill to Hunton Creek (three miles). Three miles further you join W-90. You then cross Dry Creek and the road goes under I-25 and hits US-20 at mile #162. Here you can turn west to Glenrock or east to I-25 at exit #160.

OPTION: Little Medicine or Deer Creek.

If you choose the option to continue south, the road follows along Boxelder Creek (past Lacy Mountain off to the east) toward Buck Peak. After crossing Snowshoe Creek and Keely Draw, the road turns southwest (away from an old paved road) and swings around Pole Mountain. Here the road becomes a 2-track and crosses Buck Creek, seven miles south of the C-17/C-18 junction. (The scenery becomes very nice here - as it often does on 2-track roads.)

Two miles further south, you cross Gunnysack Creek and pass Buck Peak off to the east. After a several more miles, you pass by Cherry Mountain (to the east) and in three miles, you cross Little Gunnysack Creek. The trees here are limber pine and on the slope to the east are spruce trees.

Two miles after crossing Little Gunnysack Creek, the road climbs a pretty rough hill (at least Black Irene didn't like it) and comes out on top to a junction. If you take the road to the west, it crosses Curry Creek and then follows a ridge over to Deer Creek (seven miles). There you can head southwest to a junction with the Medicine Bow Road (four miles). At that junction, you can turn south to Rock River and Medicine Bow, or you can continue west toward Casper on the Bates Hole Road (see page 38).

Back at the junction on the hill, if you turn southeast toward the Cold Springs Road, the road gets much better after two miles. There you can look north and see where Boxelder Creek makes a sharp bend to the northeast. You can also see the Snowy Range and Elk Mountain to the far south.

Three miles from the Cold Springs/Deer Creek Junction, you cross Sleepy Jack Creek and Elkhorn Creek. After three more miles (and crossing several other small creeks), you pass by the East Boxelder Creek Road (dead end) and cross Cabin Creek. One mile from Cabin Creek, you hit the Cold Springs Road (A-62) at the North Fork Little Medicine Bow River. From here you can see Twin Peaks and Squaw Mountain to the north. At this junction, you can go southwest to Medicine Bow and Rock River, or you can travel northeast to Douglas (see page 32).

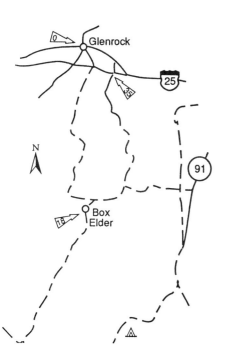

Trip Seven

Bates Creek Reservoir Loop and Option

This trip begins by turning east off W-487 at mile #63. About a half mile from the highway is a road going north, but stay on N-402 and follow Corral Creek into the Canyon. This is a beautiful drive past cedar, cottonwood, tall sagebrush, and lichen covered boulders. The road swings southeast and then south after about three miles.

Just after crossing the creek, you can see Rocky Gap off to the east a bit. You then climb over a divide and drop down to Bates Creek (six miles from Corral Creek). The road follows above the creek through a small basin. After about two miles, the creek cuts through a gorge to the northeast and you cross Chalk Creek above a nice little waterfall.

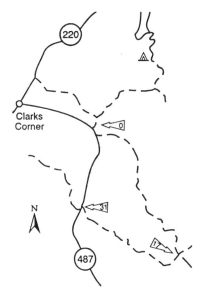

From the falls, the road climbs out of the basin and goes past a 2-track road turning north at Mud Springs Draw. Continue to the top of the rim and 100 yards past the Bates Creek Reservoir Road is a junction. Here N-402 continues southeast to the option below.

To stay on the loop trip going back to W-487, turn southwest toward the Ferris and Pedro Mountains on the Bates Hole Stock Trail (N-403). After a couple of miles the road swings northwest and, as you drop of the rim, you have a great view of the Bates Hole area. The road then winds around below a rimrock canyon and past several dry washes.

As you continue going down through Sand Draw, you can see Chalk Mountain, Horse Peak, and Bear Mountain off to the south. You then pass by Twin Buttes (off to the north) and head toward Haystack Butte to the west. Two miles further you hit W-487 at mile #57.

OPTION: To the Cold Springs Road.

If you continue southeast on N-402, the road travels along the rim for about 10 miles. Along this stretch, you can see the Shirley Mountains to the southwest; to the south are the Freezeout Mountains (below Elk Mountain), and to the southeast is the Snowy Range. To the west are the Pedro Mountains and Chalk Mountain. To the east and around to the north are the Laramie Mountains.

At the next junction you can take the road northeast over to Deer Creek (four miles) and then on over to the Boxelder Road (three more miles). There you can go north to Glenrock (4WD), or you can continue east to the Cold Springs Road (seven miles) at Little Medicine (see page 37).

Back at the junction on the rim, turn southeast and drop down over Dugway Rim. You pass by a small road turning east and continue south for about five miles to the Little Medicine Bow River. After crossing the river, you head south for five miles (and pass by a road going west to the mine) to a major junction. (N-402 is C-97 at this end).

At this junction, you can turn southwest on C-97 and hit W-487 at mile #18, north of Medicine Bow. Also at this junction, you can turn northeast on A-62 and go two miles to another junction. There you can continue northeast on A-62 to Douglas, or turn southeast on A-619 to Rock River or Wheatland (see page 32).

The original "bed and breakfast" run by young Norman and his mother is found on the short trip. After the well ran dry and the shower wouldn't work, both Norman and his mother were reported to have managed a small motel on the coast.

Trip Eight

Casper Mountain Circle Drive Road

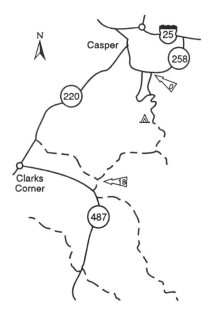

This trip begins by turning south off W-258 (Casper Outer Belt Drive) at mile #13 (accessed from W-220 mile #113, or I-25 exit #185). Here you take W-251 toward Casper Mountain. After two miles, you pass W-252 going west past Garden Creek Falls and back to Casper. Stay on W-251 and the road turns away from the falls and begins climbing switchbacks up the side of Casper Mountain.

The road travels through stands of spruce, pine, and aspen. After four miles you pass by the Hogadon Road (N-504) going west to the ski area. Here W-251 ends and N-505 continues through Casper Mountain Park and Beartrap Meadow Park for about two miles.

The road then begins to drop down the other side toward Muddy Mountain and the pavement ends. Here the road turns southwest toward the Pedro and Ferris Mountains off in the distance. As the road continues to drop down, you pass by a side road going to the summit of Muddy Mountain.

The Circle Drive Road now begins traveling past cedar trees and red bluffs to a junction (seven miles). Here you can take the Coal Mountain Road (N-401) northwest along the base of Coal Mountain to US-220 at mile #101 (seven miles). You can also turn southwest for one mile and hit W-487 at mile #64.

My cousin Sara at the Hogadon Ski Area. Sara has qualified in the western regional Junior Olympic competition for the last four years.

Trip Nine

The Natural Bridge drive and return road

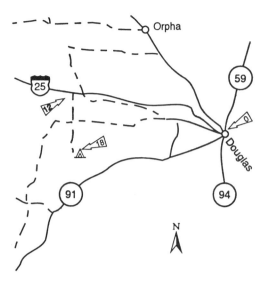

This little trip begins by turning off I-25 about 12 miles west of Douglas (exit #151) and taking C-13 south toward the foothills of the Laramie Range. Along here you can see Casper Mountain to the west and to the southeast is Table Mountain

After two miles you come to a junction with the Spring Canyon Road (C-11). Here you can turn east back to Douglas, or southwest to the Windy Ridge Road. There you can either head east to W-91, or west to the Boxelder Canyon Road (see pages 32 and 37).

Continue south for a couple miles and you drop down into a beautiful little canyon along LaPrele Creek at Ayres Natural Bridge County Park. This is a terrific place to picnic and lounge under peaceful shade trees. The birdlife here in the early spring is outstanding. The park is open between April 1 and October 31.

Krissy, Keith, Robin, and Samantha investigate aquatic invertebrates (bugs) in LaPrele Creek for a scientific research project at East Elementary.

Trip Ten

Hermosa Cutoff from Tie Siding northeast to I-80

The Ames Monument at the highest point on the trans-continental railroad.

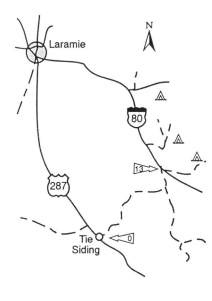

This trip begins by turning off W-287 (mile #417) at Tie Siding. The Hermosa Road (A-222) climbs up a hill to the northeast and crosses the tracks at Hermosa. Here you can see the Snowy Range and Sheep Mountain to the northwest. To the west is Boulder Ridge. After crossing the tracks, the road travels through a field of granite boulders. Up here you can see Jelm Mountain to the south of Sheep Mountain. The trees in this area are limber pine.

Five miles from Tie Siding, you get a glimpse of Dale Reservoir to the east and the road crosses Dale Creek (two more miles). After crossing the creek, you climb up a ridge to a junction at the Ames Monument.

If you take the Monument Road (A-234) south (after stopping of course), you get a good view of the Colorado Rocky Mountains. After crossing the tracks at Dale Creek, you head southeast and drop down to the East Fork Dale Creek. Two miles further, you pass by a road going south and you then cross Duck Creek. Here the road swings northeast, away from Twin Mountains, and crosses the county line (A-234 changes to RD-206). You pass by the Remount Pines Road and after crossing Lone Tree Creek, you hit pavement. Turn west on RD-103 and under the tracks to I-80 at exit #339.

Back at the junction at Ames Monument, if you turn north on the Monument Road, you head toward the Sherman Mountains. After two miles, you come to a junction at I-80 exit #329. There you can go under I-80 and travel through the Medicine Bow National Forest to the Happy Jack Road (see page 43). If you continue northwest along the old highway, you come to another junction in three miles. There you can take the Blair Road into the forest and hit the Happy Jack Road. If you continue northwest on the old highway for four more miles, you hit I-80 (exit #323) at the Lincoln Monument.

Trip Eleven

Laramie to Chugwater on the Roger Canyon-Iron Mountain Road

This trip begins by taking I-80 exit #310 into Laramie. You follow Curtis Street to the stoplight on Third Street and continue east to the stoplight at Ninth and Reynolds. Turn north on Ninth Street and after leaving Laramie, you begin traveling northeast on the Roger Canyon Road (A-17).

You head toward the Laramie Mountains for five miles and the road swings around The Spur. Here you can see Timber Canyon and Katie Brown Canyon to the east. After going around The Spur, the road turns back to the east and into Roger Canyon. This is a nice drive past mountain mahogany, limber pine, and rock walls.

You travel through the canyon for two miles and the pavement ends. Two miles further, you begin following Schoolhouse Creek and pass between Dirty Mountain on the north and Sherman Hill on the south. Here a road continues northeast toward Ragged Top, but stay on A-17 to the southeast and along the creek.

After crossing Schoolhouse Creek, the road climbs up past Sherman Hill and you can see Horse Mountain to the east. Ragged Top and Powell Mountain are to the northeast. One mile further is a small road turning east, but stay southeast on A-17 toward Green Top Mountain.

The road turns back to the east again and crosses Horse Creek. You then cross a couple of small creeks and go past Horse Mountain. Here you get a glimpse of Eagle Rock back to the southwest. About two miles further, the road crosses another small creek and you get a good view of the Horse Creek Hogback to the northeast.

The road then travels out on a finger and drops down along the creek in Fisher Canyon. (There are boxelder and cottonwood trees here - and the best tick infested area in the state.) After leaving the canyon, you join W-211 at mile #27 at the Horse Creek Post Office (A-17 is Rd-228 on this end).

If you take W-211 south, the road travels below the rim for about six miles and crosses Lodgepole Creek at mile #17 (Cheyenne Pass is to the west). There you can take Rd-109 south to Federal and join the Happy Jack Road at mile #15 (see page 43). You can also continue east on W-211, out of the valley and across the rolling prairie to I-25 (exit #16) north of Cheyenne.

Back at Horse Creek Junction, turn north on W-211 and the road goes between the rim and the Horse Creek Hogback. At mile #31 the road passes through a small saddle and drops down along Sand Creek to the Iron Mountain Post Office at Farthing. You then travel along a small razorback for two miles and begin following Chugwater Creek. After crossing the creek at mile #42, the pavement ends.

Continue north on Rd-106 for two miles where the road turns northeast for two miles to another creek crossing. As you continue down the valley, the terrain becomes progressively less rugged. After about three miles, you cross the creek one more time and begin traveling on the Iron Mountain Road. Five miles further, you cross Jacob Draw and pass below Degans Butte (two more miles). You then hit pavement and the road crosses Mendenhal Draw. Six miles further, you pass by the Diamond Road going west and hit I-25 (exit #54) at Chugwater.

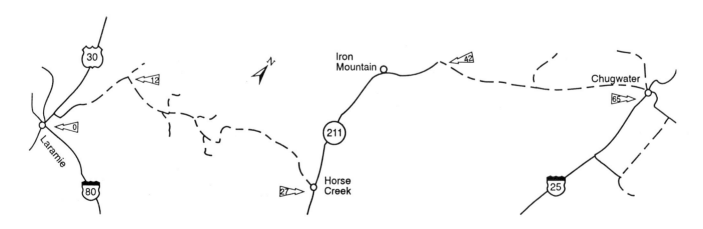

Trip Twelve

The Happy Jack Road from Cheyenne to Laramie

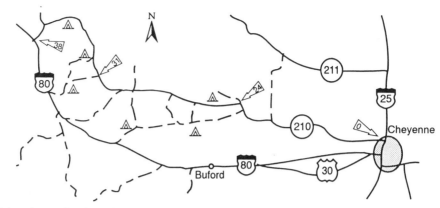

This trip begins by taking I-25 exit #10D (Missile Drive) and going west on W-210 (Happy Jack Road). You can also reach the Happy Jack Road by taking I-80 exit #358 (West Lincoln Freeway) and then turn back to the west on the Otto Road. After one mile, you turn north on W-222 and go under I-80 to the Happy Jack Road.

Now that both starting points have joined (W-210, mile #3), you head west toward the Laramie Mountains. The road climbs up a long hill to the northwest and then swings back to the west. At mile #12 you can see Table Mountain off to the northwest, and at mile #14 you cross South Fork Crow Creek to a junction. Here you can take the Crystal Reservoir Road to I-80 (exit #335) at Buford (14 miles).

Continue west on W-210 and you cross Crow Creek after one mile and come to another junction. Here you can take RD-109 north to Federal and join W-211 to either Chugwater or Laramie (see page 42).

Stay on W-210 and the road climbs up through the foothills and by a razorback to a junction at mile #24. Here you can take a side road south to Curt Gowdy State Park at Granite Reservoir. After passing by this turnoff, you go by the North Crow Creek Reservoir Road at mile #26 and enter the national forest. Here the Vedauwoo Road (NF-700) turns south where you can hit I-80 at exit #329. The trees in this area are aspen and ponderosa pine.

Continue west on W-210 toward the Sherman Mountains and you cross Brush Creek and pass by NF-707A going south to the Blair-Wallis Road. At mile #30 you cross South Branch North Fork Crow Creek and pass by NF-701 going north to the Telephone and Pilot Hill Roads. At mile #31 the Blair-Wallis Road (NF-707) goes south to some campgrounds. On this road you can travel through Hidden Valley to I-80 at exit #323, or follow along the service road to exit #329.

At mile #34 you cross South Lodgepole Creek and pass by the Telephone Road (NF-712) going to Eagle Rock. At mile #36 the Happy Jack Recreation Area Road turns off to Yellow Pine and Pole Creek Campgrounds. In this area you begin seeing lodgepole pine, spruce, and fir trees.

At the junction at mile #37 you can either take the Pilot Hill Road (NF-703) northeast to Eagle Rock, or you can turn south to the Upper and Lower Tie City Campgrounds. At mile #38 you come to the Lincoln Monument Rest Stop (I-80, exit #323). Here you can take the Hidden Valley Road (NF-705) to the Blair-Wallis Campgrounds, or go west on I-80 to Laramie (eight miles).

Shekinah, Isaac, Nikolas, Calli, and Zachary at one of the many campgrounds along the Happy Jack Road.

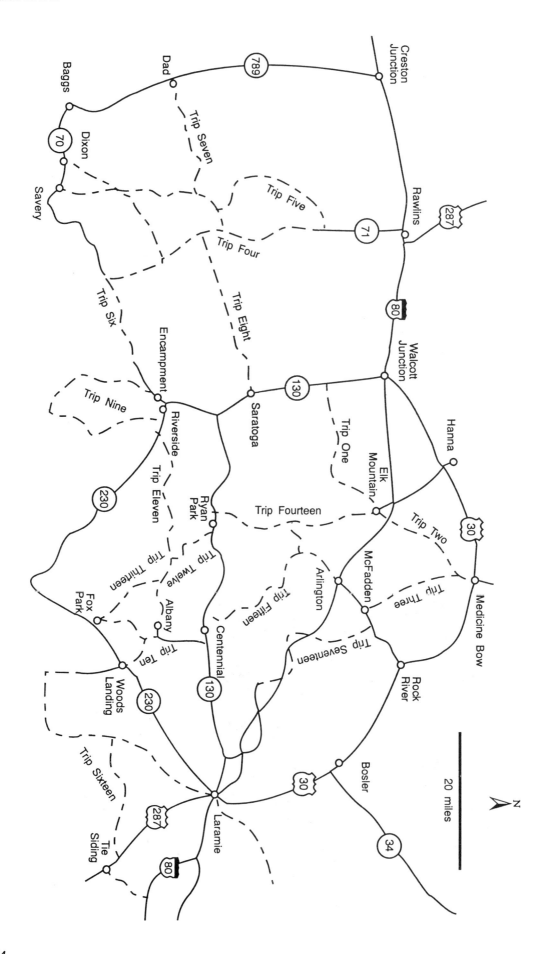

Trip One

The Pass Creek Cutoff from Elk Mountain southwest to W-130

Pass Creek Canyon between Coad Mountain and Elk Mountain.

This trip begins by turning off I-80 at exit #255 and taking W-72 toward Elk Mountain (the city). At mile #16 you turn southwest on the Pass Creek Road (C-404). As you head toward Elk Mountain (the mountain), you can see Kennaday Peak to the south. After about four miles, you pass by a small lake and cross Mill Creek. The road turns south across Fish Creek and climbs up a small hill. Here you can see Medicine Bow Peak, the Gap, and Browns Peak to the southeast. To the southwest is Pennock Mountain.

The road turns back to the southwest (past another road continuing south) and you can now see Coad Mountain, just south of Elk Mountain. You follow along Thade Creek and after crossing it, the road turns west (past a ranch road continuing southwest) toward Coad Mountain. You then begin following Pass Creek through the canyon. (Very nice drive here.)

After five miles, you cross the creek and leave the canyon where you continue following Pass Creek across the Overland Flats. Here you can see Sheephead Mountain to the north and to the southwest are the Sierra Madre Mountains. About eight miles from the mouth of the canyon is a junction. Here C-215 goes north to the Rattlesnake Pass Road. Continue west for four more miles and you hit W-130 at mile #8, between Walcott Junction and Saratoga.

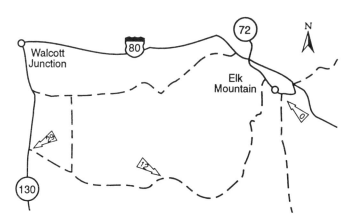

Trip Two

The Windmill Road from Elk Mountain to Medicine Bow

This trip begins in Elk Mountain (W-72 at mile #16, south of I-80 exit #255). Take the County Road across the Medicine Bow River and up the hill to a junction. Here you can turn south on C-101 to Centennial or Ryan Park (see page 60 and 61).

Turn east on C-402 and after two miles, you go under I-80 (exit #260). Stay north on C-3 and you pass by a couple of ranch roads. The road follows along the Medicine Bow River and crosses it after about five miles. You then climb over a small divide and follow along Sand Creek for seven miles to Halfway Hill. Along this stretch you can see Pine Ridge off to the east.

After going by Halfway Hill, the road travels across Spade Flats and through windmill country. To the north are the Freezeout Mountains, northwest are the Shirley Mountains, and to the far northeast is Laramie Peak. To the east is Indian Hill, south are the Snowy Range Mountains, and to the southwest is Elk Mountain.

After six miles you come to a junction. Here you can take C-1 south to W-13 at mile #11 at McFadden (see page 47). At this junction you can see East Allen Lake to the west and Como Bluffs to the east. Turn north on C-1 and after three miles you cross the tracks and enter Medicine Bow (US-30 at mile #272).

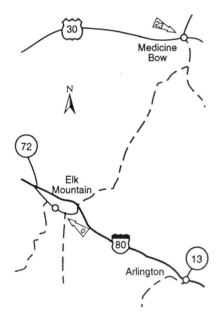

Don't expect to see any Dutch boys when traveling through windmill country in Wyoming.

Trip Three

The Windmill Road from Medicine Bow to McFadden

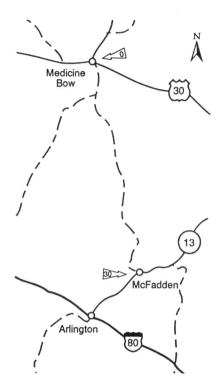

This trip begins by turning south off US-30 at mile #272 in Medicine Bow. You take C-1 over the tracks and head south for two miles to East Allen Lake (off to the west). The road then climbs a small hill to a junction. Here you can see the Snowy Range Mountains to the south, southwest is Elk Mountain, east is Como Bluffs, and northeast is Laramie Peak. At this junction, you can take C-3 southwest to I-80 near Elk Mountain (exit #260 or #255, see page 46).

Continue south on C-1 and the road crosses the Medicine Bow River (one mile). The road then swings east and then south across Horne Flats. A bit further, you pass between Indian Hill on the east and Pine Ridge on the west.

Two miles further south, you pass by a road going west toward Alligator Rock and Bible Rock (just on the other side of the ridge). Continue south and the road crosses Foote Creek and climbs up through a cut in Foote Creek Rim.

After going over the rim, the road drops down to Rock Creek and follows it south for three miles. You pass through a small oil field area and the main road turns east across the creek. You then climb up a small hill to McFadden and W-13 at mile #11.

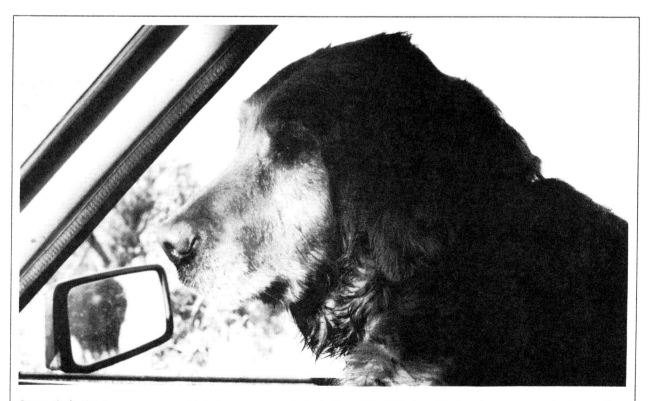

Smeagle is the barometer by which I gauge a great deal of my life. If his head is hanging out the window, or if he is wet and covered with mud, everything is going well. If he is curled up on the seat and sleeping, we need to take an "attitude adjustment" break and knock about for a bit.

Trip Four

The Aspen Alley Road from Rawlins south to Savery

This trip begins by taking I-80 exit #214 to Rawlins and then turning west on W-71. After going under the interstate, the road swings south and climbs to the top of Five-mile Ridge. Here you can see Rawlins Peak to the north. The road travels along the top for a bit and at mile #8 you can see Chokecherry Knob to the east, Atlantic Rim to the west, and Miller Hill to the southwest.

At mile #11, W-71 ends and you continue south on the pavement past Sheep Mountain (off to the east). Here you can see the Sierra Madre Mountains to the south and to the southeast are the Snowy Range Mountains.

Two and a half miles from the end of W-71, you go by the Bridger Pass Road (BLM-3301). On this road you can go over to the Cow Butte Road, the McCarty Canyon Road, and the Miller Mountain Road (see pages 50 and 52). Continue south and as you pass Teton Reservoir, you can see Pennock Mountain, Coad Mountain, and Elk Mountain to the far east. The road then crosses Miller Creek, LaMarsh Creek, Lonetree Creek, and Rasmussen Creek.

Fourteen miles south of W-71, you cross Sage Creek and the pavement ends. The road now climbs up Middlewood Hill to a junction. Here C-503 turns down the hill to the southwest. On this road, you can take the Mc-Carty Canyon Road to Dixon, the Cow Butte Road to Dad, or you can loop back to W-71 on the Muddy Creek/Bridger Pass Road (see page 50).

Stay to the south and you begin following Fish Creek down to the next junction. Here you can take C-500, up the hill to the east and on over to Saratoga (see page 53).

Continue south along Fish Creek and across North Fork Savery Creek. The road

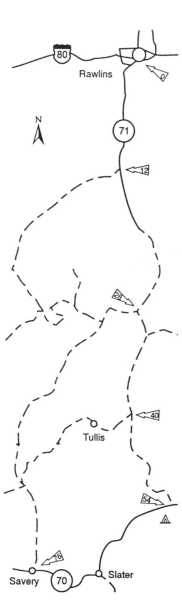

then climbs a hill and drops down to Smiley Meadows and Truckdriver Creek. You go up and over the next hill to Deep Gulch and after climbing the next hill, you can see Divide Peak off to the east and Dexter Peak to the southeast. You then drop down across East Fork Savery Creek and up and over again to Dirtyman Creek.

Just after crossing Dirtyman Creek, you come to another junction. Here you can take the road southwest to Tullis and over to Dixon (see page 53).

Continue south toward Green Ridge and just before you enter the forest, you can see Singer Peak to the east. The road swings southeast as you enter the national forest and you begin traveling on NF-801. The trees in this area are aspen, ponderosa, and lodgepole pine.

Two miles further, the road crosses Deep Creek and you begin seeing fir trees. The road drops down a steep grade to Big Sandstone Creek (a few cottonwoods here) and then gradually climbs back up again to Little Sandstone Creek (nice drive here).

After crossing the creek, you pass by the Sandstone Campground and the Divide Headquarters Road. The road then travels through a small park and you can now see Singer Peak to the northeast (beautiful drive here). About one mile further, you pass through Aspen Alley (fantastic drive here) to a junction. Here NF-801 ends and you can take the road east over to Encampment (see page 51).

Turn west toward Baggs and you pass by the Battle Creek Campground to pavement and a terrific overlook. To the south is Columbus Peak (large and domed), southwest is Battle Mountain, and to the far southwest is Hahns Peak.

From this overlook you continue west through the mixed forest for about four miles and then southwest past the Savery Stock Driveway. You then begin traveling on W-70 (mile #26).

As the road heads toward Battle Mountain, you can see Squaw Mountain between Columbus Mountain and Battle Mountain. In the foreground, east of Squaw Mountain, is Flattop. Further to the southeast is the broad Saddle Mountain and behind it a bit is Hahns Peak.

Below Saddle Mountain is the rock capped Sheep Mountain and east of it is Three Forks Mountain. (Nice view.)

At mile #20 you pass between Battle Mountain and Horse Mountain, and you then pass by C-710 going south to Steamboat (62 miles). The road travels below Sugarloaf and you begin following the Little Snake River at Slater. After crossing Savery Creek, you enter Savery, 11 miles east of Baggs. Here Bakers Peak is off to the south.

Timing is everything when it comes to fall colors in Wyoming. I missed the fantastic Aspen Alley by three days because I was in the Black Hills photographing paper birch and bur oak.

Trip Five

Dixon to Rawlins on the McCarty Canyon-Bridger Pass Road

This trip begins by turning off W-70 at mile #7 in Dixon. As you head north toward Muddy Mountain on C-503, you can see Battle Mountain to the east; southeast is Columbus Peak, and to the south, above Chalk Bluffs, is Bakers Peak. The road swings east and then north again along Cottonwood Creek. After crossing the creek and passing by Muddy Mountain, the road swings northeast of Browns Hill to a junction on top. Here C-501 turns south to Savery. Continue north along the top for one mile to another junction. Here the road to the northeast goes to Saratoga or Rawlins (see page 48).

Stay northwest on C-503 and as the road swings north, you can see Flat Top Mountain to the west and behind it on the far horizon are the Haystacks. Three miles from the last junction, a road turns northwest to the Horse Butte and Cow Butte Roads (see page 52). Stay on the main gravel road going north to Five Buttes.

After passing the buttes, the road swings northeast past several 2-track roads and drops down to Ketchum Buttes (five miles). The road drops down a bit more, into a small basin below Ketchum Buttes, and crosses a couple of small creeks. After about three miles, you pass below Rendle Butte and begin following Little Savery Creek.

After crossing Little Savery, you follow McCarty Creek up the canyon to a junction on top (four miles). Here you can continue northeast on C-503 and go down to Sage Basin and then over to Saratoga or Rawlins.

Turn northwest up the hill on the Miller Hill Road (BLM-3328). As you travel along the rim, you can see Sage Basin to the north and the Little Savery Creek drainage to the south. (If you look closely you can see Five

Buttes and Muddy Mountain to the south.) After four miles, you turn off the Miller Mountain Road (it continues to the north) and take the Muddy Creek Road (BLM-3306) west.

As you drop down on the Muddy Creek Road, it turns southwest away from the Littlefield Creek drainage. The road then loops to the southeast and back to the northwest to a junction on Muddy Creek. Here you can take the Cow Butte Road (BLM-3308) across Muddy Creek and on over to W-789 at Dad (see page 52).

Stay northwest along Muddy Creek on BLM-3306. At the second creek crossing, Littlefield Creek has joined Muddy Creek, and at the fourth creek crossing (eight miles from the Cow Butte Road), McKinney Creek has joined Muddy Creek. (This is big draw country.)

At this point the Muddy Creek Road is blocked at Sulfur Springs. Turn north on the Bridger Pass Road (BLM-3301). The road leaves Muddy Creek and climbs up above McKinney Creek and then Eagle Creek. You travel between Atlantic Rim and Miller Hill for about seven miles to Bridgers Pass.

The road then drops down a bit and you head northeast toward Sheep Mountain. Here Emigrant Creek is on the south and Atlantic Rim is still on the north. Ten miles from Bridger Pass, you hit pavement, two and a half miles south of the end of W-71. Here you can go south to Savery (see page 48). (Note: People wishing to go the other way on this route, make sure you take the road two and a half miles south of the end of W-71 and not the road two miles south.)

Turn north on W-71 and you pass by Sheep Mountain and climb up to Eight Mile Basin. Here you can see Chokecherry Knob off to the east. As you continue north, the road drops down Five Mile Ridge and you can see Rawlins Peak to the north. The road goes under I-80 and turns east one mile to I-80 (exit #214) in Rawlins.

Trip Six

The Sierra Madre Road from Riverside west to Savery

This trip begins by taking W-70 west from Riverside and Encampment. As you climb up the foothills, you can see Blackhall Mountain to the southeast and to the east above Bennet Peak is Medicine Bow Peak. To the northeast is Kennaday Mountain, Pennock Mountain, and Elk Mountain, and to the west is Vulcan Mountain. At mile #51 the pavement ends and you come to a junction. Here you can take NF-550 south on the Hog Park Road (see page 54).

Continue west past the Bottle Creek Campground and into the forest. The trees in this area are aspen and lodgepole pine. At the Beaver Creek crossing, you can see Green Mountain to the south. The trees along the road here are limber pine and a bit further you begin seeing fir trees.

Three miles from Beaver Creek, the road crosses South Fork Cow Creek and you can see Vulcan Mountain ("Captain, tricorder readings indicate . . .") above the Cow Creek drainage to the north. After two more miles, you cross over the divide at Battle Pass. Here a trail goes into the Houston Park Wilderness area. At this point, you can see the Battle Creek drainage to the west, Red Mountain is nearby to the southwest, and to the northwest is Bridger Peak.

As the road drops down below Bridger Peak at the Edison Monument, you can see Battle Lake below Red Mountain. The road heads toward Quartzite Peak and you begin passing spruce trees. To the far southwest you can see Battle Mountain. (This is a more than adequate area.)

You then go by the Haskins Creek Campground and the Lost Creek Campground. The road follows along the creek for two miles to a great overlook of the Lost Creek/Haggerty Creek confluence.

The road then crosses Haggerty Creek and you pass through a terrific stand of aspen trees. Three miles from Haggerty Creek, you come to a junction. Here you can take the Deep Creek Road (NF-801) through Aspen Alley and north to Rawlins or Saratoga (see page 48).

Continue west past the Battle Creek Campground Road and you hit pavement. Here the aspen forest becomes mixed with spruce and pine. Two miles from the Deep Creek Road, you come to a scenic overlook (simply stated). To the south is Columbus Peak (large and domed), southwest is Battle Mountain, and to the far southeast is Hahns Peak.

From this overlook, you continue west through the mixed forest for about four miles and then southwest past the Savery Stock Driveway. A bit further is W-70 at mile #26.

As the road heads toward Battle Mountain, you can see Squaw Mountain between Columbus Mountain and Battle Mountain, and in the foreground east of Squaw Mountain is Flattop. Further to the southeast is the broad topped Saddle Mountain and behind it to the east is Hahns Peak. Below Saddle Mountain is the rock capped Sheep Mountain and to the east of it is Three Forks Mountain.

At mile #20 you pass between Battle Mountain and Horse Mountain, and one mile further you pass by C-710 going south to Steamboat (62 miles). The road then travels below Sugarloaf and you begin following the Little Snake River at Slater (mile #17). After crossing Savery Creek, you enter Savery, 11 miles east of Baggs.

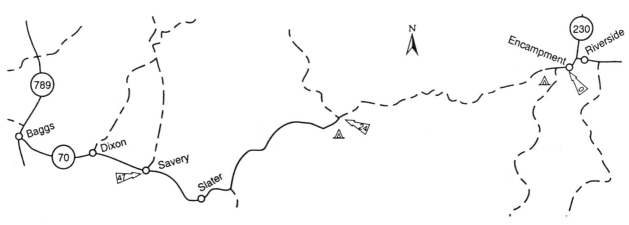

Trip Seven

Saratoga west to Dad on the Twin Grove - Cow Creek Butte Road

This trip begins by turning west off First Street in Saratoga and taking Bridge Street out of town. As you travel along on C-500, you can see Sheep Rock above the North Platte River to the north and to the northeast is Sheephead Mountain (below Elk Mountain). South of Elk Mountain is Coad Mountain, Pennock Mountain, and Kennaday Peak. To the east are the Snowy Range Mountains. (Nice view.)

The road follows along above Jack Creek to a junction (12 miles). Here you can take C-640 southeast, past Buck and Haines Reservoir, and then loop back to Saratoga. Continue west, across Jack Creek, for five more miles to the next junction. Here NF-452 goes south to the Jack Creek Campground.

Stay on C-500 and you cross Snow Draw, Willow Creek, and Spring Creek. After crossing Spring Creek, the road climbs up to Twin Grove. The road travels along the top for a bit and then drops down to a junction on Fish Creek. Here you can go south to Savery or to Dixon (see page 48).

Turn north and the road follows Fish Creek up to the next junction (three miles). Here you can continue north to Rawlins. Turn west on C-503 and the road goes down a hill (passing by a road going north toward Adams Reservoir) into Sage Basin and across South Fork Sage Creek. After about three miles, the road climbs back up to a junction on Miller Hill. Here C-503 turns south through McCarty Canyon and on over to Dixon (see page 50).

Turn west up the hill on the Miller Hill Road (BLM-3328). The road swings northwest along the top and past Sage Basin (on the north) and the Little Savery Creek drainage (on the south). Along here you get glimpses of Bakers Peak, Battle Mountain, and Columbus Peak to the south. You travel north for a bit and drop down to a junction where the Miller Road continues north.

Take the Muddy Creek Road (BLM-3306) to the northwest. After two miles, the road drops down a bit and turns southwest away from the Littlefield Creek drainage. The road then loops southeast and back to the northwest to a junction at Muddy Creek. Here the Muddy Creek Road continues northwest and cuts over to Bridger Pass and W-71 (see page 50).

Turn west across Muddy Creek on the Cow Butte Road (BLM-3308). After crossing the creek, the road climbs up through Canary Grove Draw to a small junction. Here the Rendle Road (BLM-3312) goes south toward Rendle Buttes.

Stay on the Cow Butte Road, west and then south, toward Cow Creek Butte. As the road goes out on a finger between Deep Gulch on the east and Garden Gulch on the west, you can see Battle Mountain to the southeast. The road swings almost all the way around the butte and then heads southwest. There are a couple of small side roads in this area, so stay on the main road heading southwest toward Flat Top Mountain. About eight miles from Cow Creek Butte, you cross Cow Creek, and two miles further you cross a small creek to a junction. Here the Willow Road (BLM-3305) turns northeast toward the Sand Hills area.

Stay west across Dry Cow Creek and to another junction. Here you can take the Horse Butte Road (BLM-3309) south to the roads on Browns Hill, or you can travel past Horse Butte to W-789 (mile #43).

Turn northwest for three miles and the road swings back to the southwest. (Here an unmarked road goes northeast to a well, so people traveling from W-789 to Saratoga need to turn southeast at this possible wrong turn.) You then travel southwest for about three miles to W-789 (mile #28) at Dad.

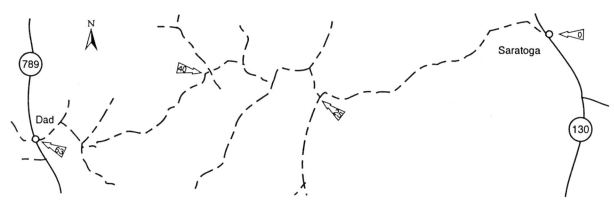

Trip Eight

The Browns Hill Road from Savery northeast to Saratoga

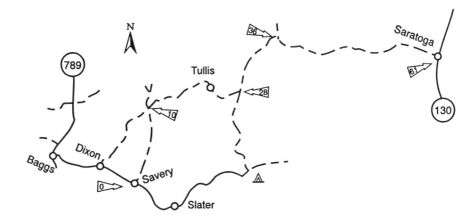

This trip begins by turning north off W-70 (mile #12) in Savery. After passing the Little Snake River Museum (nice place), the road climbs a hill and you can see Bakers Peak to the south, Columbus Peak to the southeast, and Battle Mountain to the east. One mile north of Savery, you come to junction. Here the road going northeast along Savery Creek loops back to W-70 north of Battle Mountain.

Stay to the north on C-501. (The marker was shot up pretty bad, but I think that's what it said. Poor thing!) You climb up a long hill where you can see Muddy Mountain off to the northwest. The road drops down a steep grade and heads north to the base of Browns Hill. The road then makes a long climb to the top and heads northwest to a junction. Here you can take C-503 south to Dixon.

Continue along the rim to the northwest on C-503 for one mile and you come to another junction. Here C-503 goes north through Mc-Carty Canyon. On this road you can go to Rawlins, Dad, or over to Saratoga.

Turn east off C-503 for one mile and the road swings back to the north again. The road continues to zig-zag across the top of Browns Hill and you travel above Coal Gulch to the northeast. Eight miles from the last junction, the road drops down to an area where Bird Gulch (from the west) and Coal Gulch join together at Savery Creek. (Nice place.) The road follows along the oxbow bends of Savery Creek and travels through a small valley for about two miles. You then leave the creek and make a long climb up the mountain.

The road travels southeast along the top to Tullis where it turns back to the northeast to a junction (three miles). Here you can see Dexter Peak to the east. At this junction, you can go south on the Aspen Alley Road back to Savery.

Turn north across Dirtyman Creek and you go over a hill to the East Fork Savery Creek. The road goes over another divide to Deep Gulch and then up and over to Truckdriver Creek and Smiley Meadow. As you climb over the next hill to North Fork Savery Creek, you can see Divide Peak to the east. After crossing North Fork Savery Creek, you follow along Fish Creek for a mile to the next junction. Here you can continue north to Rawlins on the Aspen Alley Road (see page 48).

Turn northeast on C-500 and the road climbs up the side of a hill to Twin Grove. Up here you can see Elk, Coad, and Pennock Mountains to the northeast and to the east is the Snowy Range. Kennaday Peak is between Pennock Mountain and the Snowy Range. The road drops down across Spring Creek and Willow Creek and then Snow Draw. Five miles from Twin Grove is a junction. Here you can turn south on NF-452 to Jack Creek Campground (eight miles).

Turn northeast and after five miles, you cross Jack Creek to another junction. Here C-640 goes southeast to Buck and Haines Reservoir and then loops around to Saratoga.

Continue up the hill and down again along Jack Creek. After about eight miles, you can see Sheep Rock to the north and to the northeast is Sheephead Mountain (northwest a bit of Elk Mountain). A bit further, you enter Saratoga on Bridge Street, about seven blocks west of First Street (W-130, mile #21).

Trip Nine

The Hog Park Loop Road from Riverside to Encampment

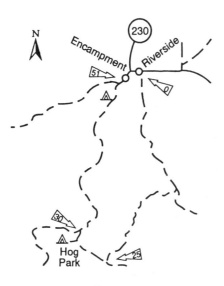

This trip begins by turning off W-230 at mile #101 east of Riverside. As you head south on the Blackhall Mountain Road (C-211), you can see Vulcan Mountain to the west, and above Baggot Rock to the north is Elk Mountain and Pennock Mountain. To the northeast is Kennaday Peak and to the east is Medicine Bow Peak and the Snowy Range Mountains. The road climbs up along Cottonwood Creek and crosses it after four miles. The road continues to climb to an overlook above Purgatory Gulch. Here you can see the Encampment River to the south. The trees here are spruce, fir, aspen, limber pine, and lodgepole pine.

Commissary Park and the trailhead into the Encampment River Wilderness.

You enter the forest boundary after one mile and begin traveling on NF-409 (beautiful overlooks along this drive). The road loops around and you begin traveling above the Dunkard Creek drainage and then above Etna Creek on the east side of the divide. The road turns back to the south where you can see Blackhall Mountain above Billie Creek. A bit further, you drop down to a junction. Here you can take NF-409 southeast to the Blackhall Lookout and Colorado #125.

Turn southwest on the Rim Road (NF-496) toward Hog Park Reservoir (15 miles). You cross a few tributaries of Billie Creek and after leaving that drainage, the road crosses Cascade Creek. Two miles further, you pass above the Box Canyon drainage and you can see Willow Mountain off to the west. After about three miles, the road drops down to the East Fork Encampment River. One mile after crossing the river, you come to a junction at Commissary Park, Colorado (a gravel road freeway). The road east (#80) goes to Cowdrey, Colorado (35 miles).

Turn west across the Encampment River on NF-496 and past the Encampment River Wilderness trailhead. After leaving the river, the road passes through some meadows, crosses South Fork Hog Park Creek, and goes by the Lake View Campground Road. Continue north past the dam and across Hog Park Creek to the next junction. Here you can take NF-550 southwest to Steamboat Springs (52 miles).

Take NF-550 north toward Encampment. The road climbs up the side of Willow Mountain where you cross Olson Creek and Brady Creek. The road continues to climb for a couple of miles and you come to a small park below Willow Mountain. Here you can see Kennaday, Pennack, and Elk Mountains to the north. To the east is Blackhall Mountain.

You then cross North Soldier Creek and the road drops down a bit to South Miners Creek. Two miles further, you cross North Fork Miners Creek and begin passing below Green Mountain to the Halfway House. Here you continue dropping down along Willow Creek to the North Fork Encampment River.

Two miles from the river crossing, you hit W-70 at mile #51. Here you can turn west, past the Bottle Creek Campground (100 yards), and travel over to Baggs (see page 51). Turn east for six miles to W-230 at Encampment.

Trip Ten

Woods Landing north to Centennial on the Fox Creek Road

This trip begins by turning off W-230 (mile #27) east of Woods Landing. The Fox Creek Road travels northwest along Fox Creek and through a small canyon for about one mile. This is a nice drive past cedar, ponderosa pine, spruce, and cottonwood trees. After crossing the creek, you begin following Owen Creek up the canyon for four about miles.

The road then travels through some mountain meadows and across the open top for three miles to a junction. Along this stretch you can see Medicine Bow Peak above the Centennial Ridge to the northwest, Jelm Mountain to the south, and Lake Mountain to the west. At the junction you can take NF-517 west to Owen Lake and Fox Park (see page 59). Continue north for two miles and you hit W-11 at mile #9. Here you can turn west to Albany and the roads to Keystone and Rob Roy Reservoir (see pages 56 and 58).

Turn north on W-11 and the road follows along the base of Sheep Mountain and the South Fork Little Laramie River for about six miles. Here the Dinwiddie Road (A-416) turns northwest and hits W-130 at mile #26. Continue on W-11 as it swings around the end of

Sheep Mountain and hits W-130 at mile #22. Here you can turn east to Laramie, or west across the Little Laramie River to Centennial (six miles).

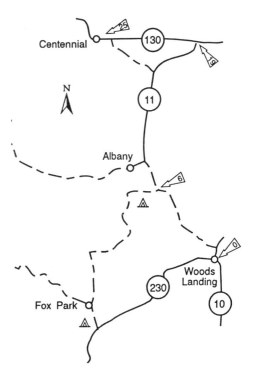

Centennial has one of the finest "scarecrow" police cars in the west!

Trip Eleven

Centennial west to Riverside on the Rob Roy Lake Road

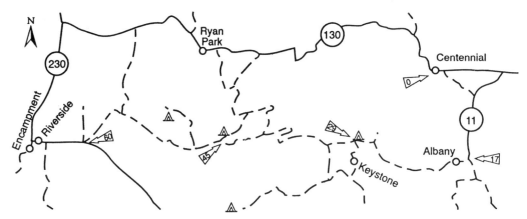

This trip begins by taking W-130 east from Centennial and crossing the North Fork Little Laramie River. Just after crossing the river, you pass by the Dinwiddie Road (A-46) going southeast. Stay on W-130 to the east and at mile #22 you cross the Little Laramie River to a junction. Here you can continue east to Laramie.

Turn south on W-11 and the road swings around the end of Sheep Mountain and follows along the Little Laramie River. At mile #3 the Dinwiddie Road comes back in from Centennial. Here you can see Medicine Bow Peak and Browns Peak rising above the Centennial Ridge and Valley. At mile #9 you come to a junction. Here you can take the Fox Creek Road to Woods Landing, Owen Lake, or Fox Park (see pages 55 and 59).

Continue on W-11 for two more miles to Albany. The pavement ends here and you begin traveling on NF-500. The road crosses the tracks and continues west up the side of Muddy Mountain (past lodgepole pine and a few aspen trees). After about two miles, you come to a couple of junctions. At the first junction, you can take NF-513 south to Dry Park and join NF-517 going to Fox Park. At the next junction (a half mile further on NF-500), you can take NF-542 southwest to Keystone (see page 58).

Continue west along Bird Creek on NF-500 and you begin seeing a few spruce and fir trees. After about three miles, you have a view of Medicine Bow Peak and Browns Peak in the Snowy Range Mountains to the north, and the Sierra Madre Mountains to the southwest. A bit further, you cross Douglas Creek at Rob Roy Reservoir and pass by NF-505 going north to

Cinnabar Park. The road goes by the Rob Roy Campground and one mile after crossing Elk Creek is a junction. Here you can take NF-543 south past the Holmes Campground to Keystone and Fox Park (see page 58).

Continue west on NF-500 toward the French Creek Campground (20 miles). You pass by NF-511 (going south to the Platte River or Fox Park), and after two more miles you come to an access trail to the Savage Run Wilderness. As you continue west, you have another good view of the Sierra Madre Mountains.

The road then makes a loop to the northeast (past a side road going east up the creek) and then back to the west, down along Mullen Creek. The trees in this area are spruce and fir. After three miles you come to another junction. Here you can take NF-225 up the hill to the north and hit W-130 near Ryan Park (see page 58).

Continue west on NF-500 toward the French Creek Campground. As the road drops down, you begin seeing more lodgepole pine and aspen trees. After five miles you come to a junction at the French Creek Campground. Here NF-206 goes back up the mountain and connects with NF-225 going to Ryan Park.

Stay on NF-500 to the west and you cross the creek and follow it past aspen, willow, cottonwood, and cedar. After three miles you come to a junction. Here you can take the side road north to Bennett Peak and the Platte River. At this junction, you can see Bennett Peak to the northwest, Barcus Peak to the west, and Blackhall Mountain to the southwest.

Stay to the west and you leave the French Creek drainage. The road drops down on C-660 (continuation of NF-500) to the North Platte River below. After crossing the river, the road travels below Barcus Peak and heads northwest, past Bennett Peak, to another junction. Here you can take C-203 over the bridge and travel north along Brush Creek to W-130 at mile #61 east of Saratoga.

Continue west along the river and then southwest for about three miles. Just after passing C-102 (going north), you hit US-230 at mile #104 east of Riverside. Here you can see Baggot Rocks to the north and to the northeast is Kennaday Peak and Pennock Mountain.

"Dead-out fires", don't leave your campsite without one!

Trip Twelve

The Keystone-French Creek Road from Fox Park north to Ryan Park

This trip begins by turning off US-230 at mile #36. As you head north toward Fox Park on NF-512, the road passes by the Evens and Miller Lake Campgrounds. The trees in this area are lodgepole pine. After going through Fox Park, you come to a junction. Here you can take NF-517 across the tracks and over to Owen Lake and Albany (see page 59).

Stay on NF-512 to the west and after about one mile the road swings northwest where you begin seeing a few spruce trees. You pass by NF-509 (looping around to rejoin this road after a couple of miles) and the road makes a sharp turn toward Keystone. One and half miles further, you cross Lake Creek to a junction (100 yards after NF-509 rejoins NF-512). Here NF-512 goes west to the North Platte River (17 miles). On this road you can also cross over on NF-511 and join this route near Holmes Campground.

Turn northwest on NF-543 and the road follows along Douglas Creek and crosses Muddy Creek after one mile (nice drive here). Three miles further, you pass the Bobby Thompson Campground and cross Little Beaver Creek to a junction at Keystone. Here NF-542 turns east toward Albany.

Stay on NF-543 to the north and the road continues along Douglas Creek. After crossing Keystone Creek, you pass by NF-111 (going west to the Platte River or back to Fox Park) and climb up to Rob Roy Reservoir. The road follows along the west shoreline and after crossing Dave Creek and Bear Creek is a junction near the Holmes Campground. Here you can take NF-500 east, past the reservoir, to Albany (see page 56).

Don't expect to see any slap-stick cops at Keystone, Wyoming.

Turn west on NF-500 toward the French Creek Campground (20 miles). You pass by NF-511 again and two miles further is an access trail to the Savage Run Wilderness. As the road continues to the west, you get a good view of the Sierra Madre Mountains.

The road then makes a loop to the northeast (past a side road going east up the creek) and then back to the west, down along Mullen Creek. The trees in this area are spruce and fir. After three miles you come to another junction. Here NF-500 continues west along the creek toward the French Creek Campground and Riverside (see page 56).

Turn north, up the hill, on NF-225. The road makes a zig-zag to the west and east as you climb up to South French Creek. Here NF-236 continues east along the creek. Stay on NF-225 for one mile to the next junction. Here NF-206 goes back down to the French Creek Campground (three miles).

Stay on NF-225 going up the hill and you have a big view of the creek below and Blackhall Mountain to the southwest. After four miles, you cross Middle French Creek and in two more miles, you come to the last junction. Here you can take NF-227 northeast along the creek to W-130 at mile #49 (four miles).

Stay northwest on NF-225 and across North French Creek. After one mile you begin following above Barret Creek and four miles further, you hit W-130 at mile #53, just east of Ryan Park and the Ryan Park Campground.

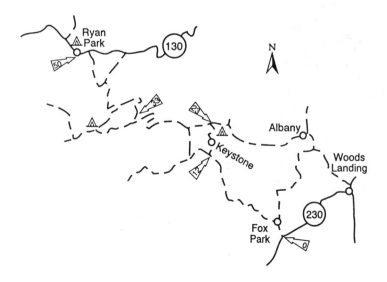

Trip Thirteen

The Albany Road from Centennial south to Fox Park

This trip begins by going east from Centennial on W-130 and crossing the North Fork Little Laramie River. Just after crossing the river, the Dinwiddie Road (A-46) turns southeast. Stay on W-130 and at mile #22 you cross the Little Laramie River to a junction. Here you can continue east to Laramie.

Turn south on W-11 and the road swings around the end of Sheep Mountain and follows along the Little Laramie River. At mile #3 the Dinwiddie Road comes back in from Centennial. Here you can see Medicine Bow Peak and Browns Peak rising above the Centennial Ridge and Valley. At mile #9 is another junction. Here you can continue on W-11 to Albany and Keystone (see page 56).

Turn south on the Fox Creek Road to the next junction in two miles. Here you can continue south on the Fox Creek Road to Woods Landing (see page 55).

Turn southwest on NF-517 toward Owen Lake and away from Sheep Mountain. The road climbs along a small creek and passes by stands of aspen. After crossing the tracks, you begin traveling past lodgepole pine and a few limber pine trees. One mile further, you come to another junction. Here you can take NF-540 to Owen Lake (two miles).

Stay on NF-517 and the road makes a couple of sharp turns and then heads southwest again. Along here you have a couple of nice overlooks of the Centennial Valley and the Snowy Range Mountains. The road then travels through Dry Park to a junction. Here NF-513 goes northwest for about two miles to the French Creek Road.

Continue southwest on NF-517 and you begin following Lake Creek. (Nice drive.) After two miles, you turn south across the creek and begin following Collins Creek. After crossing this creek the second time, you leave it and follow the tracks south to a junction at Fox Park (two miles). Here you can take NF-512 northwest to Keystone and then over to either Ryan Park or Riverside (see pages 56 and 58). Turn south on NF-517, through Fox Park and past the Miller Lake and Evens Creek Campgrounds, to US-230 at mile #36.

A change in snow conditions forces Jackie to alter the basic molecular composition (rewax) on her "skinny skis". Metal edges are almost a necessity on the wind packed snow above timberline.

Trip Fourteen

Ryan Park north to Elk Mountain on the Brush Creek Road

This trip begins by turning off W-130 at mile #56 west of Ryan Park. As you head north on the Brush Creek Road, you pass the South Brush Creek Campground and go by lodgepole pine and a few aspen trees. Two miles from W-130, you cross North Brush Creek and to the Lincoln Park Campground. Here you begin seeing spruce and fir trees. Three miles further is a junction.

If you take option NF-261 northwest (Elk Mountain 35 miles), the road crosses Middle Cedar Creek after four miles. The road then swings around Kennaday Peak to Cedar Pass (four more miles). From there, the road turns east and drops down across Rankin Creek and Lee Creek to NF-201 (seven miles from the pass). This road goes south back to the Brush Creek Road. From that junction, you continue on NF-261 across Pass Creek and East Fork Pass Creek. There you travel seven miles to Turpin Creek and the Medicine Bow River and join NF-101 south of the Bow Campground.

Back at the main junction, stay northeast on NF-100 (Elk Mountain 29 miles) and you cross Fish Creek in one mile. Here the road passes by the Kennaday Lookout Road and the cutoff road (NF-201) to Pass Creek. Stay on NF-100 and you continue to climb along North Brush Creek.

Two miles from the cutoff road, you begin traveling along the top and pass several small parks and clearings. (Nice area.) A few miles further is a tornado blowdown area, and you can see Pine Butte to the east and Kennaday Peak to the west. The road now heads north to Turpin Reservoir.

Below the reservoir, the road drops down along Turpin Creek and passes by the Tie Hack Campsite. After crossing the creek you get a good view to the west of Elk, Coad, and Pennock Mountain (north to south). You then pass by the Long Lake Road and drop down a hill to the Bow River Campground. After crossing the Medicine Bow River, you come to a junction. Here you can take the Sand Lake Road to Stillwater Park, Arlington, or Centennial (see page 61).

Turn north on NF-101 (Elk Mountain 15 miles) and the road drops down along the river for two miles to a junction at the Bow River Work Station. Here the Cedar Pass Road (NF-261) turns west and then south, back to Ryan Park. Stay north on C-101 (NF-101) and after a couple of miles you can look back to the southwest and see Kennaday Peak. To the southeast is Medicine Bow Peak and Browns Peak.

As you continue north, you can see Laramie Peak to the far northeast, the Freezeout Mountains to the north, and the Shirley Mountains to the northwest. On top of the bench above Elk Mountain (city), C-3 turns east to I-80 at exit #260. Turn northwest down the hill and across the river to Elk Mountain.

The Wood Frog is a relic species left behind in the Snowy Range and Big Horn Mountains during the retreat of the glaciers from the last ice age (about 10,000 years ago).

Trip Fifteen

Arlington south to Centennial on the Sand Lake Road

I wasn't allowed to disclose the identity of these hunters, or the location of this hunting camp in the Snowy Range. (I think a couple of the hunters were married with children.)

This trip begins by taking I-80 exit #272 to Arlington. You head west along the south side of I-80 and go past the Rock Creek Trail to the top of a hill. Here you turn southwest on the Sand Lake Road. The road swings south and you pass below Conical Peak (off to the east) after about two miles. The road travels up a small valley lined with aspen trees and a bit further you begin traveling past lodgepole pine on NF-111.

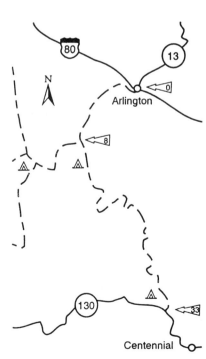

One mile after entering the national forest you can see Elk Mountain above White Rock to the west. You now begin seeing limber pine and fir trees. About three miles further is a junction. Here NF-120 turns west and joins the Brush Creek Road (NF-101) near the Bow River Campground.

Continue south on NF-111 toward Sand Lake (seven miles). About one mile from the junction, you can look west across the clear cuts and see Elk Mountain, Coad Mountain, Pennock Mountain, and Kennaday Peak (north to south). To the east is Rock Mountain. As the road travels south, you pass by

NF-113 going southeast toward Crater Lake, and in two miles you come to another junction. Here you can take NF-101 northwest for eight miles to the Bow River Campground. There you can go to either Stillwater Park, I-80 at Elk Mountain, or W-130 at Ryan Park (see pages 59 and 60).

Turn southeast on NF-101 and after passing by the other end of the Crater Lake Road, you come to the Deep Creek Campground and the side road to Sand Lake. Stay on the main road to the east and across Deep Creek.

The road then swings northeast above the Deep Creek drainage, and you can see Lookout Mountain to the north. As the road loops back to the southeast above North Fork Rock Creek, you can see Coyote Hill to the east. After crossing North Fork Rock Creek, the road makes another large loop to the northeast and back to the southeast above the Rock Creek drainage. Three miles further you cross Trail Creek.

Four miles after crossing Trail Creek is the North Fork Observation Point. Here you can see Medicine Bow Peak and Browns Peak to the west and to the northwest is Rock Creek Knoll. From this overlook the road drops down to the North Fork Little Laramie River and Campground. You then cross the river and continue down to W-130 (mile #31) west of Centennial.

Trip Sixteen

Laramie to Woods Landing the hard way: Sand Creek Pass

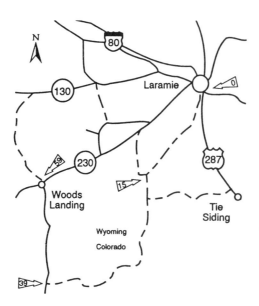

This trip begins by taking I-80 exit #313 to Laramie. Turn south on W-287 for about a half mile and then turn west on Blackfoot Street. You follow the pavement around the bend and then south on Fort Sanders Drive. After about two miles, you turn west across the tracks and then south again on the Sand Creek Road (A-34). Here you can see the Laramie Range to the east. To the west is Sheep Mountain and the Snowy Range Mountains, and to the southwest is Jelm Mountain.

After four miles you cross Five-mile Creek and begin traveling southwest across the Laramie Basin. One mile further, you pass by a small lake off to the north and you can see Red Buttes to the southeast. You pass by the next road (two miles) going north, and two miles further is a small junction. Here the road to the Hutton Lake Wildlife Refuge turns west.

Chimney Rock at the Wyoming-Colorado border.

Stay on the main road as it swings south of Hutton Lake to another junction at Antelope Creek (four miles). Here you can take the Brubaker Lane (A-37) west for one mile and then north along Sand Creek. That road then crosses the Laramie River and joins W-230 at mile #12.

Turn south at Antelope Junction and you pass by Lone Tree Reservoir #1 and #2 (off to the west) after about three miles. You then come to another junction. Here you can take the Sportsman Lake Road (A-316) east across Antelope Creek (three miles) and Lone Tree Creek (two more miles). That road then swings around part of Boulder Ridge and goes by Sportsman Lake. The road then crosses Government Creek and Willow Creek and hits W-287 at mile #416 north of Tie Siding (14 miles total trip).

Turn southwest on the Sand Creek Road and after crossing Sand Creek, you pass by a road (A-322) going west that ends on private land. Continue south and the road travels through a beautiful area of swirled and convoluted sandstone. The road follows along the creek again and heads toward Chimney Rock (very nice drive here).

As you pass below Chimney Rock, you enter Colorado. (It's still a nice drive though.) The road now climbs up Boulder Ridge to a junction (six miles). Here you can go southeast on L80C to Fort Collins (64 miles).

Turn west toward Sand Creek Pass on L80C (three miles). After going over the pass, the road drops back down again (I guess that's the way passes work) and follows along Jimmy Creek. You go by the Red Feather Lakes Road and come to a junction on the Laramie River. Here you can go south to Colorado-14 (21 miles). The road continuing west loops past Glendevey and rejoins the main road south to Colorado-14.

Turn north toward the Snowy Range Mountains on L103 and along the Laramie River. After about six miles, you pass by the Hohnholz Lakes and five miles further, you hit pavement on W-10. From here the road continues to follow the river and travels along the base of Jelm Mountain. Ten miles from the state line, you cross the river at Woods Landing and hit W-230 at mile #28.

Trip Seventeen

McFadden south to Laramie via Diamond Lake - Bamforth Lake

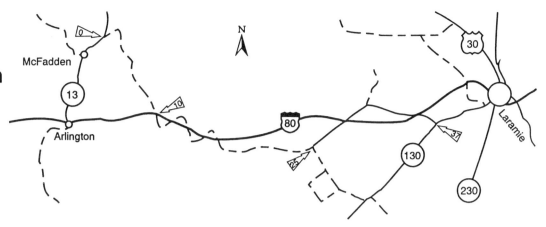

This trip begins by turning off W-13 at mile #9 east of McFadden. You head east on C-15 and after climbing to the top of the hill, you can see Laramie Peak to the northeast and Elk Mountain to the southwest. The road travels across the top for a mile and then turns south, down to Coal Bank Creek.

The road climbs back on top again and after about three miles, you pass between Diamond Lake on the west and King Reservoir on the east. You then cross Jimmy Creek and Dutton Creek and after three miles the road goes under I-80 at exit #279.

The Wyoming Toad (Bufo hemiophrys baxteri) is found only in the Laramie Basin and is currently listed as a Rare and Endangered Species. This little critter was the main focus of my graduate studies at the University of Wyoming.

Here you continue southeast on C-15 and after crossing the county line, you begin traveling on the Dutton Creek Road (A-57). The road crosses Cooper Creek and then goes under I-80 again. You climb up Bengough Hill and after about three miles, the road goes under I-80 one more time.

The road crosses Four-mile Creek and climbs up a bit where you can see James Lake to the northeast. After crossing Seven-mile Creek, you hit pavement and travel across the Laramie Basin to a junction. Here you can see Signal Hill to the north and to the northwest is Seven-mile Hill. At this junction, you can take the Hunt Road (A-59) north to I-80 at exit #290.

Continue on the pavement for three miles and you join W-12 at a junction. Here you can see Sheep Mountain and the smaller Jelm Mountain to the south. At this junction, you can take the Mandel Lane (A-57) south across the Little Laramie River and hit W-130 at mile #14 across from the Big Hollow. On this route you can also take the McGill Lane (A-513) one mile west to the Millbrook Road. This road will hit W-130 at mile #20 across from Porter Lake.

Continue east on W-12 (Herrick Lane) and at mile #10 you cross the Little Laramie River. The road then goes under I-80 to a junction at mile #6. Here you can take Sprague Lane (A-54) north to the Little Laramie River, or you can go east on A-53 toward Carroll Lake.

Continue on W-12 and you pass by Alsop Lake on the south and Lore Lake on the east. At mile #5, you can see Bamforth Lake Wildlife Refuge in Big Basin on the east and Knadler Lake off to the south. At mile #3 you go under I-80 (for the last time) and after climbing a small hill, you hit W-130 at mile #5 west of Laramie.

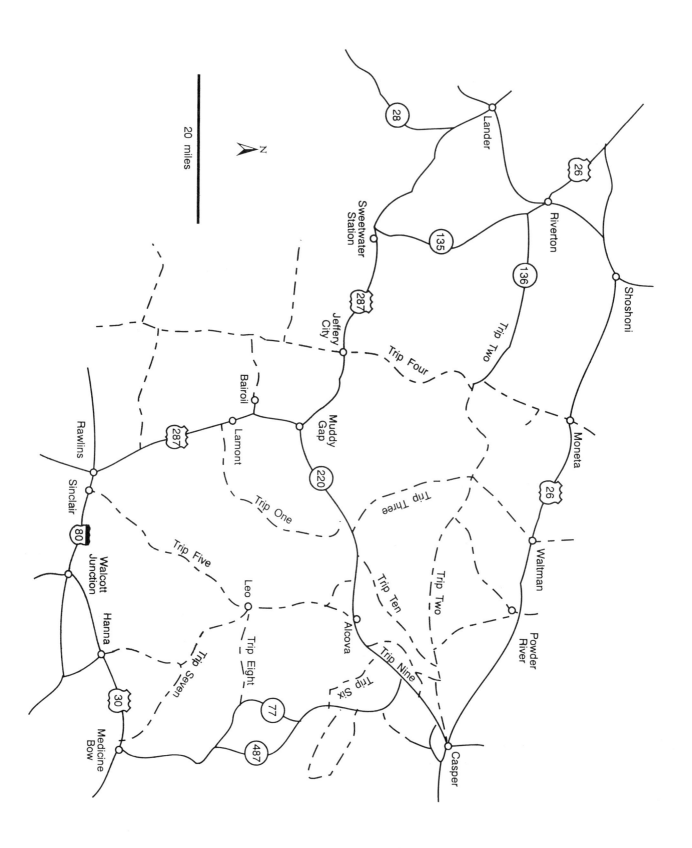

Trip One

The Buzzard Road from Lamont northeast to US-220

With the sand dunes and Ferris Mountains as a backdrop, the ghost town of Ferris is like a setting from an old western movie.

This trip begins by turning off US-287 at mile #29 south of Lamont. As you head east toward the Seminoe Mountains, you can see Bull Springs Rim to the west, Separation Flats to the south, Green Mountain to the northwest, and the Ferris Mountains to the northeast. After traveling past several OFR's, is a junction six miles from the highway.

Turn southeast under the powerlines and then east again for one mile to a small spring. Stay to the east on the main road and you begin traveling through some vegetated sand dunes. (Note: This area from the dunes to the mouth of the canyon below requires a high clearance vehicle.) Seven miles further is Ferris. Here you can see the Haystacks to the south and the Seminoe Mountains to the east. To the northeast is the top of Bear Mountain and to the north are the Ferris Mountains. (This area is just plain pretty.)

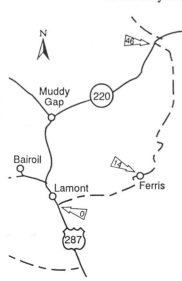

Leaving Ferris, you head northeast toward the gap between Bear Mountain and Ferris Mountain. The road passes by some small lakes and sand dunes for the next five miles and enters a beautiful little canyon. Here you

follow Sand Creek for about three miles to the mouth of the canyon.

After leaving the canyon you have a great view of the Pedro Mountains. The road heads northeast along the side of a hill and then drops down to a ranch (two miles). Just past the ranch you go up a steep hill where the road turns west and then north again.

As the road travels north along Arkansas Creek, you can see Bear Mountain to the southeast and the Ferris Mountains to the southwest. On the west side of the road is the Arkansas Basin and on the east side is Castle Basin (below the Pedro Mountains).

About 13 miles from the ranch, the road crosses Arkansas Creek. Here you can see the Shirley Mountains to the far southeast. Behind the Pedro Mountains to the east, is the Laramie Range. The road then passes by the eastern edge of Sentinel Rocks and crosses the Sweetwater River (five miles from Arkansas Creek).

After crossing the river, you head northwest and hit US-220 at mile #65, between Alcova and Muddy Gap Junction. (The county road on this end is N-410.) From here you can see Independence Rock and Devils Gate to the southwest (below the Ferris Mountains). To the northwest are the Granite Mountains and to the east is Steamboat Rock.

Trip Two

Casper to Riverton on the Poison Spider- Gas Hills Road

This trip begins by going west on the Poison Spider Road (N-201) on the west side of Casper. You can access this road by turning off W-220 at mile #111 and taking the Robertson Road (N-305) north for two miles. You can also turn off US-20 at mile #6.5 and take the Zero Road (N-202) southwest for one mile. You then turn south on the Robertson Road for one mile to the Poison Spider Road.

As you travel west on the Poison Spider Road, you pass by N-204 and N-205 going north to the Zero Road. Three miles further west, the pavement ends at a small junction. Here N-206 also goes north to the Zero Road and US-20 (mile #13).

Continue west on N-201 and the road passes by an interpretive site at Emigrant Gap (two miles) and two miles further, another junction. Here you can take N-306 south and join N-308 going to Bessemer Bend and W-220 (mile #105). Also at the junction, you can take the Zero Road (N-202) northeast to Casper.

Turn west, past the Poison Spider School, and after two miles you come to the next junction. Here the Ryan Hill Road (N-319) turns south. This route goes past Oil Mountain and hits W-220 (mile #73) west of Alcova (see page 75). At this junction you can see the western end of Casper Mountain and Coal Mountain to the southeast. To the south is Bessemer Mountain and the peaks on the horizon, to the southwest, are the Pedro Mountains.

Stay on N-201 and the road goes by Oil Mountain (off to the south) and then travels through an area of broken table rock. The road then crosses Poison Spider Creek and three miles further, you come to another junction where the pavement ends. Here the Powder River Road turns northwest around Pine

Mountain to US-20 at either Natrona at mile #30 or Powder River at mile #38.

As you continue west on N-201, the road follows along the creek and passes several small lakes and a hogback ridge. You then begin to follow a ridge (off to the south) and head toward the Rattlesnake Range. Sixteen miles after crossing Poison Spider Creek, you come to a small junction. Here N-320 turns south and ends at Horse Heaven.

Stay to the west and after seven more miles, you pass by an OFR running north and south. Continue west past some outbuildings and toward Garfield Peak in the Rattlesnake Mountains. The road travels along for about five more miles and crosses Stinking Water Creek. Along here you have a terrific view of Snider Basin below Garfield Peak to the south. To the north you can see the Bighorn Mountains and to the northwest is Lysite Mountain. After a couple of miles, N-211 turns north to Powder River and US-20 (23 miles).

Stay on the Poison Spider Road and you cross several small creeks and go by Fales Rocks (off to the north) after four miles. The road then crosses Stone Cabin Creek (four more miles) and passes between a series of hogbacks on the north and the Rattlesnake Range on the south to a junction. Here you can take the Dry Creek Road north along the South Fork Powder River to Waltman and US-20 at mile #51 (see page 68).

Turn west on the Gas Hills Road (N-212) and after three miles you cross Deer Creek and leave the Rattlesnake Range. To the far west are the Wind River Mountains. Just after crossing the creek is another junction. Here you can take the Dry Creek Road (N-321) south to W-220 at mile #67 (see page 68).

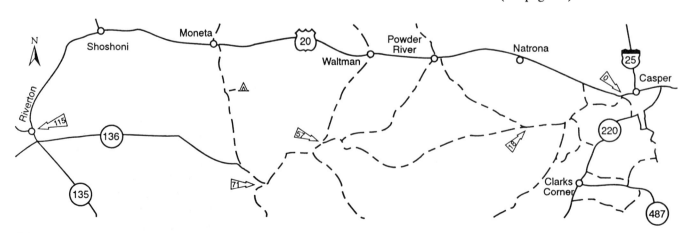

Stay on the Gas Hills Road and it enters a mining area for the next ten miles. After winding around through the mining area, you join W-136 at a junction. Here you can take the Ore Road, west and then south, through Muskrat Basin. That road then climbs over the Beaver Divide and passes through the Granite Mountains to Jeffery City (see page 69).

Turn northwest on W-136 and go past Sarcophagus Butte. After about six miles (at mile #38), you come to another junction. Here the Castle Garden Road turns north to Moneta and US-20 at mile #78 (see page 69 for this great little trip).

Continuing on W-136, you cross Muskrat Creek at mile #37 and at mile #35 your cross Mahoney Draw. Here you can see the Beaver Divide off to the south. At mile #29, you cross Horseshoe Creek and the road swings west across Conant Creek (mile #23).

After traveling west for 12 miles, you enter the Wind River Indian Reservation. To the north you can see where the Wind River Canyon cuts through the Owl Creek and Bridger Mountains. To the far east are the Gas Hills and to the south is the Beaver Divide. At mile #1 you pass by W-135 going south to US-287 and you cross the Little Wind River. The road then joins W-789 south of Riverton.

My good friends from the Taucher Ranch, Molly, Bret, Amy, and little Betsy got together for this photo to say, "Please remember that kids are found on dirt roads too!"

Trip Three

The Dry Creek Road from Waltman south to W-220

Sometimes called "a horny toad", the Eastern Short-horned Lizard is common throughout most of Wyoming. These cute little critters are often collected as pets by young children, but they really do much better when left to roam in the wilds on their own.

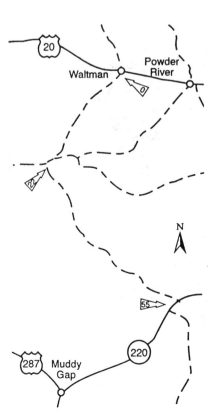

This trip begins by turning off US-20 at mile #51 in Waltman. As you head south toward the Rattlesnake Hills on N-212, you can see Pine Mountain to the east and Lysite Mountain to the north. After crossing Sand Draw (one mile), the road swings southwest and begins following the South Fork Powder River. About 13 miles from Waltman, you pass Wild Horse Butte (off to the east) and cross the river.

Take the pavement through the Coal Hills and, after passing through Hoff Gap, you can see Maverick Butte off to the west. The road then travels south for three miles to a junction where the pavement ends. Here you can take the Poison Spider Road east to Casper (see page 66).

Turn west on the Gas Hills Road (N-212) and after about three miles you cross Deer Creek. One mile west of Deer Creek is another junction. Here you can take the Gas Hills Road west to the Castle Garden/Ore Road and W-136 (see pages 66 and 69).

Turn south on the Dry Creek Road (N-321) and you follow along Deer Creek for a couple of miles and cross Holiday Creek. The road then climbs for the next three miles to where you can see French Rocks to the east.

The road then leaves the Deer Creek drainage and drops over to Dry Creek. About five miles further south, you pass by Bald Mountain and then Goat Mountain (off to the east). As the road leaves the Rattlesnake Hills, you can see the Green Mountains, above the peaks of the Granite Mountains, to the southwest.

The road follows along Dry Creek for about ten miles and then crosses it. You then travel southeast for 11 miles to W-220 at mile #67. Here you can see the Granite Mountains to the west. To the southwest is Independence Rock, Devil's Gate, and the Ferris Mountains. To the south are the Pedro Mountains and to the southeast is Steamboat Rock and Steamboat Lake.

Trip Four

Moneta to Jeffery City on the Castle Garden - Ore Road

This trip begins by turning off US-20 at mile #78 just east of Moneta. As you head south on the Castle Garden Road, you pass by the Buck Camp Road going southeast. Stay on the main road southwest. Along this stretch you can see the Bighorn Mountains to the northeast, Lysite Mountain to the north, and Cooper Mountain to the northwest.

After about eight miles you hit the top of the Moneta Divide. Here the Wind River Range is to the west, the Owl Creek Mountains are northwest, and the Beaver Divide is around to the south. Below the divide you begin traveling through some shallow depressions and soap holes called the Buffalo Wallows. Fifteen miles south of Moneta is a junction. Here a side road to Castle Gardens turns east for six miles. (Take this journey! The road travels along the base of some bluffs and fractured rock. The jumbled rock figures, broken country, and twisted trees are fantastic and builds a certain amount of anticipation of what the gardens will look like. The road ends at a picnic area and you will not be disappointed. The raw beauty and power of this site will not soon leave you!)

Continuing south from the Castle Garden turnoff, the road follows along Muskrat Creek for about four miles and then winds around a small hill. Up here you can see the Gas Hills to the southeast. The road then drops down for one mile and hits W-136 at mile #38. Here you can turn west to Riverton and W-789 (see page 66).

Turn southeast and after passing by Sarcophagus Butte is a junction at mile #44. Here you can turn northeast on the Gas Hills Road and connect with either the Dry Creek Road to Waltman, or the Poison Spider Road to Casper (see pages 66 and 68).

Turn southwest on the Ore Road and the road travels through a mining area for about two miles. The road then swings south and after five miles you begin traveling through Muskrat Basin (below Beaver Rim, stretching from the east, around to the south, and over to the west).

On top of the divide you can see Crooks Gap to the south (Crooks Mountain is on the west side and the Green Mountains are on the east side). To the west is the top of Tin Cup Mountain and back to the north are the Bighorn Mountains and Owl Creek Mountains. If you look across Black Rock Creek to the southeast you can see the peaks of the Granite Mountains. Behind them in the distance are the Ferris Mountains. (Nice view.)

The road begins to drop down a bit and you can see where the creek runs through Black Rock Gap off to the east. Further down the road you begin traveling past the domed hills of the Granite Mountains. Along here you get a better view of Crooks Gap, with Crooks Peak (small flat top) on the west side and Sheep Mountain (broad and rounded) on the east side. After crossing the Sweetwater River, the road goes by a small mine site and you enter Jeffery City on the Ore Road (US-287, mile #23).

The side road to Castle Garden is well worth the trip!

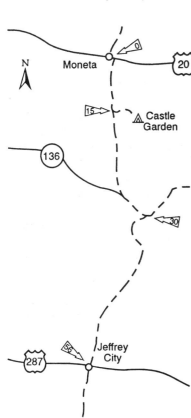

Trip Five

Pathfinder south from W-220 to Sinclair

This trip begins by turning off W-220 at mile #81 between Muddy Gap Junction and Alcova. As you head south on N-409 (toward Pathfinder Reservoir), you can see Pyramid Peak in the Pedro Mountains to the south, the Ferris Mountains to the southwest, the Granite Mountains to the west, and to the northeast is Flat Top and Casper Mountain. After about four miles, a side road turns west to Bishop Point and part of the Pathfinder National Wildlife Refuge.

Stay to the south and the road travels through an area of lichen covered rocks and juniper trees. The road drops down the hill past Swede Spring to a junction at an interpretive area. Here you can go down to the marina and recreation area, or you can loop back to Bishop Point (six miles).

Turn toward Alcova Dam on N-408 and the road winds down through the switchbacks where you have a nice view of the North Platte River and Pathfinder Dam. This scenic area is lined with cottonwood, willow, and juniper trees and contains a variety of birdlife.

The road leaves the river after a half mile and you begin following along the edge of Fremont Canyon. At the next junction, the tunnel road turns off to the power plant. If you get out and knock around here a bit, you can hear wrens singing in the gorge and you'll probably see some marmots and rock climbers (human).

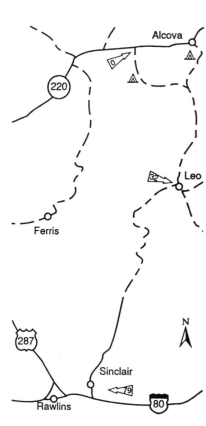

Turn south across the bridge and away from the river. The road climbs up to an overlook of Alcova Reservoir and another junction. Here you can go north on N-407 (along the edge of Alcova Reservoir) and loop back to W-220 at mile #87 at Alcova.

Turn south on N-407 toward the Miracle Mile. After three miles, you cross the county line and begin traveling on C-291. The road then crosses Canyon Creek (four miles) and the pavement ends. After a few miles, the road swings southwest a bit and you can see The Chimneys and Heath Peak to the near southwest (to the west is Pyramid Peak). Along here you can also see the Shirley Mountains to the south and the Seminoe Mountains to the southwest. A couple of miles down the road, you pass by Dome Rock off to the east.

About four miles from Dome Rock, the road crosses Sage Creek to a junction at Leo. Here you can take C-291 south to US-30 at Hanna or Medicine Bow. You can also take the cutoff through Shirley Basin to W-77 (see pages 72 and 73).

Turn southwest toward Seminoe Dam on C-351 and at the Miracle Mile is another junction. Here you can take the road south to Kortes Dam (dead end), or you can follow the river north back to Pathfinder Reservoir and Sage Creek.

Stay west across the river and the road climbs along Hamilton Creek and through the Seminoe Mountains. (Nice drive.) The road winds around through the mountains and passes numerous rocky craigs. Along here you see chokecherry, aspen, cedar, limber pine, and ponderosa pine trees. As you travel down Morgan Creek on the other side of the divide, the road swings back to the southwest. After two miles a side road continues down to an overlook and Seminoe Dam.

Turn south toward the state park and you climb up a steep hill to an overlook of Seminoe Reservoir. Here you can see Elk Mountain to the south. As you leave the park, you begin traveling on pavement again and the road passes by some sand dunes (stretching east from Rock Springs). You now begin traveling toward the Haystack Mountains through the northeastern edge of the Great Divide Basin.

The road continues southwest across the arid flats for about 15 miles where it drops down along the North Platte River. You travel through a canyon lined with fragmented boulders and rimrock (Fort Steele Breaks) for three miles to the Dugway Recreation Site. The road leaves the river and eight miles further you enter Sinclair (I-80, exit #219).

Trip Six

The Stock Trail Road from Bates Hole to Government Bridge

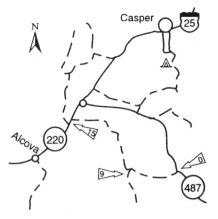

This trip begins by turning off W-487 at mile #57. As you head west on the Bates Hole Stock Trail (N-403), you can see the white topped Twin Buttes to the east. After crossing Stinking Creek, the road climbs up a bit and you can see Bear Mountain, Horse Peak, and Chalk Mountain to the south. The road then turns north toward Casper Mountain and Bessemer Mountain and passes Haystack Butte.

After passing the butte, the road turns back to the west (toward Clarkson Hill, white bluff off in the distance) and drops down into a basin. Three miles further, you pass by the Bolton Creek EEA Road and cross Bolton Creek to a junction. Here you can turn south for one mile to another junction. There you can take the Spindle Top Road (N-405) along Bear Creek, or continue south toward Bear Mountain on the Bolton Creek Road. (These roads join each other near Bear Mountain.)

Turn northwest on the Bolton Creek Road (N-404) and the road travels between Bolton Creek on the north and Bear Creek on the south. After about three miles you cross Bolton Creek again and hit W-220 at mile #95, just north of Government Bridge. Here you can see the Pedro Mountains to the south and Bessemer Mountain to the north.

Smeagle and Black Irene try to dissipate solar radiation at the Bolton Creek bridge.

Trip Seven

Hana and Medicine Bow north to the Miracle Mile

This route has two starting points. **Trip number one begins** by turning off US-30 at mile #252. Here you take W-72 north for one mile to Hanna. After crossing the tracks, you turn east for a half mile to Jefferson Street. Turn north on Jefferson Street (C-291). As you leave Hanna, the road travels through a mining area and the pavement ends after three miles. You continue through the mining area for another five miles and travel through Hanna Draw to the Medicine Bow River (four more miles). After crossing the river, the road follows along Troublesome Creek to a junction with C-270 from Medicine Bow.

Trip number two begins by turning off US-30 at mile #269 west of Medicine Bow. As you head north on C-121, you can see the Snowy Range Mountains to the south, Elk Mountain to the southwest, and to the north are the Freezeout Mountains. The road passes Allen Lake and swings northwest toward the Shirley Mountains.

After a couple of miles, you pass by a road going north and you can see Pine Butte behind Fossil Ridge to the northeast. The road then crosses Pine Draw and drops down below Wildcat Top to the Medicine Bow River (10 miles from the highway). Three miles from the river crossing is a junction. Here C-121 turns north and goes past Beer Mug Mountain to Difficulty.

Continue west on C-270 and across Difficulty Creek. After five miles (and passing by two ranch roads going north), you come to a junction with C-291 from Hanna at Troublesome Creek.

Now that both routes have joined, you turn north on C-291 and cross the creek. One mile further, you go by a road continuing north. Stay west and the road travels along a razorback ridge (part of Schneider Ridge) for about 10 miles. As the road turns north, you can see Seminoe Reservoir to the west and the Seminoe Mountains off to the northwest. The road climbs Schneider Ridge and drops down to the Austin Creek School.

After crossing Austin Creek, the road swings around the end Horseshoe Ridge and begins to climb up a bit. At the top, a small road turns west along the ridge and toward Seminoe Reservoir.

Stay on the main road north and you go through a pass between the Shirley Mountains and the Seminoe Mountains. Here you lose sight of Elk Mountain to the south, but you can now see the Pedro Mountains to the north. To the far northwest are the Granite Mountains. About three miles further, you cross Lost Creek and in four miles are two junctions at Leo. Along this stretch you can now see the Ferris Mountains to the west.

At the first junction you can take the road east and travel past the Shirley Mountains and Freezeout Mountains to W-77 at mile #132 (see page 73). Continue north for one mile to the second junction. Here you can go north on C-291 to W-220 at Alcova.

Turn west on C-351 for four miles to the Miracle Mile on the North Platte River. From here you can travel through the Seminoe Mountains to I-80 at Sinclair (see page 70).

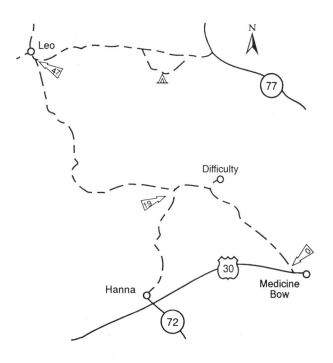

A photo of a snow storm in Shirley Basin.

Trip Eight

The Miracle Mile cutoff to W-77

Performing a simple operation like this required only a few instruments and a local anes- thetic for Black Irene. See page 135 for a more complicated surgical procedure.

This short trip begins at the Miracle Mile on North Platte River. You head east away from the river and the Seminoe Mountains on C-351 for four miles to a junction at Leo. Here you can take C-291 north to W-220 (mile #87) at Alcova (see page 70). Take C-291 south for one mile to the next junction. Here you can continue south on C-291 to US-30 at either Hanna or Medicine Bow.

Turn east and the road passes through a small cut in the hill. You then follow along a ridge on the north side of the Shirley Mountains for about three miles to South Fork Cave Creek. Along here you can see the Pedro Mountains to the north, the Granite Mountains to the far northwest, the Ferris Mountains to the west, and the Seminoe Mountains to the southwest. The road then climbs over the other side and begins following the Middle Fork Cave Creek. Here Fourmile Ridge is off to the north.

Six miles further east, the road crosses the creek and you can see Fourmile Point to the north and Chalk Mountain to the northeast. After one more mile, you come to a small junction. Here you can take the Shirley Mountain Loop Road to the Pryor Flat Recreation Area and then rejoin this road further to the east.

Continue east and as you lose sight of the Ferris and Pedro Mountains to the west, you begin traveling across Shirley Basin toward Laramie Peak in the Laramie Mountains. After passing the other end of the loop road, you hit W-77 at mile #132, between Casper and Medicine Bow. From here you can see the Freezeout Mountains to the south.

Trip Nine

The Bessemer Bend Road south to the Government Bridge

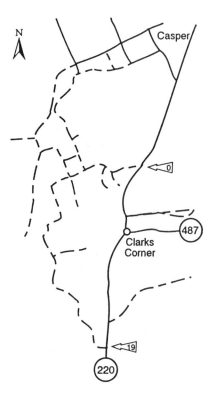

This trip begins by turning off US-220 at mile #105 south of Casper. As you head west on the Bessemer Road (N-308), you can see Bessemer Mountain to the southwest and to the east is Casper Mountain and Coal Mountain.

After two miles you cross the river and come to a junction. Here N-111 turns south to a fish hatchery.

Continue west on N-308 for two miles (past N-306 going north toward Casper) to another major junction. Here N-308 turns north and hits the Ryan Hill Road (N-319), one mile south of the Poison Spider Road.

Take N-314 west for one and a half miles (past N-312 going south to a dead end) and the road makes a sharp turn to the south. Here N-314 ends and you travel south for two miles on N-315 to Rasmus Lee Lake. The road then turns west for two miles to a junction. Here you can take the Trapper Road (N-316) north for one mile to the Ryan Hill Road. At this junction, you can see Oil Mountain to the north and to the east is Casper Mountain and Bessemer Mountain.

Turn south on N-316 and after crossing Willow Creek, the road drops down to the east and the river below. The road then follows the river below Clarkson Hill. Here you can see Muddy Mountain to the east and to the northeast is Coal Mountain (below Casper Mountain). After four miles you hit W-220 at mile #94 at the Government Bridge.

Government Bridge is a popular access point on the North Platte River. Thanks for the pretty picture Riley!

Trip Ten

The Ryan Hill Road from Casper southwest to W-220

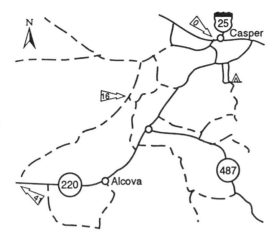

This trip begins by going west on the Poison Spider Road (N-201) on the west side of Casper. You can access this by turning off W-220 at mile #111 and taking the Robertson Road (N-305) two and a half miles north. You can also turn off US-20 at mile #6.5 and take the Zero Road (N-202) south for one mile. You then turn south on the Robertson Road for one mile to the Poison Spider Road.

As you travel west on the Poison Spider Road, you pass by N-204 going north to the Zero Road and US-20 at mile #9. Three miles further west the pavement ends at a junction. Here you can take N-206 north to the Zero Road and US-20 at mile #13.

As you continue west on N-201, the road passes by an interpretive site at Emigrant Gap (two miles). About two miles further is a junction. Here N-306 goes south and joins N-308 going to Bessemer Bend and W-220 at mile #105. Also at this junction, you can take the Zero Road (N-202) back to Casper.

Turn west past the Poison Spider School and after two miles you come to another junction. Here the Poison Spider Road continues west. On this road you can hit the Dry Creek Road, Castle Garden/Ore Road, and W-135 (see pages 66 and 68). At this junction you can see the western end of Casper Mountain and Coal Mountain to the southeast and to the south is Bessemer Mountain.

Turn south on the Ryan Hill Road (N-319). After one mile you pass by N-308 going southeast to the Bessemer Bend and W-220. Continue on N-319 and the road swings southwest along the base of Oil Mountain. Four miles further, you come to another junction. Here N-316 goes southeast toward Bessemer Mountain. At this junction you can see Muddy Mountain to the south of Casper Mountain.

Continue southwest on N-319 and after three miles you cross Poison Springs Creek. Here you can see Clarkson Hill off to the south. After crossing Willow Creek (seven miles), the road climbs to the top of Ryan Hill and a BLM Interpretive Site. Up here you can see the Rattlesnake Hills to the west, the Ferris and Granite Mountains to the southwest, and the Pedro Mountains to the south.

Two miles from the interpretive site, you cross Fish Creek. The road follows Fish Creek past McCleary Reservoir and then crosses Shell Creek. You continue to follow Fish Creek for another five miles and cross it near the confluence with Horse Creek. After following Horse Creek for three miles, you hit W-220 at mile #73, between Alcova and Muddy Gap Junction. Here you can see the Granite Mountains to the west, the Ferris Mountains to the southwest, the Seminoe Mountains to the south, and the Pedro Mountains to the southeast.

A student at Casper College, Sharon spends a beautiful afternoon combining artistic expression with a rustic setting.

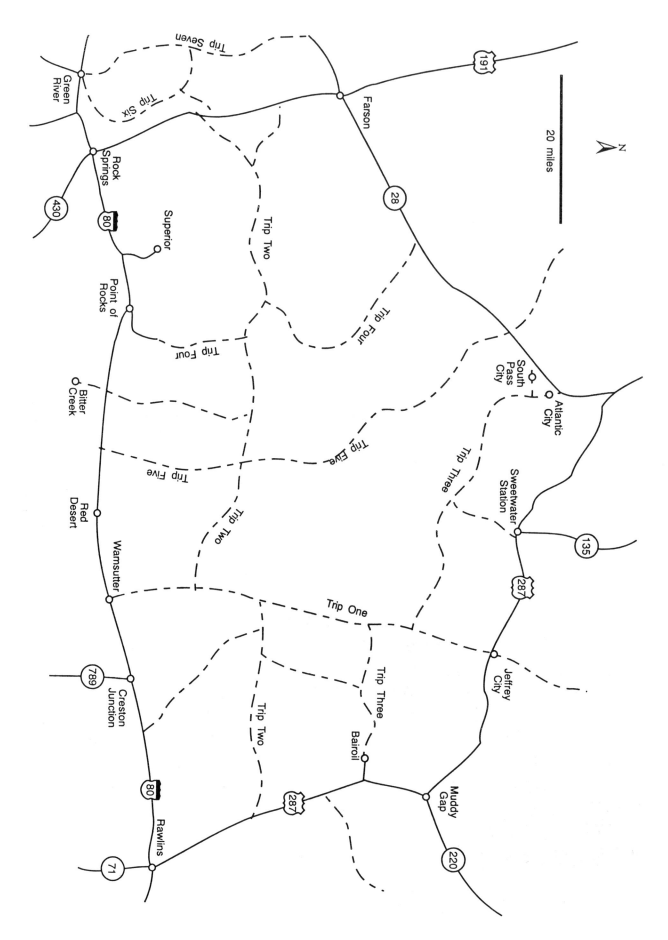

Trip One

Jeffery City south to Wamsutter on the Crooks Gap Road

This trip begins by turning off US-287 at mile #23 in Jeffery City. As you head south on the Crooks Gap Road, you can see the gap between Crooks Peak and Crooks Mountain on the west side and Sheep Mountain and the Green Mountains on the east side. To the northeast are the Granite Mountains and off to the distant east are the Ferris Mountains.

After crossing Crooks Creek there are several roads turning east, but continue south toward the gap. About eight miles from Jeffery City is a junction. Here the road south goes to a mine site.

Take the sharp turn west and across the creek again. After passing through the gap, a small road takes off toward Crooks Mountain, but continue south into the Great Divide Basin. After about four miles you come to a junction. Here you can take the Three Fork Road west to Atlantic City and W-28 (see page 78).

Continue south and you cross the county line and begin traveling on S-23. Here you can see Bare Ring Butte to the east. After three miles you come to another junction. Here you can see the Wind River Mountains to the northwest, Continental Peak and Oregon Buttes to the west, and Steamboat and South Table Mountain to the southwest. At this junction you can turn east to another junction in 10 miles. There you can continue east to Bairoil and W-287, or you can go south on the Sooner Road and hit the Dunes Road (see page 78).

Continue south toward Wamsutter to the next junction in three miles. Here the Osborne

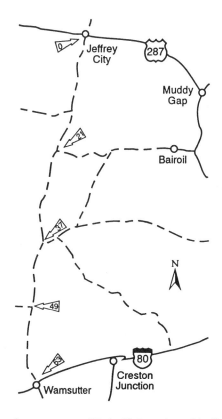

Road turns west to Hadsell Crossing. (I believe this road may connect with the Luman Ranch Road and the Atlantic City Road, but I have not traveled this route.) From this point you can see the Ferris Mountains and the Seminoe Mountains to the east.

Continue south and you pass by the Hadsell Road going west. Two miles further is a junction with the Dunes Road going east to W-287 north of Rawlins (see page 80).

Stay south on S-23 for three miles and the road goes by Circle Bar Lake to the near east, and you can see the Chain Lakes to the far east. A few miles further south, you pass by the Government Reservoir Road (looping over to the Luman Road on S-20 going west), and a bit further you pass by Coal Butte (off to the east).

Five miles from Coal Butte is a junction on the Siberian Ridge. Here you can turn west on the Luman Road to the Killpecker Sand Dunes north of Rock Springs (see page 80).

Continue south on S-23 for 14 miles to Wamsutter. Along this stretch of the road, you can see Delaney Rim to the south and Table Rock off to the southwest. The road goes under I-80 (exit #173) and you enter the east side of Wamsutter on McCormick Street, just north of the Post Office on Broadway.

An old windmill near Coal Butte in the Chain Lake Flats area.

Trip Two

The Three Fork Road from Bairoil to Atlantic City

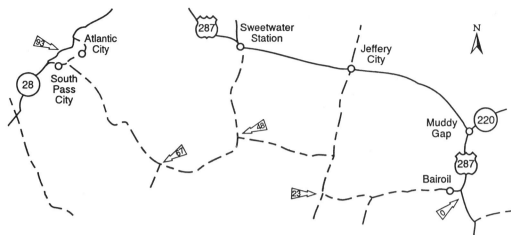

This trip begins by turning off US-287 at mile #33 and taking W-73 west toward Bairoil. After three miles, and just before entering Bairoil, you turn south toward Bull Springs Rim on S-22. The county road then turns west and you begin following along Lost Soldier Creek below Twin Buttes. The eight miles to the top of the divide is pretty rocky - but it gets better. On top you can see the Ferris and Seminoe Mountains to the east.

You pass by a 2-track road going north to A&M Reservoir and come to a junction. Here you can turn south on the Sooner Road . Continue west toward the Wind River Mountains and across wild horse country.

Eleven miles from the Sooner Road is the junction with the Wamsutter Road (S-23). Here you can see Crooks Gap to the north, Continental Peak and Oregon Buttes to the west, and Steamboat and South Table Mountain to the southwest. At this junction you can turn south to Wamsutter or swing west to Rock Springs (see pages 77 and 80).

Turn north past Three Ring Butte and in three miles you come to the next junction. Here you can continue north to Jeffery City. Turn west on the Three Fork Road (BLM-2317) to Atlantic City and the road travels along the base of Crooks Mountain.

After three miles a small road turns south, but continue west through some curves and across Arapaho Creek. (The road is now a 2-track, but it is fairly wide and in good shape.) The road climbs up a bit and you have a good view of the Wind River Mountains to the west (near Atlantic City) and the Great Basin to the south. From here the road swings out along a ridge overlooking part of Buffalo Basin on the south.

You follow along a divide for about five miles and just past a small road turning south you drop down along East Alkali Creek and cross Stinking Spring Draw. Here the Three Forks Road turns north for one mile and then west again. Two miles from this zig-zag is a sheep camp. (This should be used as a reference point for people traveling in the opposite direction through this area.)

Three miles west of the sheep camp is a junction with the Bison Basin Road. Here you can turn north across East Alkali Creek and follow a ridge above the creek. That road then drops down into Sweeny Basin and hits US-287 at mile #42, a half mile east of Sweetwater Station.

Turn south and the road follows along the rim for three miles to the Hadsell Crossing Road. Stay to the west for two miles and you pass by the turn off to the Bison Basin Oil Camp. The road then drops down and crosses West Alkali Creek (three miles). Here you continue west and begin following Sulfur Creek for a bit.

The road travels along a divide for five miles and you can see Daley Lake to the south. The road then passes north of a small uranium plant. (Here you take the 2-track road west along the side of a ridge.) Along this stretch, you can see the pink and white bluffs of Honeycomb Buttes to the southwest and beyond them is Steamboat Mountain. To the west is Continental Peak and to the south is McKay Lake.

As you travel further west, you can see Scotty Lake south of McKay and to the west a bit is the larger Picket Lake. After about one mile you come to a junction. Here the road north goes toward Horse Track Ridge. The Red

Creek Road going south splits after two miles. There you can turn southwest past Honeycomb Buttes toward the Oregon Buttes Road, or you can turn southeast past Red Lake to the Dunes Road.

Take the road to the northwest and head toward the Wind River Mountains. After six miles, you can see Continental Peak, Oregon Buttes, and Pacific Butte (long broad mountain) to the west. Five miles further, you begin following the Sweetwater River. After two more miles, the road swings north across Long Slough to the Sweetwater Bridge.

After crossing the river, you follow Willow Creek north for six miles and pass by the Lewiston Road going southeast to Willies Hand Cart Site. Three miles further, you pass by the Pickaxe Road going northwest. Stay northeast and you get a terrific view of the Atlantic City area. The road then drops down some switchbacks to Atlantic City.

Turn west toward W-28 to a junction in one mile. Here you can go northwest for two miles and hit W-28 at mile #45. Turn west for two miles to a junction at South Pass City. After visiting the historical site, you can turn north for two miles and hit W-28 at mile #43.

The South Pass City Historical Site is one of many interesting places to visit in the Atlantic City area.

Trip Three

The Great Divide Basin Road from W-287 to Rock Springs

This trip begins by turning off US-287 at mile #15 at the base of Willow Hill. As the road heads west across Separation Flats, you can see the Seminoe Mountains to the east, the Ferris Mountains to the northeast, and to the northwest are the Green Mountains. The first series of hogback ridges you pass is Separation Rim. As you continue west and climb up a small divide (southern end of Bull Rim), you can see the Mahoney Lakes and Mud Flat Lakes off to the south. These lakes are located in a large depression and dust devils are frequently seen in this area.

About 26 miles from US-287 is a junction with the Sooner Road (BLM-3215). On this road you can travel north to the Crooks Gap Road going to US-287 at Jeffery City, or you can loop back to US-287 at Bairoil. If you turn south on the Sooner Road, it crosses the Chain Lake Flats and joins the Riner Road going to I-80 at exit #196.

Continue west on S-63 for four miles and the pavement ends near a mine site. From this point you can just barely see Steamboat Mountain to the west. Oregon Buttes are north of Steamboat and a bit further north is Continental Peak. To the northwest are the Wind River Mountains near South Pass.

Two miles from the end of the pavement is a junction. Here the Riner Road (BLM-3203) cuts sharply to the southeast. This road travels past the Chain Lakes to a junction at Mud Springs (15 miles). There you can turn northeast to US-287, or you can continue south through Buck Draw, climb over Windy Ridge, and then travel through Creston Draw to I-80 at exit #196 (32 total miles).

Continue west for two miles to another junction. Here you can take the Crooks Gap Road north to Jeffery City and W-287 (or after about 15 miles, you can take the side road back to Bairoil, see page 78).

Turn south on S-23 and after three miles you pass by Circle Bar Lake (off to the east). A few miles further south, you go by the Government Reservoir Road (looping over to the Luman Road) and you then pass Coal Butte. Six miles from Coal Butte is a junction on the Siberian Ridge. Here you can continue south for 15 miles to Wamsutter and I-80.

Turn west on S-20 and follow the Luman Road along the Siberian Ridge. Along this stretch you can now see North and South Table Mountain to the west (just south of Steamboat Mountain). To the southwest is Black Butte and to the south is Delaney Rim. After eight miles you come to the next junction. Here you can turn south on the Red Desert Road (BLM #3207) for one mile to a small junction. There you can continue south (not southwest) for 20 miles to I-80 (exit #165) at Red Desert.

Back at the main junction, continue west toward Continental Peak and you have a good view of Lost Creek Basin. As the road travels across the greasewood flats, you see a lot of alkali deposits. Five miles past the Lost Lake Road (BLM #3208) is a tricky area and unmarked junction. Here S-67 turns south to I-80 near Tipton. Continue west for one mile to the next junction. The main road (S-67) turns sharply north toward Hay Reservoir and a small OFR turns south to I-80 near Tipton.

Take the road going straight west and toward Steamboat. The road follows along a low vegetated dune on the north and open flatland on the south. After about six miles of wondering whether your on the right road, you pass by Chalk Butte off to the south. Steamboat

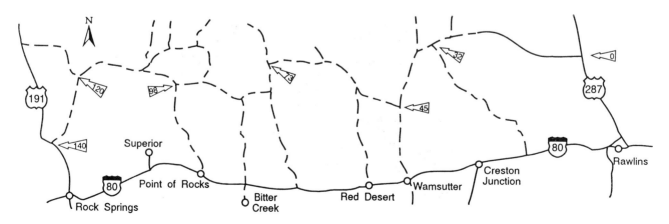

The Boars Tusk is a most powerful figure that stands like an ancient guardian and seems to influence the entire area.

Back at the main junction on the Great Basin Road, stay to the west and head toward Black Rock and Spring Butte. A couple of miles after passing Black Rock is another junction. Here you can turn south to the Jim Bridger Power Plant and I-80 (exit #130) at Point of Rocks (see page 82).

Turn northwest for seven miles to the next junction. Here you can take the Steamboat Road (S-83) north to W-28 near Farson.

Continue west and the road passes between Steamboat Mountain on the north and the two Table Mountains on the south. As the road drops down the other side, you can see the Boars Tusk and the Chicken Springs area to the west. To the north you can look through Indian Gap (Steamboat on the east and Essex Mountain on the west) and see the Wind River Mountains.

A few miles further at the Chilton Ranch, you can take a washboard road northeast to a parking area at the Sand Dunes ORV area. Two miles further is another road going north into the sand dunes. Both of these roads offer places to picnic and play in the sand.

From here the main road swings south of the Boars Tusk. Just after passing the Pine Canyon Road (beautiful drive and return trip to the east) is a junction at Fifteen-mile Knoll.

If you turn northwest here, the road climbs along the side of White Mountain near Chicken Springs (seven miles). If you stop at the pole fence around the springs you have a nice place to picnic and view the Killpecker Sand Dunes and the Boars Tusk. The road then travels through some vegetated sand dunes (tricky driving) and hits W-191 at mile #33 south of Farson (16 miles total).

Turn south on S-17 and the road follows along Killpecker Creek. Along this stretch, you can see White Mountain to the west and the Leucite Hills to the east. Three miles south of Fifteen-mile Knoll is a small junction. Here you can take a side road east to Cedar Canyon, or you can turn west to the White Mountain Petroglyphs (real nice).

Continue south for seven miles and you pass by a side road turning east to Long Canyon. Stay south on S-17 for five more miles to W-191 at mile #10. Here you can continue south to Rock Springs or turn north to Farson.

is still ahead of you to the west. Three miles past Chalk Butte you can breathe easy again when you hit S-21 (a much better road). At this junction, you can go north to Oregon Buttes and W-28 (see page 83).

Turn south on S-21 for four miles to another junction. Here you can continue south on S-21 to I-80 exit #152 at Table Rock.

Stay west toward Steamboat on the Twelve-mile Well Road. After about seven miles is a small junction. Here you can take S-19 south to I-80 at exit #142 (16 miles).

Continue west on S-19 and during the next eight miles you have a nice view of the Wind River Mountains (looking north across Black Rock Flats). At the next junction you can turn north toward the Bar X Ranch. On this route you come to another junction in six miles. There you can turn northwest and hit the Steamboat Road (S-83) going to Farson. Also at that junction, you can travel northeast to the Bar X Ranch where you have the option of looping southeast back to the Great Divide Basin Road, or turning north to Oregon Buttes and W-28 (see pages 82 and 83).

Trip Four

Point of Rocks north to Farson on the Steamboat Road

This trip begins by taking I-80 exit #130 to Point of Rocks. You follow the pavement east along I-80 for two miles and then north through Deadman Wash. After eight miles, you pass by the power plant and the pavement ends. Continue north for one mile and the road swings west, below a small ridge, and travels through Potash Wash to a junction. Here you can take S-18 west toward Zirkel Mesa to Superior.

Turn northwest on S-15 and the road climbs up to the top of the rim. Here you can see Six-mile Ridge and Black Butte to the south. As you continue north, you can see Black Rock to the northeast, the Wind River Mountains to the north, and to the northwest a bit is Spring Butte. Further to the northwest is North Table Mountain, South Table Mountain, and Steamboat Mountain.

The road travels between Black Rock and Spring Butte, and after crossing Black Rock Creek you come to a junction. Here you can turn east on the Dunes Road to US-287 (and a variety of other choices, see page 80).

Stay northwest for seven miles to the next junction. Here the Dunes Road continues west, between Steamboat Mountain and North Table Mountain, to Rock Springs.

Turn north on S-83 and the road crosses the Killpecker Sand Dunes and winds around to a small junction at the base of Steamboat. Here a side road takes a sharp cut to the northwest and climbs along the side of Steamboat to the top. This road is quite steep and should not be attempted if it's wet.

If you can make the trip, you get a fantastic look at the Steamboat buttress and the lookout from the top offers an exceptional view of the basin to the south. From there you can see the sand dunes stretching east to the Ferris Mountains. There are aspen, willow, and pine trees up here and you can see bands of horses, herds of mule deer, antelope, and possibly elk. As this side road travels north

Rock Cabin Springs—a good place to picnic and swat desert mosquitos.

past the Tri-Territory Historical Site to rejoin S-83, you get a view of Oregon Buttes and the Wind River Mountains.

Back at the base of Steamboat, if you choose to stay on the more traveled S-83, the road winds along past knobby hills and sandstone and follows along a rim to the east. After about three miles, the road turns north and you climb a bit to Freighter Gap. After passing through the gap, the road crosses Split Rock Canyon and rejoins the side road going over Steamboat.

Now that both travel options have joined, you head northwest on S-83 and drop down to Jack Marrow Creek. The road follows along the creek for a seven miles to another junction. Here a dead end road continues west.

Turn north toward Rock Cabin Springs (three miles). There is part of the old cabin still standing and the spring is a great place to picnic and watch muskrats working around their lodge. About a half a mile north of the springs is a junction. Here you can take S-21 east to the Oregon Buttes Road.

Take the road going west and as you work your way toward W-28, you have a nice view of Sweetwater Gap in the Wind River Mountains to the north, Oregon Buttes and Continental Peak to the east, and the Wyoming Range to far the west. The large flat topped mountain just off to the southwest is Buffalo Hump. About 15 miles from Rock Cabin, you cross Pacific Creek and hit W-28 (mile #13) east of Farson.

Trip Five

South Pass to Table Rock on the Oregon Buttes-Bar X Road

This trip begins by turning off W-28 (mile #33) at South Pass. As you head south on S-58, Pacific Butte is the broad flat mountain immediately to the southwest; the broken Oregon Buttes are a bit further to the south, and the pointed Continental Peak is off to the southeast. After about nine miles, you cross the county line and begin traveling on S-74. The road winds down the hill and passes between Continental Peak and Oregon Buttes. Here you have a spectacular view of Edmund Springs and the basin to the south. (The springs are nice place to picnic and to watch hawks, waterfowl, and shorebirds.)

After leaving the springs, the road heads out into the flats and you can see the pink and white bluffs of Honeycomb Buttes to the east. To the southwest is Joe Hay Rim and behind it is Steamboat. The road continues southeast and you pass through a seemingly endless, but beautiful, wasteland of alkali, dried lakes, and blow outs. Watch for dust storms and dust devils all over this area.

A few miles after crossing Bush Creek (15 miles from Edmund Springs) is a junction. Here you can turn west to a junction near Rock Cabin Springs. There you can take the road north to Farson or south to the Dunes Road (see page 82).

Turn east on S-21 and after four miles you pass by two small roads going south to the Bar X Ranch. Both of these routes will connect with the Dunes Road (see page 80).

Stay on the main road southeast into Alkali Flats. After passing through these flats for about six miles, you come to a junction. Here a road turns northeast toward Buffalo Hump Basin and Hay Reservoir.

Continue south on S-21 and the road passes by Red Lake (actually a large red basin that is almost always dry) off to the east. The road then passes through some vegetated sand dunes where you can see Steamboat Mountain, North and South Table, and Black Rock off to the west. Eight miles south of the Buffalo Hump Road is a junction. (This road is easy to miss - so watch your odometer reading.) Here you can take the Dunes Road east to the Crooks Gap Road and US-287.

Continue south four more miles to the next junction. Here you can turn west on the Twelve-mile Road (Dunes Road) to Steamboat Mountain and Rock Springs.

Stay south on S-21 and you cross Twelve-mile Gulch and Black Rock Creek. The road then travels past many OFR's, so stay on the main road going south. Along this stretch you can see Black Butte to the southwest, Table Rock to the south, and Delaney Rim to the southeast. Twenty miles after turning off the Dunes Road, you hit I-80 at exit #152.

Oregon Buttes is a desolate place with a unique beauty of its own.

Trip Six

The White Mountain Road from W-191 southwest to Green River

This short trip begins by turning off W-191 at mile #13 north of Rock Springs. Turn west on S-14 for two miles to a junction. Here you can take the road continuing west and join the Blue Rim Road (see page 85).

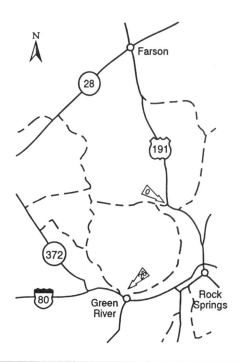

Turn south toward the top of White Mountain and after a couple of miles you can see Pilot Butte to the southwest and Aspen Mountain to the southeast. To the northeast is South Table, Steamboat Mountain, Indian Gap, and Essex Mountain (from east to west). You can also see the Wind River Mountains to the distant northeast, with the Killpecker Sand Dunes and Boars Tusk in the foreground. (Nice view.)

About six miles further south, you pass by a road turning west to the base of Pilot Butte (with a trail leading to the top). Along this stretch you can now see the Wyoming Range to the northwest, the Uinta Mountains to the southwest, Pine Mountain to the south, and Black Butte to the east.

Four miles south of Pilot Butte you pass by a tower and the road swings west. Here you can see the nearby Wilkin Peak across to the south. After six more miles the road drops down the mountain and goes under I-80. Here you enter Green River at Trona Drive and Hillcrest Way. Take Hillcrest Way to the Flaming Gorge Highway near I-80 and exit #89.

Depending on when the last BLM roundup was, wildhorses can be seen throughout most of the Red Desert.

Trip Seven

The Blue Rim Road from Green River to W-28 west of Farson

This trip begins by turning off on to W-374 on the west side of Green River (I-80, exit #89). The road travels past the base of Tollgate Rock and follows along the Green River below Palisades Cliff. After three miles you turn

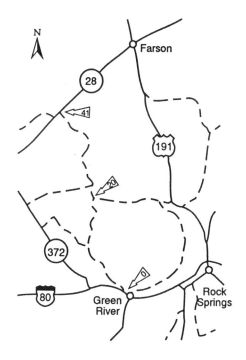

northwest on the Blue Rim Road (S-5) and go under I-80. Here the road climbs up past Greasewood Gulch (running northeast toward Pilot Butte) and then drops down along the river. A few miles further, you cross Alkali Creek and the road climbs up to a junction 11 miles from Green River. Here S-7 drops down across the river and hits W-372 at mile #12 (S-6 on that end).

Stay north along the top and after nine miles you come to another junction. Here you can turn east on S-14 to the White Mountain Road and US-191 (see page 84).

Continue north toward the Wind River Mountains and you have a great view of the Blue Rim and the basin to the west. After three miles, you pass by S-4 going west to W-372 at mile #17. (Note: The bridge across the Green River is closed on this road and has been for quite some time.)

Stay along the rim for the next five miles where the road drops down through part of the Badland Hills and across the flats to the Big Sandy River (11 miles from S-4). Two miles further you hit W-28 at mile #110.

Looking over the edge of the Blue Rim and along the Green River drainage.

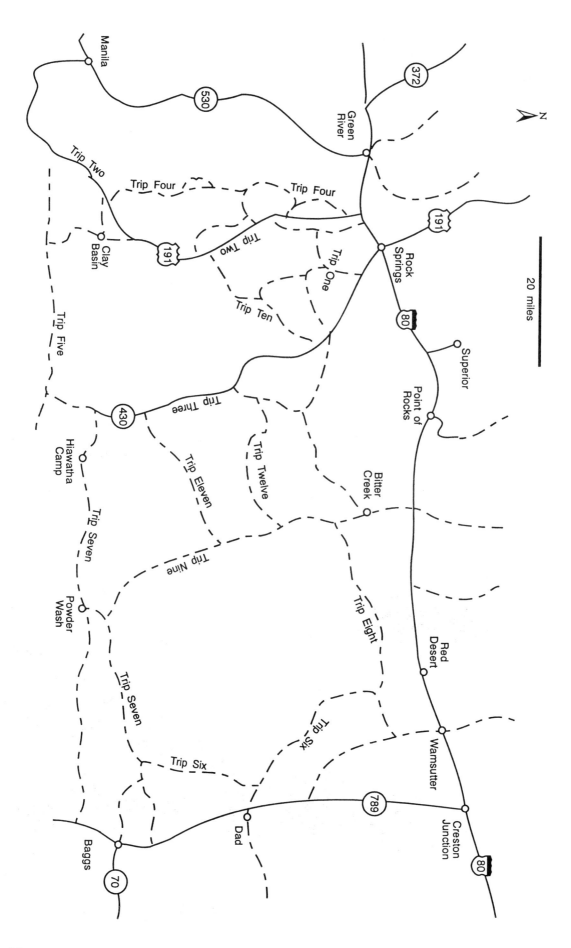

Trip One

The Little Bitter Creek Road from Rock Springs to Aspen Mountain, South Baxter, and W-430

Besides the Prairie Rattlesnake, the Midget Faded Rattlesnake is Wyoming's only other venomous reptile. It is found only in a small area of southwestern Sweetwater County.

This trip begins by turning off I-80 at exit #99 and going south on W-191. Just after crossing the railroad tracks and Bitter Creek, turn east back toward Rock Springs on S-51. After one and a half miles is a junction. Here you can continue east to Rock Springs.

Turn south on the Little Bitter Creek Road (S-29) and the road follows along the creek through a small, boulder lined canyon. After four miles, you cross the creek and pass by a 4WD road turning east up Rock Canyon. Here you can see Wilkin Peak to the west.

Continue south for five miles to a junction. Here you can continue south on S-29. This route travels past Antelope Butte (on the east) after three miles and then Earnest Butte (two more miles). The road then goes by a 4WD road turning east to Dry Canyon and crosses the creek again. From that point, S-29 climbs a hill to the southwest and rejoins W-191 at mile #517.

Turn east on S-31 and the road passes through Barney Canyon for a couple of miles. The road then swings northeast and climbs up the base of Aspen Mountain to a junc-

tion. Here you can turn north for about six miles and hit W-430 at mile #6 south of Rock Springs.

Turn south on the Aspen Mountain Road (S-27) and you go past a tower road and come to a small lookout. Here you can see the Wind River Mountains to the north and below them is the Boars Tusk and Killpecker Sand Dunes. To the northwest is White Mountain and rising above it is Pilot Butte. To the far southwest are the Uinta Mountains and before them is Mass Mountain, the Devils Playground, Black Mountain, Twin Buttes, and Cedar Mountain. Little Mountain is to the south and to the southeast is Pine Mountain above Titsworth Gap. (Nice view.)

Continue south on S-27 for two miles to a road going to Three Patches (a great place to picnic). Here you can now see Sand Butte and Pine Butte to the east. The road drops down the mountain for three miles and you come to another junction. Here you can continue south on S-27 to Tommy James Basin and the Titsworth Gap area (see page 99).

Turn east and after passing South Baxter (one mile) the road follows Circle Creek for four miles. The road then climbs over a small divide and follows Pretty Water Creek to W-430 at mile #26. There you can travel north to Rock Springs or south to the state line (see page 89).

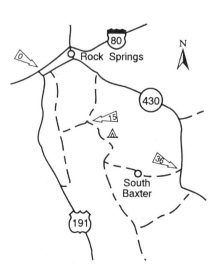

Trip Two

Wyoming #191 south from Rock Springs to the Utah State Line

This trip begins by turning off I-80 at exit #99 and going south on W-191. At mile #504 the Little Firehole Road turns southwest. This road travels through the Little and Middle Firehole Canyons and joins the Big Firehole Road. There you can either loop back to W-191, or continue south on Flaming Gorge Drive to W-191 at Minnies Gap (see page 90). At this mile marker, you can see Wilkin Peak to the west and to the east is Aspen Mountain.

Nine miles south on W-191, you can look back to the north and see Pilot Butte above White Mountain, and off in the distance north are the Wind River Mountains. In the foreground below the Wind Rivers, you can just make out the black figure of the Boars Tusk against the Killpecker Sand Dunes. Off to the west are the three drainages of the Firehole Canyons and Flat Top Mountain. To the south is Little Mountain and southwest are the towering Uinta Mountains.

After passing by the Big Firehole Road at mile #513 (going west to Flaming Gorge, see page 90), you come to a junction with the Little Bitter Creek Road. Here you can turn northeast and drop down the hill to the creek below. On this route you can loop back to Rock Springs, or cut to the east through Barney Canyon and travel over to W-430 (see page 89).

At mile #520 the Lower Sage Creek Road (S-36) heads west. On this route you can either join Flaming Gorge Drive (S-33), or take the Upper Sage Creek Road (S-34) and loop back to W-191 at Little Mountain.

After climbing over the top of Miller Mountain, you drop down to mile #531 and the Salt Wells Creek Road (S-34). This route will take you through McCorts Canyon to Titsworth Gap. There you can go south to Red Creek Basin, north to Baxter and Aspen Mountain, or continue east over to W-430 (see page 99).

As you continue south past the Upper Sage Creek Road at mile #532, the road climbs to a summit on Little Mountain. Here a small road

Tepee Mountains and the Red Creek Badlands (once a proposed wilderness area).

turns off to the side where you can park and get a fantastic overview of the Red Creek Basin. Richards Gap is due south, with the Richards Mountains on the west side and the Tepee Mountains on the east side. Across the badlands to the east is Pine Mountain.

At mile #541 the Clay Basin Road turns south through Richards Gap. On this road you can travel west to Minnies Gap, or you can head east to Browns Park and over to W-430 (see page 91).

After winding down to the base of the mountain, you come to a junction with Flaming Gorge Drive (mile #551). Here S-33 travels northwest along the gorge and back to Rock Springs (see page 90). At this point you can also turn west to the Clay Basin Road and the Irish Canyon Road to W-430.

A couple of miles further south (and after passing through Minnies Gap), you cross the state line at mile #552. Here you can continue south into Utah and cross Flaming Gorge Dam. There you can take U-191 to either Vernal, Utah (about 60 miles), or take U-44 through the fantastic Sheep Canyon to Manilla, Utah (about 40 miles). From Manilla, you can either head west to Mckinnon and Evanston, or follow W-530 along the west side of the gorge to I-80 at Green River (see page 103).

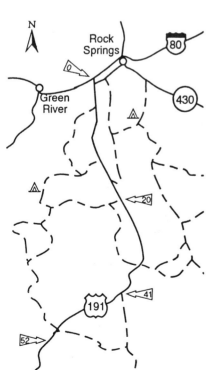

Trip Three

Wyoming #430 from Rock Springs south to Colorado

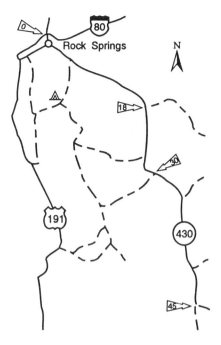

This trip begins by turning off I-80 at exit #107 and going into Rock Springs. You then follow the W-430 signs around the east side of town and head southeast out of Rock Springs. At mile #6, S-27 turns south to the top of Aspen Mountain and a picnic area at Three Patches (11 miles). On this road you can also travel to South Baxter, Titsworth Gap, and Little Bitter Creek (see page 87). Just past this mile marker, you can see Wilkin Peak to the west and Aspen Mountain to the southeast. As you look across Baxter Basin to the east, you can see the top of Black Butte and Cooper Ridge.

Even a little view of Cooper Rim and the Salt Wells Creek drainage makes me want to drag out the old tin billy and brew some cowboy coffee.

At mile #15 you cross Salt Wells Creek and at mile #18 is a junction. Here S-26 goes east through Cutthroat Draw to the Patrick Draw Road and Bitter Creek Road (see page 98). Continuing on W-430, the road follows along Cooper Rim and Salt Wells Creek and you pass Camel Rock at mile #23. Three miles south of Camel Rock, a road turns west along Pretty Water Creek to South Baxter (see page 87).

At mile #30, S-32 turns west to junctions at Tommy James Basin and Titsworth Gap. There you can go north to Aspen Mountain and Rock Springs, or west to W-191 at Minnies Gap (see page 99).

As you continue south on W-430, you get a nice view of Sand Butte and Pine Butte off to the east. At mile #35, S-24 turns east to either the Patrick Draw Road, the Sand Butte Road, or the loop road back through Cutthroat Draw to W-430 (see page 101).

At the base of Rifes Rim, a road turns west to Potter Mountain (12 miles) and Red Creek Basin (17 miles). A bit further south at mile #45, a road turns southwest to Pine Mountain (12 miles) and Vermilion Creek (4 miles).

After climbing to the top of Rifes Rim, you can see Kinney Rim to the east, Aspen Mountain to the north, and Pine Mountain to the west. Potter Mountain is a bit north of Pine Mountain and is barely a rise on the horizon from here. The two mountains south of Pine Mountain are Middle Mountain and Diamond Mountain (both in Colorado).

At mile #47 you can take the Kinney Rim Road east to Carson Springs and then hit the Bitter Creek Road. From there you can either go north to Bitter Creek and I-80, or you can travel south and hit the Powder Rim Road, running from Baggs to Hiawatha (see pages 98 and 100).

As you continue south on W-430, you pass by a road going west to 4-J Basin. At mile #52 a road turns southeast to Hiawatha, Colorado, and the Powder Rim Road.

At mile #55, W-430 ends at the Wyoming-Colorado state line. Here you can continue south on Moffat County #10 and travel through Irish Canyon to C-318 near Browns Park. There you can turn west for a bit and take the Clay Basin Road to W-191 near Minnies Gap (see page 91).

Trip Four

The Firehole Road/East Gorge Drive south from Rock Springs

This trip begins by turning off I-80 at exit #99 and taking W-191 south. At mile #504 you come to a junction. Here you can continue south on W-191 to Flaming Gorge Dam. At this junction you can see Wilkin Peak to the west and Aspen Mountain to the east.

Turn off onto the Little Firehole Road the road swings south past a tumbled assortment of sandstone outcroppings and cedar breaks for about six miles. It then follows along the edge of a beautiful little canyon for another mile to Little Firehole Creek. Here the Little Firehole Canyon runs from the horizon on the east to Flaming Gorge on the west.

After crossing the creek, you continue traveling south and climb over a small divide into Middle Firehole Canyon. As you cross the creek at the bottom, Flat Top Mountain is immediately before you to the south. The road then climbs up a steep hill and you come to a junction on top (11 miles from W-191). Here you can turn east and hit W-191 at mile #513. From this junction on the Big Firehole Road, you can look back to the north and view the Little and Middle Firehole Canyons that you have just passed through.

Turn southwest and the road drops down through the canyon below. After going below South Chimney Rock and passing the campground turnoff, the pavement ends. Here you can see both North and South Chimney Rock to the north.

Continue south on Flaming Gorge Drive (S-33) and the road climbs a long steep hill. At the top you have a spectacular view of Flaming Gorge Reservoir. The road then swings away from the lake and about six miles further you come to a junction at Sage Creek. Here you can go east along the creek and hit W-191 at either mile #520 (via S-36, Lower Sage Creek Road) or mile #532 (via S-34, Upper Sage Creek Road). Both of these are nice drives.

Stay to the south and after climbing the hill and leaving Sage Creek, you have another good view of the gorge to the west. To the southwest you can see (looking form north to south) Mass Mountain behind the badlands of the Devils Playground, and Cedar Mountain behind Black Mountain and Twin Butte. Off to the southeast is Little Mountain.

The road then drops down to bottom of the hill to a junction on Current Creek. Here S-38 branches off to the southwest and follows along the gorge. This route has several access roads leading to the lake and will connect back with S-33 after nine miles.

Turn southeast on S-33 and you follow Current Creek upstream for about two miles. You then leave the creek bottom and the road climbs up to a small junction on Current Creek Ridge. Here a road follows along the ridge to the east toward Little Mountain.

Continue south on S-33 for five miles to the next junction. Here an access road turns west to the lake, and S-38 turns north along the lake and back to the junction at Current Creek.

Stay south toward the Unita Mountains and the road drops down a steep hill and crosses Upper Marsh Creek. You then climb a steep hill to a small junction on top. Here another small road turns east toward Little Mountain. At this junction, you can see the top of Richards Mountain to the southeast.

Continuing south, you go down another steep hill and cross Middle Marsh Creek. Here the road climbs up the side of Iron Mountain and travels through a thick forest of cedar trees. (Beautiful area. Watch for deer and possibly elk through here.) Five miles from Middle Marsh Creek is a road turning east across the top of Iron Mountain. Take the main road sharply to the south and down to Minnies Gap (five miles). At Minnies Gap (W-191, mile #551) you can head north to Rock Springs, south to Vernal and Manilla, Utah, or east through Clay Basin to W-430 (see pages 88 and 91).

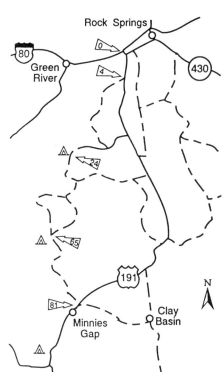

Trip Five

The Irish Canyon-Clay Basin Road from W-430 to W-191

Looking north from Clay Basin, through Richards Gap, to Little Mountain.

This trip begins at the Wyoming-Colorado state line at the end of W-430 at mile #55 (see page 89 for a description to this point). Most of this trip is in Colorado and Utah, but it is a very scenic route connecting two of Wyoming's back highways. As you travel south on Moffat-10, you go past a road turning west to Middle and Diamond Mountain (south of Pine Mountain). Three miles further south, you pass by a road going east to the Hiawatha Camp and another road going west to Cold Spring Mountain.

You now have a beautiful drive through canyons, foothills, and overlooks of the Vermilion Creek Bluffs. After about eight miles, the road drops down and winds through Irish Canyon. This is a spectacular area. At the bottom of the canyon is small turnout where you can stop and look at some petroglyphs. Four miles from the petroglyphs is the junction with Colorado-318 (mile #19). Here you can go east to Maybell and US-40 (40 miles).

Turn west and you travel along Vermilion Creek and then along the Green River at Browns Park National Wildlife Refuge. At mile #12 you can see the red rock entrance to Ladora Canyon to the south. On the east side of the "Gates" is Douglas Mountain and on the west side is Diamond Mountain. To the north is Cold Spring Mountain. After traveling 20 miles on C-318, you enter Utah and the pavement ends. You pass by several side roads during the next seven miles, but keep on the main road toward Flaming Gorge.

At the Taylor Flat Bridge Junction, you turn north and leave the river. This route cuts through the mountains on a good, but very steep road. This is a terrific little canyon lined with cedar, cottonwood, and boxelder trees.

After climbing to the summit, the road drops down into Clay Basin (nice little pocket). Five miles from the summit are a couple of junctions. Pass by the first one (turning off to the Clay Basin Camp) and go one mile further west. Here you can go north past the Clay Basin Camp to Rock Springs (54 miles). This route travels through Richards Gap and hits W-191 at mile #541. This is a very nice drive and it offers a great view of the Richards Mountains and the Red Creek Basin. Also at this junction, you can continue west toward Flaming Gorge (24 miles) and hit W-191 at mile #551 near Minnies Gap.

Trip Six

Wamsutter south to Baggs on the Barrel Springs Road

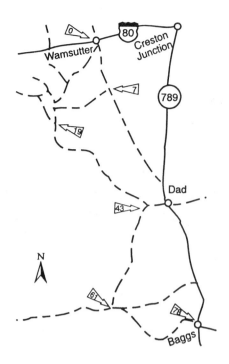

This trip begins in Wamsutter (I-80, exit #173) by taking Broadway past the Post Office and across the railroad tracks to S-23. You go south (past the Echo Springs Road turnoff) on S-23 for seven miles to a junction. Here you can continue south on S-23 and C-701 to W-789 at mile #28 at Dad.

Turn southwest on the Barrel Springs Road (BLM-3310) and after three miles the road swings to the west. From up here you can see Flat Top Mountain to the south and to the southwest (above Delaney Rim) are the gray bluffs of the Haystacks. Seven miles further west are two junctions at North Barrel Springs.

At the first junction you can take the Red Desert Road north along Delaney Rim and loop back to Wamsutter (a rough road). About 100 yards further west is the second junction. Here you can continue west and go past an old building to a pumping unit where the road splits. There, the main road to the north goes up a hill and follows along the rim toward Tipton. The small road to the southwest crosses the creek and goes up a hill to the LaClede Road (see page 96).

At this second junction, turn south on the Barrel Springs Road and toward the Windmill Draw Road. Two miles south of the junction, an OFR turns northwest past a couple of pumping units and hits the LaClede Road going west.

Continue south and you can see the Haystacks to the southwest. To the west are the Man and Boy Buttes and to the far southeast is Battle Mountain. Five miles from the North Barrel Springs-Tipton Road junction, you drop down to the Barrel Springs-Eureka junction. Here you can take the Eureka HDQR-Wamsutter Road east for eight miles and join C-701 (S-23 has become C-701 at the county line), 15 miles south of Wamsutter.

Continue south on the Barrel Springs Road. After crossing the creek and climbing a hill, the road travels south for about six miles to a small junction. Here you can take the road to the southwest and climb through some rimrock to the top of Willow Creek Rim (about two miles). That road then passes through some blowouts and soap holes for about three miles to another junction. There the road south dead ends at a pumping unit, so you can either take the road west into Horseshoe Bend (The Haystacks), or follow the rim road southeast to a crossing at Sand Creek and hit the Powder Rim Road. (Both of these are 4WD roads, see page 94.)

Stay southeast toward Flat Top on the Windmill Draw Road and after five miles you cross Windmill Draw. Three miles further is another small junction. The road up the hill to the west goes past Courthouse Butte and over near Church Butte.

Turn southeast down the hill and you get a glimpse of Dad Dail Reservoir. At the bottom, the road swings east through South Barrel Springs Draw and travels across the Mexican Flats to a small junction (six miles). Here a road continues east through Red Wash and hits W-789 at Dad (six miles). Turn south for one mile and the Windmill Draw Road joins the Standard Road at a main junction. Here you can take the road east and hit W-789 at mile #30 just south of Dad.

Continue south on the Standard Road and the road winds around to the southwest. After six miles, the road turns south past an OFR going west and you climb to the top of West Flat Top. Here you can see North Flat Top off to the east. As the road drops down the other side, you can see East Flat Top to the east, to the southwest is Powder Rim, and to the far west is Kinney Rim.

The road continues to drop down along Hangout Wash to a junction with the Powder Rim Road. Here you can see Cherokee Rim to the south. If you go west across Sand Creek (one mile), you can travel past Powder Mountain and hit the Bitter Creek Road, north of Powder Wash, Colorado (see page 94).

Turn east for two miles to the next junction. Here the Powder Rim Road continues east to W-789 at mile #43 north of Baggs.

Turn southeast and the road drops down across Red Creek at the eastern tip of Cherokee Rim. You then follow along Sand Creek for a bit and the road climbs a ridge above the Little Snake River on the south and Red Creek Basin on the north. The road continues along the ridge toward Battle Mountain and Bakers Peak. After passing by a road going northwest, you drop down past Poison Buttes into the basin below.

The road travels through the basin for about four miles (past OFR's with poison gas warnings) and then drops down through a cut in The Bluffs. You follow along the base of The Bluffs for about four miles to W-789, one mile north of Baggs.

Asking for local information is sometimes fun. When I inquired about these "dugouts" near McPherson Springs, the reply was "They must be for something 'cause people 'round here don't dig holes in the ground for nothing".

Trip Seven

The Powder Rim Road from W-430 east to Baggs

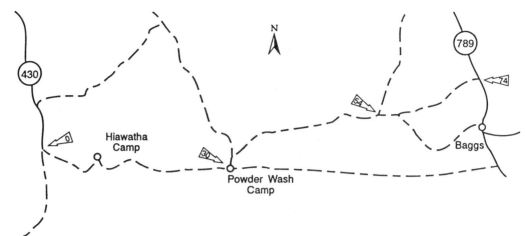

Hiawatha Camp

Powder Wash Camp

Baggs

This trip begins by turning off W-430 at mile #52 south of Rock Springs. (See page 89 for a trip description to this point.) You turn east toward the Hiawatha Camp for five miles and the pavement ends as you enter Colorado (Moffat-4). Two miles further, you hit pavement again when you swing back into Wyoming. Here the road passes through a pretty little canyon where it crosses Horseshoe Creek and Vermilion Creek. The pavement ends again as you pass by the Hiawatha Camp in Colorado.

Just after passing the camp is a small unmarked junction. Here the Gap Road goes north across Alkali Creek and joins the Kinney Rim Road (see page 100).

Stay to the east and the road once again enters Wyoming for about four miles. The road then swings back into Colorado, crosses Shell Creek, and climbs up the northern end of Lookout Mountain. From the summit you can see Kinney Rim along to the north. To the northeast is Powder Mountain and off in the distant east is part of the Sierra Madra Mountains. In Wyoming to the west is Pine Mountain and southwest a bit in Colorado is Middle Mountain and Diamond Mountain.

You travel east on Moffat-4 for five miles to a junction at the Powder Wash Camp (30 miles from W-430). Here you can continue east on M-4 (13 miles of dirt, 26 miles paved) and hit Colorado-13 at mile #126, four miles south of Baggs.

Turn north at Powder Wash. After crossing over into Wyoming (four miles), you come to a junction. Here the Bitter Creek Road turns northwest. On this route you can hit the Kinney Rim, Sand Butte, and LaClede Roads, or you can continue north to I-80 at exit #142 (see page 98).

Turn sharply to the northeast on the Powder Rim Road and across the North Fork Powder Wash. The road climbs through some cedar breaks and passes on the north side of Powder Mountain. You then climb a steep hill to the edge of the rim. Here a small road drops down into the basin below. From this overlook you can see Skull Creek Rim and East Fork Point to the northwest, and beyond them are the Haystacks. To the northwest is the top edge of Kinney Rim and Sand Butte.

The road winds around and up and down for three miles to Anthill Knob (off to the south a bit). Two miles past the knob is another good view to the north. Here you can look north into the Horseshoe Bend area of the Haystacks. To the northwest, behind Skull Creek Rim and East Fork Point, is Adobe Town Rim. In the foreground to the north is Prehistoric Ridge and to the northeast are the three Flat Top Mountains.

The road continues along the rim for five miles to a junction. Here the road going south drops down to Cherokee Basin and joins M-4, running east and west in Colorado.

Continue east for about two more miles to the next junction. Here a small road turns north into the basin below. If you take this road to Rotten Springs, you can go west back to the first Powder Rim overlook, join the Bitter Creek Road at the Skull Creek Rim overlook, or cross Sand Creek and follow Willow Creek Rim to either Horseshoe Bend or the Barrel Springs Road (all of these are 4WD roads, see also page 92).

Continue east for five miles and the road winds down through some cedar breaks, passes by McPherson Springs, and crosses Sand Creek. (Since the bridge is out on Sand Creek, so you have to ford the creek.) A half mile east of the crossing is another junction. Here you can take the Standard Road north over West Flat Top to the Barrel Springs Road, about one mile from W-789 (see page 92).

Continue east for two miles to the next junction. Here you can turn south on the Poison Butte Road to Baggs. Stay east and you pass by a BLM Waterfowl Enclosure. Along this stretch you can see Muddy Mountain to the east, the top of Battle Mountain is southeast a bit, and further to the southeast is Bakers Peak. The road then drops below Flat Top Mountain and follows along Red Creek for about five miles. You then climb to an overlook of Cottonwood Creek and drop down two more miles to W-789 at mile #43, seven miles north of Baggs.

The Skull Creek drainage and badlands on the north side of Powder Mountain.

Trip Eight

The Fort LaClede Road going east from Bitter Creek to Wamsutter

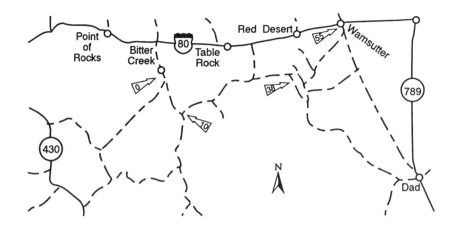

This trip begins by turning off I-80 at exit #142. You turn south on S-19 for seven miles to a junction at Bitter Creek. Along this stretch you can see Black Butte to the west, Table Rock to the southeast, and to the south is Pine Butte and Sand Butte. At the junction, you can take the Patrick Draw Road (S-24) southwest to W-430 or the Sand Butte Road (see page 101).

Continue south on the Bitter Creek Road and you pass by Table Rock. Ten miles from Bitter Creek you come to a junction. Here you can see Delaney Rim along to the east and Sand Butte Rim to the west. At this junction you can continue south on the Bitter Creek Road and hit the Sand Butte, Kinney Rim, or the Powder Wash Roads (see page 98).

Turn east on the Fort LaClede Road and the road travels past the edge of Delaney Rim and begins following Bitter Creek to the southeast. (Due to the road ruts along this stretch, you may spend more time alongside the road rather than on it.) After five miles, you come to the LaClede Stage Station ruins. This is a great place to picnic and knock around.

One mile south of the LaClede ruins is a small junction. Here you can see The Haystacks to the southeast. At this junction you can take the road south to Manuel Gap (nine miles) and Adobe Town Rim. Also along this road, you can loop back over to the Bitter Creek Road.

Continue east for one mile to Fort LaClede at the Bitter Creek crossing. If you didn't stop at the stage station you'll just about have to at the fort. This is a great spot. After leaving the fort, the road meanders off to the east and in

five miles, you come to another small junction. Here you can take the "Dugway Road" over Delaney Rim and hit I-80 at exit #152 near Table Rock.

Continue east on the main road and you travel past the Haystacks and through an area of vegetated sand dunes. Eight miles further you can see Man and Boy Buttes to the north and the road swings away from the Haystacks. A few miles further (and about 11 miles from the Dugway junction), you pass an OFR going northwest toward the Man and Boy Buttes. (People going in the opposite direction, do not take this road, but stay to the southwest.)

Three miles east from this side road is a junction. Here another OFR heads west back toward the Man and Boy Buttes. (People going the other way should once again stay to the southwest.) About 100 yards east of this side road, the road splits at the top of a hill. The road following along the ridge goes to a well unit (two miles) and then drops down to the Barrel Springs Road. (If you take this road, you will need to turn north on the Barrel Springs Road for three miles to the North Barrel Springs Junction, see also page 92.)

Turn northeast on the road going down the hill. At the bottom is a small junction at a pumping unit. Here you can turn north up the hill and then west to Tipton. Stay to the east, past an old building, to a main junction at North Barrel Springs. Here you can turn south on the Barrel Springs Road to the Windmill Draw, Eureka, or Standard Roads (see page 92).

Continue east for 100 yards to the next junction. Here you can take the Red Desert

Road (BLM-3323) north along the base of Delaney Rim for about seven miles. That road then turns away from the rim and does a little zig-zag to the top of a hill near the power lines. There the road becomes a 2-track as it drops down a steep hill to Wamsutter.

The best choice is to continue east (away from Delaney Rim) toward the Wamsutter Road (10 miles). The road travels east for about seven miles and passes several small lakes. Along here you can see the gray bluffs of the Haystacks rising above Delaney Rim to the southwest, and to the south you can see Flat Top Mountain. The road then swings northeast and drops down a bit to the Wamsutter Road.

Here you can go south to W-789 at Dad (19 miles) and then continue south to Baggs. Turn north on S-23 and after 8 miles you enter Wamsutter and hit I-80 (exit #173).

NOTE: People wishing to take the Fort LaClede Road west from Wamsutter and North Barrel Springs, take I-80 exit #173. You go through town, past the Post Office, and across the railroad tracks. Continue south (past the Echo Springs Road) on S-23 for eight miles to the Barrel Springs Road. There you turn west for 10 miles to the junction at North Barrel Springs. Then you continue west (not northwest) up the hill to the LaClede Road.

Both the LaClede Stage Station and Fort LaClede (shown here) are great places to picnic and knock about.

Trip Nine

The Bitter Creek Road from I-80 south to Powder Wash, Colorado

This trip begins by turning off I-80 at exit #142 and going south for seven miles to Bitter Creek. Along this stretch of the road, you can see Black Butte to the west, Sand Butte and Pine Butte to the south, Table Rock to the southeast, and Steamboat and South Table Mountain to the north.

After crossing the tracks at Bitter Creek, you come to a junction. Here you can take the Patrick Draw Road (S-24) southwest for seven miles to another junction. There you can either go west on S-26 through Cutthroat Draw to W-430 at mile #18, or you can continue south on S-24 and go past the Sand Butte Road (five miles) to W-430 at mile #35 (see page 101).

Continue south on the Bitter Creek Road (S-19) and you pass by Table Rock (off to the east). After about 10 miles you come to a junction. Here Delaney Rim is off to the east and Sand Butte Rim is around to the west. At this junction the LaClede Road turns east around Delaney Rim and travels over to the Barrel Springs Road between Wamsutter and Baggs (see page 96).

Stay south and the road follows Antelope Creek into a small canyon. After passing several old wooden pump houses, you come to a small junction with a possible error (five and a half miles from the LaClede road). Here a BLM sign indicates that the road west goes to Sand Butte and on over to W-430. While this is true, it is a poor road. I believe the sign should have been placed two and a half miles further south where a better road goes over to both Pine Butte and Sand Butte (see page 101).

Continue south of this sign for four miles and you come to another junction (10 miles south of the LaClede Road). Here you can take the road going east and join the LaClede Road north of Manuel Gap and Adobe Town Rim.

Continue south on S-19 and after two miles you pass by a ranch (stay to the southeast here). Two miles further is an unmarked junction. Here the Kinney Rim Road turns west and joins W-430 at mile #47 (six miles to Carson Springs and 16 miles more to W-430, see page 100).

Continue south and the road begins traveling through soaphole country. Stay on the roads here or you stand a good chance of getting stuck. After about four miles, you pass by a small road (4WD) going east that drops down over Adobe Town Rim to Sand Creek and beyond. The main road crosses Shell Creek and climbs a small ridge. From here you can see Cow Creek Reservoir to the southwest and Powder Mountain to the southeast. Three miles further, you pass by a small road going northeast to East Fork Point on Skull Creek Rim (10 miles).

As you continue south on the Bitter Creek Road, you pass the Cow Creek Headquarters and three miles further is another small junction. Here you can turn east and drop down into the Skull Creek drainage. There you can connect with the Powder Rim or Barrel Springs Roads (4WD, see pages 92 and 94). If you don't drive this road, you'll at least want to grab some picnic stuff and walk out on the point for a bit. The view from there is fantastic.

Continue south from this 2-track and after one mile the road swings by the head of Skull Creek. Here you can look north along the rim and see the plateau at East Fork Point. Rising above it in the distance are the Haystacks.

The road then turns southeast for seven miles (passing by Powder Mountain off to the east) to a junction. Here you can go east along Powder Rim to Baggs (see page 94).

Continue south for one mile to the state line and then three miles further to a junction at Powder Wash, Colorado. From Powder Wash, you can either go west to Hiawatha Camp and W-430 at mile #52 (30 miles), or you can travel east to Colorado-13 at mile #126, four miles south of Baggs (39 miles).

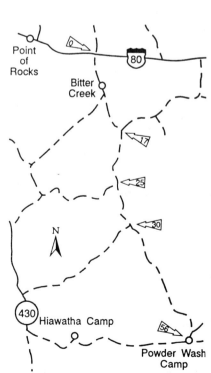

Trip Ten

The Salt Wells Creek Road from W-191 east to W-430

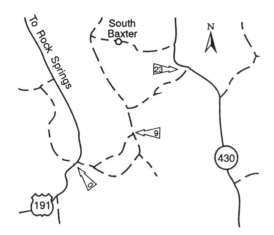

This trip begins by turning east off W-191 at mile #531 (see page 88 for a trip description of W-191 to this point). Here the Salt Wells Road (S-34) travels along the base of Miller Mountain for two miles to a small junction. If you continue east on S-34 to Pine Mountain, the road can get pretty bad at Buffalo Springs.

Turn northeast on S-71 and continue along the base of Miller Mountain. As the road gradually swings back to the east, you can see Potter Mountain to the far east.

About four miles from the first junction, you pass by Bean Springs and the road turns toward Titsworth Gap. This section of the road through McCort Canyon is one of the prettiest areas around and well worth the trip. There are willows and huge sagebrush along Bean Spring Creek and the steep canyon walls are dotted with juniper trees and patches of aspen. At the gap is a junction with S-34. Here you can follow Gap Creek south to Buffalo Springs and Pine Mountain.

Turn north for three miles and you come to another junction in the Tommy James Basin. Here you can continue north on S-34 to Baxter and Aspen Mountain (see page 87). At this junction, you can see Aspen Mountain to the north and Miller Mountain to the west. Along to the southeast is Laney Rim and to the east is the top of Pine Butte and Sand Butte.

Turn east on S-32 and the road follows along Gap Creek for six miles to the base of a ridge. Here Salt Wells Creek comes in from the southwest and you follow it through a shallow canyon for four miles to W-430 at mile #30. There you can turn north to Rock Springs or south to the Colorado state line (see page 99).

Just north of Titsworth Gap and looking east along Gap Creek and Laney Rim.

Trip Eleven

The Kinney Rim Road from W-430 to the Bitter Creek Road

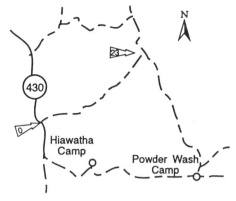

This trip begins by turning off W-430 at mile #47 (see page 89 for a trip description to this point). After traveling east toward Kinney Rim for six miles, you come to a junction. Here you can turn southeast to Alkali Creek (four miles) and then follow along the base of the rim to the Powder Rim Road (see page 94).

Continue east toward Kinney Rim and Carson Springs (10 miles). After two miles you come to a small junction. Here a road turns northeast and drops over into Chicken Springs Basin.

Continue east and you can see where the two-track road climbs over the rim. After passing Chicken Springs, you begin the steep climb up. The road here can have some pretty deep ruts in it and a 4WD is recommended.

At the top of the rim you can see Pine Mountain to the west, and as you look across Crow Creek Reservoir to the southeast, you can see Powder Mountain. To the east is the top edge of Adobe Town Rim and Skull Creek Rim, and to the northeast are the Haystacks.

The road then drops down the other side to Carson Springs. Depending on the amount of water at this little oasis, you can often see a variety of waterfowl and shore birds. There are also bands of wild horses in the area.

Six miles east of Carson Springs, you hit the Bitter Creek Road (S-19). Here you can travel south to the Powder Rim Road and Powder Wash, Colorado. Also here, you can take the road north to Bitter Creek and I-80 (see pages 94 and 98).

After slipping and sliding over Kinney Rim in a spring rainstorm, Black Irene calms her engine with a nitro-tab under the hood.

Trip Twelve

The Sand Butte Road from W-430 to the Bitter Creek Road

Part of Dripping Rock Draw between Pine Butte and Sand Butte.

This trip begins by turning off W-430 at mile #35 (see page 89 for a trip description to this point). The road travels east through Scheggs Draw and then swings northeast along part of Rifes Rim. Eight miles from the highway is a junction. Here you can continue north toward the Brady Unit to another junction (five miles). There you can either travel through Patrick Draw to Bitter Creek and I-80, or you can loop back to W-430 at mile #18 through Cutthroat Draw.

Turn east toward Sand Butte and the Bitter Creek Road. The road climbs up along Dripping Rock Draw and past the base of Sand Butte where it then swings over toward Pine Butte. There are a few 2-track roads along this route, but stay on the main road with the reflector poles. After traveling between the two buttes and through Pine Butte Basin, the road makes a steep climb to a small saddle (eight miles from the Brady Draw Road). Here you can see Aspen Mountain and Pilot Butte to the northwest and to the northeast is Table Rock. Southeast is Powder Mountain and to the east is Flat Top and the Haystacks.

From the saddle the road turns south along the back side of Pine Butte to a small junction. Here a spur road turns off to the radio tower on Pine Butte and a great view. There you can also see the Wind River Mountains, Steamboat Mountain, South Table Mountain, and Black Butte to the north. To the south is Pine Mountain and Chicken Springs Basin below Kinney Rim. Southwest is Little Mountain and the Unita's.

Turn east and the road drops down the other side above Pine Creek Wash and joins the Bitter Creek Road (10 miles). Here you can go south to the Powder Rim Road or north to Bitter Creek and I-80 (see page 98).

NOTE: For those people wishing to go from the Bitter Creek Road west past Sand Butte and over to W-430, **do not** take the turn at the BLM sign reading Sand Butte (10 miles) and W-430 (19 miles). This road will get you there, but it is in poor shape. Instead, continue south on the Bitter Creek Road for two and a half miles and then turn west following the reflector pole markers. (In case they move the sign to correct this error, the proper turn is eight miles south of the LaClede Road.)

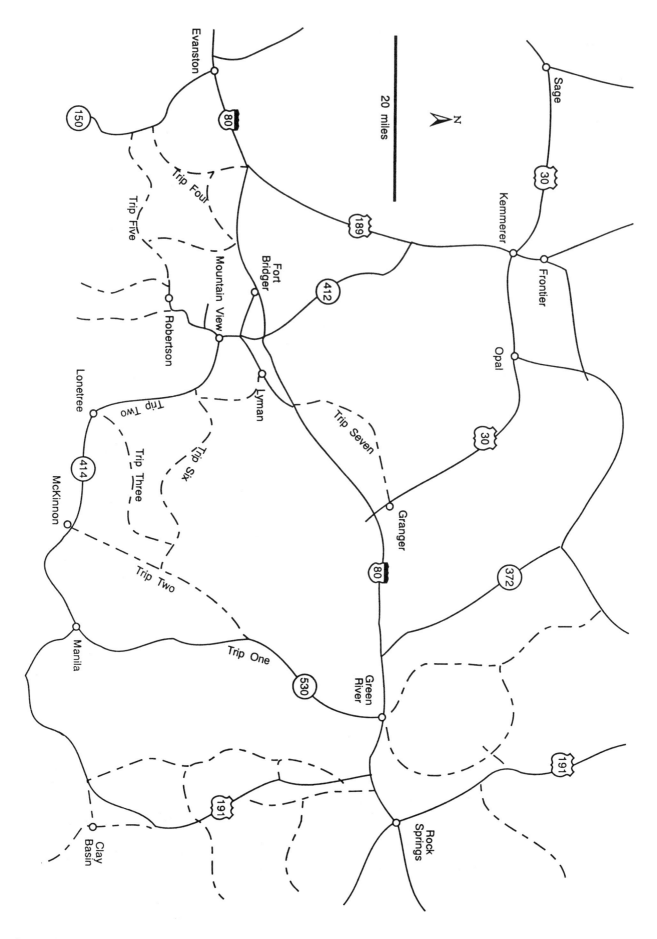

Trip One

Green River south to the State Line on W-530

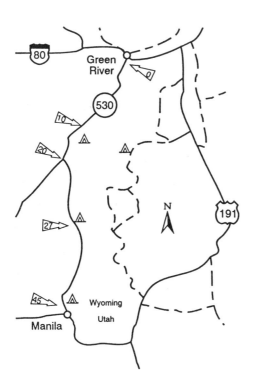

This trip begins by taking I-80 exit #91 into Green River and going south on W-530. After passing through town, the road climbs to the top of Green River Hill and a scenic overlook at mile #9. Here you have a good view to the east of Big Firehole Canyon, North and South Chimney Rock, and Flat Top Mountain. To the far south are the Uinta Mountains and to the southeast is Little Mountain.

At mile #10 is the Lost Dog Road going to the confluence. A few miles down the road, you cross the Blacks Fork River (upstream from the confluence with the Green River). Here you can see the sand covered Massacre Hill to the west.

At mile #20 you come to McKinnon Junction. Here you can turn southwest on S-1 to McKinnon (29 miles). Along this route you can take the Cedar Mountain Road or Dry Creek Road west to Lonetree or Mountain View. At McKinnon you can loop over to Manilla, Utah and rejoin W-530. You can also continue west to Mountain View and Evanston (see pages 104, 105 and 108).

Continuing south on W-530, you pass by several roads that turn east and access Flaming Gorge Reservoir. At mile #29, you can see the badlands called the Devils Playground to the west and behind them is Black Mountain. South of Black Mountain is Twin Buttes (two points on the same mountain). If you look back to the northeast you can still see South Chimney Rock and Flat Top Mountain.

Near mile #34, you pass by the dome shaped hills of Haystack Buttes and on the other side of the gorge to the east is Little Mountain. At mile #42 you begin to drop down through Linwood Canyon and, as you cross the Henrys Fork River, you have a fantastic view of the Uinta Mountains. At mile #45 you cross the state line, two miles north of Manila, Utah.

From Manila you can continue west on U-43 to Mckinnon and then over to Mountain View on W-414. You can also take U-44 south through Sheep Canyon to U-191 (nice drive). There you can either go south to Vernal, Utah, or go north across Flaming Gorge Dam to Rock Springs (see page 88).

A Swainson's Hawk nest in the badlands of the Devils Playground.

Trip Two

The McKinnon Road from W-530 west to Mountain View and I-80

Southwestern Wyoming is a good place to find reptiles. Shown here is a nasty little Plateau Lizard.

This trip begins by turning off W-530 at McKinnon Junction (mile #20, see page 103 for a trip description to this point). Here you head southwest on S-1 where the road travels along the side of the Devils Playground and Black Mountain.

Nine miles from W-530 is a small junction. Here you can see Mass Mountain to the west and south of it is Cedar Mountain. At this junction you can turn west one mile to another junction. There you can go southwest on the Cedar Mountain Road to Lonetree, or you can continue west on the Dry Creek Road to Mountain View (see pages 105 and 108).

As you continue further south, the Uinta Mountains loom up before you and to the east you can see the northern point of Twin Buttes. The road then cuts through the cedar breaks at the base of Cedar Mountain and crosses the

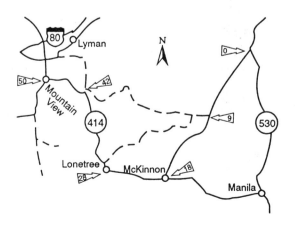

Henrys Fork River to McKinnon (W-414). Here you can turn east to Manilla, Utah, and then either take W-530 back to Green River, or you can travel further east to Minnies Gap on W-191 (see page 88).

Turn west on W-414 and the road follows along the Henrys Fork River and the base of Cedar Mountain to Lonetree. (Nice drive.) Here U-290 turns southwest toward Table Mountain and the Wasatch National Forest.

After leaving Lonetree, you cross the Henrys Fork and pass by the Cedar Mountain Road going northeast back to S-1. Continue north and the road passes between Hickey Mountain on the west and Sage Creek Mountain on the east. This is a pretty area here, with the high mountains striking a strong contrast to the arid badlands.

As you continue toward Mountain View, the road travels along the Cottonwood Creek Bench and at mile #108 you come to a junction. Here you can take the Dry Creek Road east to S-1, or head north on the Cottonwood Bench Road to Lyman.

Continue on W-414 and you drop down to Poverty Flats. At mile #100 the road crosses the Smiths Fork River to a junction in Mountain View. Here you can turn north on W-414 and hit I-80 at exit #39 (five miles), or you can take W-410 to Robertson and then travel over to I-80 at Evanston on the Piedmont Road (see page 107).

Trip Three

The Cedar Mountain Road from S-1 to W-414 at Lonetree

A twisted and solitary cedar tree demonstrating the art of raw beauty.

This trip begins by turning off S-1, nine miles southwest of McKinnon Junction. (See page 103 for a trip description to this starting point.) Turn west toward Cedar Mountain and after two miles you come to a small junction. Here the Dry Creek Road continues west to W-414 on the Cottonwood Bench near Mountain View (see page 108).

Turn southwest toward Cedar Mountain and after about seven miles, you pass by a road going south back toward S-1. Continue southwest and you can see where the road climbs up the side of the mountain.

The road climbs up a couple of steep switchbacks to a terrific view on top. To the north are the Wind River Mountains. To the

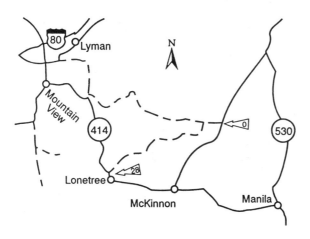

northwest is Round Mountain and the Wyoming Range, and to the west is Medicine Peak and Sage Creek Mountain. The Uinta Mountains are off to the south. Behind Black Mountain to the east is Little Mountain and behind it is Pine Mountain. You can also see the Richards Mountains behind Twin Buttes to the east. Finally, off to the northeast is Aspen Mountain, Wilkin Peak, and Pilot Butte.

One mile west of this lookout, you pass by a 4WD road going down the side of the mountain to Box Springs. On this road you can take the 2-track over to the Dry Creek Road.

Stay southwest on the North Rim Road and you travel across the top of Cedar Mountain. After five miles, the road goes down a couple of switchbacks and follows along the side of the mountain above Big Hollow in the Dry Creek drainage. Along this beautiful stretch of the road, you pass by patches of aspen trees (nice picnic areas).

The road then heads toward the gap between Sage Creek Mountain and Hickly Mountain. After a few miles, you pass by a small road going to Sage Creek Mountain. The main road drops down through some badlands to the flats along the Henry's Fork River (about three miles). You then turn west along the river and hit W-414 at mile #120 north of Lonetree.

Trip Four

The Aspen Mountain Road from Bear City to I-80

This trip begins by turning off W-150 at mile #10 south of Evanston. Here you turn northeast on the road going behind the Bear River City Historical Site. After one mile, you pass by a small road turning east around Oyster Ridge to Barrel Springs.

Stay on the main road and after about three miles you begin traveling north along the base of Aspen Mountain. After passing Alamont, the road climbs up the side of the mountain above the railroad tunnel to a junction on top. Here a dead end road drops over the other side to Aspen (two miles) and the other end of the tunnel.

Stay on the main road going north along the top of the ridge. Up here you can see Medicine Peak to the northwest and Chapman Butte to the southeast. After three miles the road drops down the mountain and two miles further you come to a junction. Here you can turn northwest to another junction (two miles). There you can turn north one mile to I-80 (exit #18) and join W-189 going north to Kemmerer. Also at that junction, you can turn southwest and go past the Eagle Rock Ski Area to I-80 at exit #10.

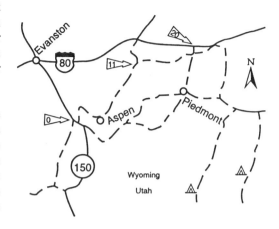

Back at the junction at the base of the mountain, turn east and the road climbs a long hill. As you drop down the other side, you pass by an old building containing a huge boiler (the ridge off to the north is called The Boilers). Five miles further east, you cross Muddy Creek to a junction. Here you can turn northwest to I-80 at exit #24, or you can turn northeast to I-80 at exit #30. Also at this junction, you can turn south on the Piedmont Road and travel to either Mountain View or Evanston (see page 107).

My cousin Tom (an extremely knowledgeable person in Wyoming history that could hold the interest of anyone fond of the old west) tells me this old boiler is the remains of an oil well steam powered pumping unit .

Trip Five

Mountain View west to W-150 and Evanston on the Piedmont Road

This trip begins by turning off I-80 at exit #39 and going south on W-414 to Mountain View. In Mountain View, you turn southwest on W-410 and after winding along the Tipperary Bench (above the Smiths Fork and Blacks Fork Rivers), you come to a junction. Here U-283 turns south to the Wasatch National Forest. Stay on W-410 and across the Smiths Fork River in Robertson. Here you can turn south on U-279 to the national forest.

Continue west on W-410 and you can see Cap White Ridge to the south. The road then crosses the Blacks Fork River travels through a beautiful area containing stands of aspen, cottonwood, willow, cedar, and spruce trees.

One mile west of the Blacks Fork River is a junction where the pavement ends (mile #16). Here you can take U-271 south to Meeks Cabin Reservoir and the national forest in Utah.

Continue west on U-204 and the road climbs up a switchback to a junction on the top of Bigelow Bench. Here you can see the top of Sugarloaf Butte and Haystack Butte to the north. To the east is Cottonwood Bench and Leavite Bench. At this junction you can turn north along the Bigelow Bench and hit U-202, two miles south of I-80 (exit #30). Also at this junction is a road going south toward Meeks Cabin.

Continue east toward a radio tower and the road drops down off the bench to Little Creek. Along here you can see Chapman Butte to the south, Medicine Peak to the northwest, Aspen Mountain to the west, and Meyer Ridge around to the north. Eight miles from the end of the pavement, you cross Muddy Creek and Piedmont Creek to a junction at Piedmont. (This is a great place to picnic and knock around a bit.) Here you can go north along Muddy Creek to I-80 at exit #24 near Byrnes Crossing.

These charcoal kilns at Piedmont are located about six miles south of I-80 exit #24. The charcoal produced here was shipped to smelters near Salt Lake City.

Turn south and after passing a few buildings, you come to a junction below a small reservoir. The road to the southwest will take you over to Aspen Mountain and Hilliard, but this route can be a disaster if the road is wet.

Turn south on U-171 and away from the reservoir for the safer and more scenic route. The road follows Muddy Creek and then Moss Creek for about six miles. At Chapman Butte the road leaves the creek. You pass between Byme Reservoir on the south and Guild Reservoir on the north and after five miles you come to a junction. Here the good weather road from Piedmont turns back to the northeast.

Turn southwest on U-171 and the road follows Aspen Creek along the base of Aspen Mountain. After three miles, you pass by U-167 going south to Rocky Point and W-150. One mile further is a junction at Hilliard. Here U-165 also turns south to Rocky Point.

Turn west on the paved U-171 and the road swings around the south side of Sulfur Creek Reservoir to W-150 (mile #11). Here you can turn south to the Wasatch National Forest and the state line (12 miles). There Utah-189 will continue on to Heber City.

Turn north on W-150 and the road passes by the Bear River City Historical Site and Oyster Shell Ridge (off to the east at mile #10). As you continue to travel north to Evanston, the road follows the Bear River and you can see Medicine Butte to the north.

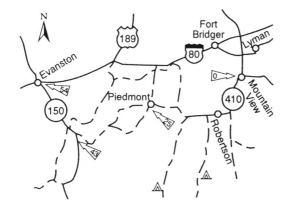

Trip Six

The Dry Creek Road from Mountain View east to McKinnon Junction

Cattail Draw and eroded badlands on the Dry Creek Road.

This trip begins by turning off W-414 at mile #108, about half way between Lonetree and Mountain View. About 100 yards after turning east on U-254 is a junction. Here the Cottonwood Bench Road continues north past Turtle Hill to Lyman.

Turn east and after crossing Cottonwood Creek, the road swings southeast toward Sage Creek Mountain. After climbing up a small hill, the road turns back to the east (away from Sage Mountain) and you head toward an old gas plant. The road passes south of the plant turnoff and two and a half miles further east is a junction. Here you can take the main road north toward a tower on the ridge (about 10 miles). After going by the tower, that road passes by a small refinery to I-80 at exit #59.

Continue east on the smaller road and after crossing Dry Creek you come to another junction. Here you can take the 4WD road up the hill to the south and follow along the Big Hollow for eight miles to Box Springs. There the road climbs to the top of Cedar Mountain and hits the Cedar Mountain Road going to Lonetree or S-1 (see page 105).

Take the road to the east. After crossing a small creek (H2S warning), you climb on to the Big Hollow Bench where you can see Pilot Butte and Wilkin Peak to the east, Mass Mountain and Cedar Mountain to the southeast, and Sage Creek Mountain to the southwest. Here a 2-track road turns east, but stay northeast and the road drops down through some badlands and crosses Big Dry Creek (five miles from Little Dry Creek).

About two miles from Big Dry Creek, you cross Cattail Draw and one mile further is a small reservoir. You come to another junction after about 10 miles of traveling past gullies, washes, and blowouts. Here you can take the Cedar Mountain Road southwest to W-414 at Lonetree.

Continue east for one mile and you come to a junction with S-1. Here you can either go south to W-414 at McKinnon, or north to McKinnon Junction (W-530 at mile #20, see page 103).

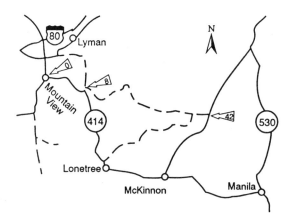

Trip Seven

Lyman to Granger on the Church Butte Road

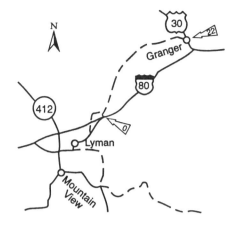

This trip begins by going east from Lyman on US-80. Three miles out of town, you turn north at mile #46. Here you can see the Uinta Mountains to the south. To the southwest is Sugarloaf Butte and Haystack Butte. After about two miles (of not so pretty scenery), you hit pavement and the road follows along I-80 for one mile. The road then goes under the interstate and crosses the Blacks Fork River. Here you begin traveling on a better road and pass by Moss Agate Cut.

You can also hit the Church Butte Road and avoid the broken pavement by taking I-80 exit #48. Here a good gravel road travels northwest across the Blacks Fork River and joins the Church Butte Road a couple of miles north of Moss Agate Cut.

Now that both routes have joined, the road continues along the river and you pass by U-235 going northwest to a pumping station. Two miles further, you cross the river again and you begin following along the base of an eroded rim toward Church Butte.

After passing by Church Butte, the road turns away from the river and you continue to follow the rim for one more mile. The road then travels through a small basin (Porter Hollow) and crosses the county line. Two miles further, you pass by Moss Agate Knoll (off to the north). After three more miles, you cross a small creek to a junction.

Here you can turn east for one and a half miles to US-30 at mile #98. There you can go south to I-80 exit #66 or exit #61. Also at this junction, you can turn north for one mile to the Blacks Fork River in Granger. There you can take W-375 east to US-30 (mile #95).

The Church Butte area is a great place to hike around looking for nothing inparticular.

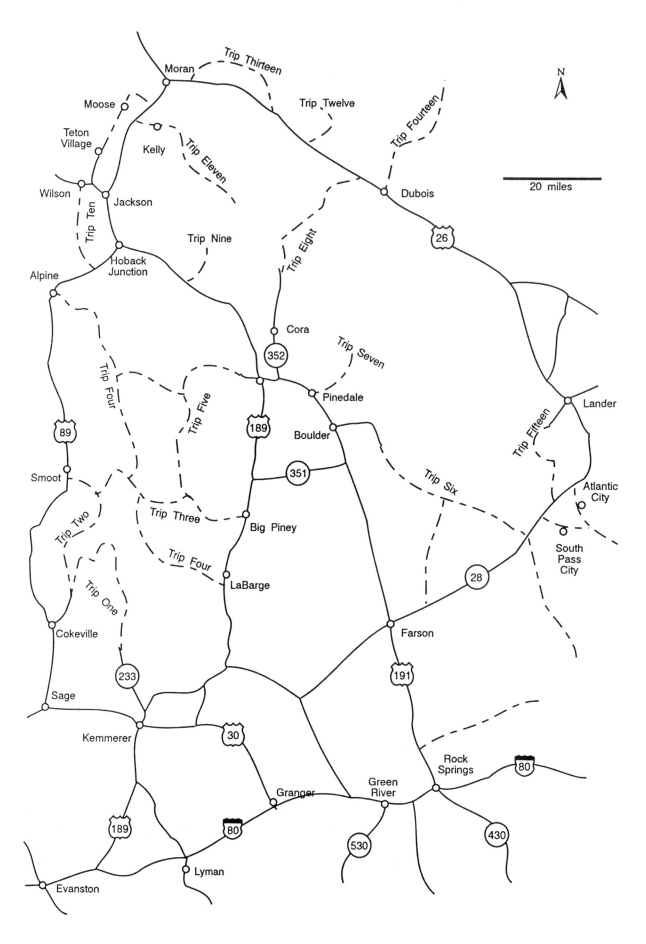

Trip One

Kemmerer to Cokeville the hard way: Hams Fork River Road

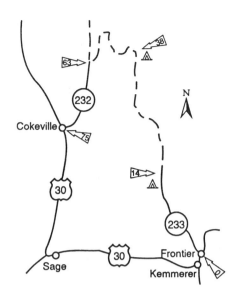

This trip begins by turning west on W-233 on the north side of Kemmerer. The Hams Fork River Road passes through Frontier and then crosses the river. The road climbs up a bit (past the airport and community park) and at mile #4 you cross the river again. You now begin traveling through a small valley between the Hams Fork Plateau on the west and Commissary Ridge on the east.

You pass by several fishing access points and at mile #13 you go by Kemmerer Reservoir and Viva Naughton Lake. At mile #20 the pavement ends. Here Commissary Ridge is

Teddy Bear Corner is one of the best stories around! Inquire locally about the little girl and the nice man.

along to the east and to the north. You can also see Dempsey Ridge and Coke Mountain to the west. Four miles from the end of the pavement you cross Beaver Creek and go by Teddy Bear Corner. A bit further is Pole Creek and the valley begins to narrow.

Three miles after crossing Pole Creek, the road crosses Carl Creek. Here you can look west and see where the West Fork Hams Fork River joins the Hams Fork River. One mile further north you enter the national forest and pass through a stand of aspen trees. Here Commissary Ridge is still to the east and the Hams Fork Ridge is to the west.

About two miles after entering the forest, you cross the East Fork and pass by a trailhead to Fontenelle Creek. Here you begin seeing lodgepole pine, fir trees and possibly moose. After a few more miles, you pass the old Elk Creek Ranger Station and come to the Hams Fork Campground (one more mile).

Turn northwest across the river and the road makes a steep climb to the top of Middle Ridge (a few spruce trees here). You then come to a junction at Basin Creek. Here a 4WD road north goes to Green Knoll and Big Park.

Continue west along Basin Creek and you pass by the Nugent Park Road going south. The road then drops down for two miles where you cross the West Fork Hams Fork River and Kelly Creek. One mile further, you pass by another road going south to Nugent Park. Stay north and along Kelly Creek for one mile to a junction. Here the road to the ranger station continues along the creek.

Turn northwest up the hill and you have a good view of the Smiths Fork drainage to the west. As you continue north, the road drops down a bit where a 4WD road turns off along Sam's Creek to the Hobbie Creek Road and the Alice Lake Trail.

Continue north and then southwest and down along Coal Creek. You then leave the national forest and four miles further is a junction. Here you can take the Smiths Fork River Road north to US-89 at Smoot (see page 112).

Turn south and you join W-232 at mile #12. The road follows along the river and down through the valley to Cokeville. On this stretch of the road, you can see the Tunp Range to the east and the Sublette Range to the west.

Trip Two

The Smiths Fork River Road from Cokeville to Smoot

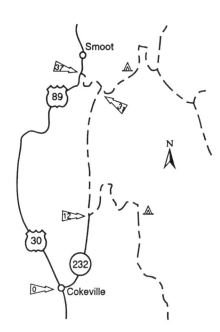

This trip begins by turning off US-30 in Cokeville and going north on W-232 (Smiths Fork River Road). As you follow along the river, the road passes below the southern end of the Sublette Range on the west and the Tunp Range on the east. To the north is Mount Wagner. At mile #12 the pavement ends at a junc-

tion. Here you can take the Hams Fork River Road east and then south to Kemmerer (see page 111).

Stay north toward the Dry Fork Road and along the river. Here Muddy Ridge is to the west and to the east is the Tunp Range. After eight miles the road crosses the river and two miles further you begin following the Dry Fork. Here a side road turns east toward the Smiths Fork, but continue along the creek toward Mount Wagner.

After about six miles the road begins climbing through a small canyon and enters the national forest. Here you see a few fir trees. Three miles further you come to a junction on the North Fork Smiths Fork River. Here you can turn east to US-189 at LaBarge or Big Piney (see pages 113 and 114).

Turn northwest up the hill. The road then swings west (past lodgepole pine) and you have a great overlook of Mount Wagner and Red Top to the north. The road turns back to the northwest again and follows along above the Salt River. To the north is Star Valley. Six miles from the last junction, you hit US-89 at mile #71, six miles south of Smoot.

Although travel conditions are certainly more ideal than those depicted in the photograph on page 113—accidents still happen. Please drive carefully on all roads!

Trip Three

The Smiths Fork River - Piney Creek Road from Smoot to Big Piney

This trip begins by going south from Smoot on US-89. As you travel through Star Valley, the Gannett Hills are to the west and to the east is the Salt River Range. At mile #72 you cross the Salt River and the road begins to climb up a bit. One mile further you turn off US-89 and head southeast on the Smiths Fork Road. The road continues to climb and you begin traveling past aspen, fir, and lodgepole pine trees.

After two miles, the road swings east and you have a great view of Star Valley, Red Top, and Mount Wagner to the north. The road then turns back to the southeast and drops down to a junction on the Smiths Fork River drainage. Here you can take the Dry Fork Road south to Cokeville (see page 112).

Stay to the southeast and across the North Fork Smiths Fork. One mile further, the road turns east and then north along the Smith Fork. (Nice drive.) After four more miles, you cross the river at Poker Hollow and begin seeing spruce trees. The road follows along the river for a bit and then climbs up a steep grade (nice area) to the top of Commissary Ridge (six miles from Poker Hollow).

The road drops down along LaBarge Creek to a junction in the LaBarge Meadows (six miles). Here you can turn north, over the Tri-Basin Divide, and follow the Greys River to US-89 at Alpine (see page 114).

Stay to the south and along the creek toward Graham Peak. After crossing a couple of small creeks, you come to a trailhead to Fontenelle Lake. Here you can see Deadline Ridge to the southeast. Three miles further, you cross Road Creek and come to a junction on Coyote Park Creek. Here you can continue south along LaBarge Creek to LaBarge.

Turn northeast and up Packsaddle Ridge toward Snider Basin and Mount Thompson. After three miles, you go through Witherspoon Pass and pass by a logging road turning south along the ridge. Stay to the east and you drop down past another logging road that goes south.

The main road continues east down to South Piney Creek in Snider Basin. Here you can see Mount Thompson to the west, Mount Darby to the northwest, North Mountain to the north, and Riley Ridge to the east. One mile after crossing South Piney is a junction at Coal Creek. Here the Middle Piney Creek Road turns north to Daniel Junction and US-189.

Stay east along South Piney Creek. The road passes between North Mountain and Riley Ridge and then leaves the national forest. As you continue to drop down, the surrounding area becomes increasingly arid. Six miles after leaving the forest, the road crosses Fish Creek. Here you can see Wyoming Peak to the west, Rand Butte to the near east, and to the far east are the Wind River Mountains.

Three miles further, you cross Middle Pine Creek to a junction. Here S-111 goes west to Middle Piney Lake and over to Daniel Junction (see page 116). Turn east on the pavement and after six miles you join W-350, five miles west of Big Piney.

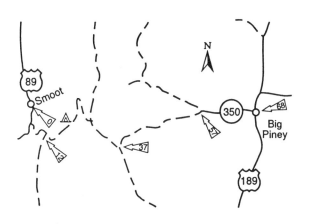

This is one of many signs indicating the conditions early travelers faced navigating this section of the Lander Cutoff.

Trip Four

LaBarge to Alpine on the LaBarge Creek - Greys River Road

This trip begins by turning off US-189 (mile #84), one mile south of LaBarge. As you head west on L-315, you can see the Little Colorado Desert to the east, the Hogback Ridge to the northwest, and to the south is LaBarge Creek.

After about six miles, you begin following LaBarge Creek northwest toward Deadline Ridge. After passing through Viola, the pavement ends (11 miles from the highway) and you follow the creek through a small valley, between Miller Mountain on the south and Lae Mountain on the north. Along here, the bottom land is filled with willow and aspen, and the hillsides are lined with limber pine, spruce, fir, and cedar trees. (A just plain pretty drive.)

After traveling through the valley for about eight miles, the road crosses Sheep Creek. The canyon now lies between Deadline Ridge on the northeast and Absaroka Ridge on the southwest. You then pass by the Fontenelle Creek road going south to Kemmerer (45 miles). Two miles further is the national forest and you cross Big Fall Creek.

Along this stretch, you can see Mount Thompson to the north. Upstream a bit you pass by a trailhead to Commissary Ridge and Indian Springs. A bit further, you pass by the Scaler Cabin Road (going west) and come to a junction between Packsaddle Ridge and Commissary Ridge. Here you can go east to Snider Basin and Big Piney (see page 113).

Continue north across Coyote Park Creek and along LaBarge Creek. Here the road passes between Mount Thompson on the east and Graham Peak on the west. Four miles from the last junction, you cross Clear Creek and pass by a trailhead to Commissary Ridge and Fontenelle Lakes.

After four more miles, you come to a junction in the LaBarge Meadows. Here you can turn northwest, over Commissary Ridge, to the Smiths Fork Road. On this road you can go south to Cokeville or west to Smoot (see pages 112 and 113).

Stay north on the Greys River Road and you climb a small saddle on the Tri-Basin Divide. The road then drops down, past spruce and fir trees, and you begin following the Greys River. (Nice drive.) Here you can see Wyoming Peak to the north, the Wyoming Range to the east, and to the west is the Salt River Range. You go by a couple of 4WD roads during the next few miles and seven miles from LaBarge Meadows is Shot Hole Spring. The road then passes below Mount Coffin (next to Wyoming Peak) and three miles further, you pass by the Spring Creek Road and enter an old burn area.

Continue north and you go past a trailhead to Swift Creek and the Cazier Guard Station (three miles). The next 10 miles down to the Three Forks Road to Barstow Lake travels along one of the prettiest stretches of Wyoming rivers. In this area you begin seeing a few cottonwood trees and the canyon widens. The road then travels through the Forest Park Feedground and you come to the Forest Park Campground.

Three miles from the campground is a junction at Sheep Creek. Here you can turn east on the McDougal Gap Road, to Daniel Junction or Big Piney (see page 116).

Continue north toward Alpine (35 miles). After about three miles, you pass the Meadows Guard Station. Here you can see Sherman Peak to the west. A couple of miles further, you leave the national forest and the road swings northwest, away from Middle Ridge, and goes around The Elbow toward Man Peak. The road enters the national forest again (one mile) and you can see Virgina Peak to the southwest.

After two miles, the road swings back to the north again and you travel through Moose Flats to the Moose Flats Campground. Here you can see Star Peaks to the northwest. After six more miles, you pass Kennington Flat (and Smeagle didn't care much for the name of the next creek you cross—Dead Dog Creek). After passing the Stewart Trailhead, you go by the Deer Creek Guard Station and Murphy Creek Campground. Two miles further is the Lynx Creek Campground.

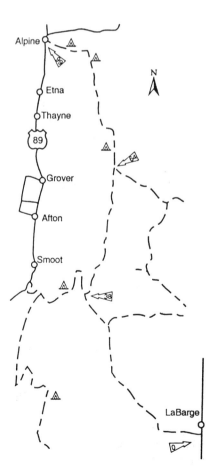

Four miles from the campground is a trailhead to Middle Ridge and the road crosses the Little Greys River. Here a road turns northeast to McCain Meadows (12 miles).

Stay on the main road as it swings west between Bradley Mountain on the north and the Salt River Range on the south. Six miles further, you pass by the Bridge Campground and begin seeing big tooth maple trees. You then leave the national forest and enter Alpine (on L-102) to a junction with US-89 at mile #118. Here you can go north one mile (across the Snake River) to Alpine Junction.

A logging truck on a straight stretch of road is a welcome sight; one coming around the bend is not! Watch your speed and drive with care.

Trip Five

Big Piney to Daniel on the Middle Piney Creek Road (with an option to Alpine on the MDougal Gap Road)

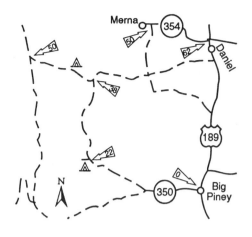

This trip begins by turning off US-189 in Big Piney and heading west on W-350. As you head toward the Wyoming Range, you can see Riley Ridge and Deadline Ridge to the southwest, Triple Peak and Bare Mountain to the northwest, and to the east are the Wind River Mountains.

At mile #5, W-350 ends and you continue west on the pavement to a junction (six miles). Here you can turn southwest on S-142 to Snider Basin and then over to the LaBarge Creek Road. There you can either go south to LaBarge or west to Smoot (see pages 112 and 113).

Stay northwest on S-111 and the road follows along Middle Piney Creek below Johnson Ridge. After about 10 miles, you enter the national forest and come to a junction. Here you can turn south toward North Mountain and travel to Snider Basin.

Continue west and you begin passing aspen, fir, and limber pine trees. After two more miles you come to another junction. Here you can continue west to Middle Piney Lake and the Sacagawea Campground. From this junction you can see Fish Creek Mountain to the southwest and to the west is Wyoming Peak.

Turn northwest along Straight Creek and you begin seeing lodgepole pine. After passing through a small saddle, the road drops down along Edwards Creek to North Piney Creek. Here Mount Schideler is to the west and to the northeast is Bald Mountain. Also at this crossing is a trailhead to North Piney Lake and the Wyoming Range Trail.

After crossing North Piney Creek the road crosses Apperson Creek (two miles), and a bit further you can see Coal Mine Mountain off to the west. The road then climbs past Red Castles to Bare Pass. Here you can see Triple Peak and Lander Peak to the northwest and to the far north is the Gros Ventre Range.

As the road drops down from the pass, you begin following South Fork Bare Creek. Five miles from the pass you come to a small junction. Here the road west follows along South Cottonwood Creek.

Turn east and after crossing South Fork Creek and South Cottonwood Creek, you leave the national forest. About two miles further, you come to a junction with the North Cottonwood Creek Road. Here you can turn west on the McDougal Gap Road to Alpine. (See option below.)

Turn east toward the Wind River Mountains and the road follows along a bench above North Cottonwood Creek. After about 10 miles you come to Ryegrass Junction. Here you can go southeast to US-189 at mile #119 (16 miles).

Turn north across the creek and toward North Horse Creek. Along this stretch you can see Bare Mountain and Triple Peak to the west and to the northwest is Prospect Peak and Lookout Mountain. After one mile you pass by S-117 going east to US-189. Stay north on S-116 and after four miles you come to the next junction. Here you can turn east and join S-117 near US-189. Also at this junction you can turn west to South Horse Creek.

Continue north on S-116 and the road crosses Horse Creek (one mile). Here you can see Prospect Peak to the west and to the northwest is Horse Mountain (next to Lookout Mountain). Three miles further, you come to a junction at the base of Beaver Divide. Here you can go three miles west to Merna and then over to North Horse Creek.

Turn east on S-112 and after six miles you join W-354 at mile #6. Here Horse Creek is on the west and the Green River is on the east. After a few miles, you pass Old Fort Bonniville and cross the river to US-191 at Daniel Junction (mile #111).

OPTION: McDougal Gap Road to the Greys River Road.

Turn west toward Alpine (50 miles) and you enter the national forest again. The road follows along North Cottonwood Creek and travels past Lander Peak and Triple Peak toward Mount McDougal. After about two miles, you cross Hardin Creek and two miles further you cross Ole Creek and North Cottonwood Creek.

Eight miles from the junction on North Cottonwood Creek, you come to McDougal Gap and a trailhead to the Wyoming Range Trail. (Very nice area.) The road drops down a couple of switchbacks to a meadow on Sheep Creek. You then follow the creek down through a steep, rugged canyon cutting through the Wyoming Range. (Fantastic drive.)

After five miles, North Fork Sheep Creek joins Sheep Creek in the run down the canyon. (Just plain beautiful.) A bit further the canyon widens to a small park and then closes in again. Nine miles from the gap, you come to a junction at the Greys River. Here you can turn south to LaBarge or north to Alpine (see page 114).

A cold milk, sandwich, and chocolate chip cookie break at Bare Pass. In the distance is Triple Peak and Lander Peak.

Trip Six

Boulder to South Pass or Farson on the Big Sandy Road

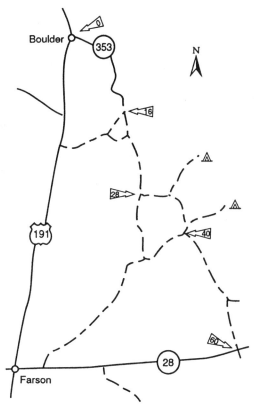

This trip begins by turning off US-191 at Boulder (mile #88) and going east on W-353. As you head toward the Wind River Mountains, you can see the top of Temple Peak to the southeast, Pyramid Peak to the east, and Fremont Peak to the northeast. At mile #2, S-125 turns north to Boulder Lake (and the Boulder Lake Trailhead) and at mile #5 you begin following the East Fork River. Here the road swings southeast toward Muddy Ridge.

Looking north at Buckskin Crossing on the Big Sandy River.

At mile #7 you pass by the Scab Creek Access Road going east. At mile #15 is a junction where W-353 ends. Here you can take S-133 southwest to Muddy Creek and join S-113 going west to US-191 at mile #73.

Continue southeast on S-118 and after two miles the pavement ends. One mile further you come to a junction at Big Sandy. Here you can take S-133 west to Muddy Creek and then take S-113 over to US-191.

Stay southeast on S-118 and you pass by a road going east to the Muddy Feedground. As you continue southeast, you can see Elk Mountain and Tabernacle Butte to the south. After five miles, you cross the Big Sandy River at Buckskin Crossing to another junction. Here you can take S-118 south to W-28 at mile #4 near Farson. This road swings around the base of Elk Mountain to Elk Horn Junction (11 miles). There you can turn north and rejoin the Big Sandy Road, or continue south to W-28 (23 more miles).

Turn east on S-132 and head toward Little Prospect Mountain. Along this stretch of the road you can see Elk Mountain and Tabernacle Butte to the south and to the northeast is Wind River Peak, Mount Nystrom, and Roaring Fork Mountain. After swinging around the mountain, the road follows along the Big Sandy River and you have a great view of the mountains. Eight miles from Buckskin Crossing is another junction. Here you can go north to the Big Sandy Campground and a trailhead into the Jim Bridger Wilderness (10 miles).

Stay southeast and after three miles you cross the Little Sandy River. Two miles further is a junction near Prospect Mountain. Here you can turn south to Elk Horn Junction and then go over to Farson.

Turn east and the road travels along Lander Creek and the base of Prospect Mountain. After five miles, you come to the next junction. Here you can go north to the Sweetwater Gap Campground and another trailhead to the wilderness.

Stay southeast along Lander Creek. Along here you can see Continental Peak, Pacific Butte, and Oregon Buttes to the southeast. To the far south is Steamboat Mountain and to the north is Atlantic Peak, Sweetwater Gap, and Mount Nystrom. Fifteen miles from the last junction you hit W-28 at mile #33.

Trip Seven

The drive and return road from Pinedale to Elkhart Park

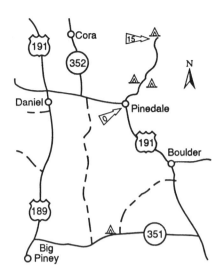

This trip begins on the south side of Pinedale where you turn northeast on to the Fremont and Half Moon Lake Road (S-154). The road climbs up past the museum and medical center and then heads toward the Wind River Mountains. After about two miles, you have a good view of Fremont Lake to the northeast and the Wyoming Range to the far west. One mile further is a junction. Here you can turn north to Sandy Beach or continue along the shoreline to the Fremont Lake Campground (five miles).

Turn northeast on the road to Half Moon Lake and you continue to climb up to another junction (four miles). Here you can turn south down to Half Moon Lake.

Continue east and you have a good view of Fremont Ridge to the northwest. Half Moon Lake, Half Moon Mountain, and Mud Lake are to the south, and to the northeast is Fortification Mountain. In this area you begin passing by lodgepole pine and aspen trees. After three miles you pass by a turnoff to the ski area. As you continue to climb, you begin seeing a few spruce and fir trees.

The road passes by an overlook of Fremont Lake and Soda Lake, and three miles further you then have a fantastic overlook of the Wind River Mountains. After one more mile is the end of the road at the Elkhart Trailhead to the Jim Bridger Wilderness and the Trails End Campground.

Jamie, John, Mike, Julia, and Jim loading equipment after a backpacking trip in the Bridger Wilderness.

Trip Eight

The Union Pass Road from Pinedale to Dubois

This trip begins by turning off US-191 (mile #105) north of Pinedale. As you head north on W-352, the Wyoming Range is to the west and the Gros Ventre Mountains are to the north. In the Wind River Mountains, you can see Temple Peak to the far southeast and Fremont Peak to the east. On the south side of Fremont Peak is Jackson Peak and on the north side is Mount Sacagawea. As you pass by Cora (mile #4), you can see Triple Peak and Bare Mountain to the far west.

At mile #8 the Willow Creek Road turns east to Willow Lake, and at mile #12 you have a nice overlook of the New Fork River. At mile #14 the New Fork Lake Road turns east to the Narrows Campground and a trailhead into the wilderness.

The main road then passes between Black Butte on the west and Middle Butte on the east. You now begin dropping down past stands of aspen to the Green River. (Nice drive.) Here you can see Big Sheep Mountain to the northeast. Just before the pavement ends at mile #25 is the Moose Gypsum Road going east to Big Bend Lookout and Little Sheep Mountain.

Continue north into the national forest. Just after passing the Whiskey Grove Campground is a junction. Here you continue northeast on the Green River Road. This route follows along the river and ends at the Green River Campground and a trailhead to the Jim Bridger Wilderness. (This is a very nice drive and the view of Square Top and the lakes is worth the trip.)

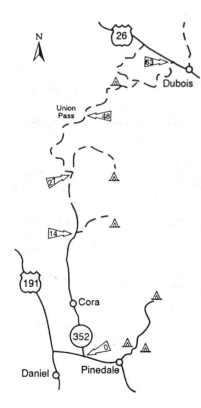

Turn north on the Union Pass Road and across the Green River. Three miles after crossing the river is a junction on Tosi Creek. Here you can see Klondike Hill to the northwest and to the northeast is Little Sheep Mountain. The road to the north follows along the river for a bit.

Turn northwest along Tosi Creek and you can see Triangle Peak to the west.

After about three miles, the road climbs up Bacon Ridge above Tepee Creek to a junction. Here the Kinky Creek Road continues northwest.

Stay east (around the ridge) and then north on the Union Pass Road. The road follows along a small creek and you begin seeing lodgepole pine and spruce trees. Four miles further, you pass by Mosquito Lake and the road travels along the edge of a large park. Here you have a good view of the Wind River Mountains (Sourdough and Connie Glaciers near Yukon Peak). A few miles further, the road crosses Wagon Creek to a junction in Buffalo Meadows. Here the road north goes to Park Creek Meadows.

Stay to the east and after two miles you cross Raspberry Creek. The road then passes through another park where you can see the top of Squaretop Mountain to the south and Downs Mountain to the southeast. You then cross Strawberry Creek and South Fish Creek. (This area is just plain pretty.) The road travels along the north side of Fish Creek Park to a junction. Here a road turns north to Leeds Creek (seven miles).

Continue east toward Union Pass and you go by a small road going south to Fish Creek Park. You then pass by the road to Lake of the Woods and come to the Union Pass Historical Site. (This is worth stopping for.) As you continue northeast from the pass, you can see Sawtooth, Darwin, and Triangle Peaks to the west and the Rams Horn to the north. The trees in this area are white pine.

The road then drops down past lodgepole pine, spruce, and fir trees. Here you have a great view of the Rams Horn to the north and the Pinnacles to the northwest. After about three miles, you pass by NF-554 going east above Warm Springs Canyon. Continue north along the creek to the next junction. Here you can take the Warm Springs Creek Road, northwest along the creek, to US-287 at mile #38. This is a nice drive if you are heading north, or if you are not ready to the hit the pavement yet (17 miles).

Turn northeast on the Union Pass Road and you begin dropping down Warm Springs Mountain. This road has a few steep switchbacks, but the view is great. Five miles from the junction on top the mountain, you hit US-287 (mile #46) north of Dubois.

Trip Nine

The drive and return road from US-191 to Granite Falls

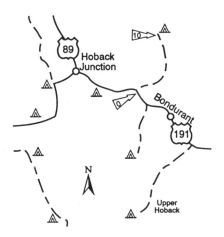

This short trip begins by turning off US-191 at mile #152, between Hoback Junction and Bondurant. As you head northeast on the Granite Springs Road and follow along Granite Creek, you can see Palmer Peak and Corner Peak ahead of you, and Battle Mountain is across the creek to the east. The trees in this area are lodgepole pine and spruce. After about two miles, you pass by a road turning north along Little Granite Creek to a trailhead.

Continue northeast along Granite Creek and after about five miles the road swings north where you pass by a road going east across the creek. Here you can see the Open Door and Corner Peak to the north, and to the northeast is Steamboat Peak and Palmer Peak.

You pass by the High Line Trailhead and then by another road going east across the creek to the Swift Creek Trailhead. One mile further is the Granite Campground. Here you can see Pyramid Peak up the canyon to the north and Pinnacle Peak off to the west.

Just past the campground is the turn to Granite Falls (nice) and you go below the Open Door. One half mile further the road ends at a parking area. Here you have a short walk to the hot springs and a trailhead to Turquoise Lake and Granite Creek.

Granite Creek Falls are located at the end of the main road and just below the Granite Creek Hot Springs.

Trip Ten

Hoback Junction to Moose Junction: the back way

Julia and her daughter Mary make time to relax and appreciate a peaceful evening view. The other visitors I saw during the hour were in such a hurry that they only peered over the edge and then rushed away in their cars.

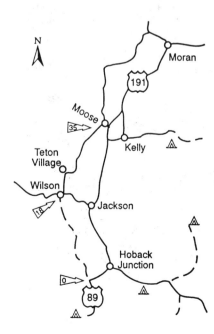

This trip begins by turning north off US-89 at mile #137, five miles west of Hoback Junction. After traveling through the cottonwood bottoms for a bit, the Wilson/Fall Creek Road climbs up to Pritchard Pass (two miles). Here you see lodgepole pine trees. As the road drop downs to Fall Creek, you also see a few spruce and fir trees. The road follows along the creek to the north, between Munger Mountain on the east and the Snake River Range on the west.

After a couple of miles, the road leaves the creek and climbs up a bit to a small park (developed area). You then drop down past aspen trees to the Snake River below. After traveling along sands of cottonwoods for two miles, the road climbs up a small bench and then drops down again to pavement. Four more miles and you hit W-22 at Wilson.

Turn east on W-22 for two miles and then north on W-390. The road follows along the Snake River on the east and travels below Rendezvous Mountain on the west. You pass West Gros Ventre Butte off to the east and then cross Lake Creek. Here you can see Table Mountain in the Gros Ventre Mountains to the far east. At mile #7 you pass by the turnoff to Teton Village and you continue north for one mile where the pavement ends.

Stay north toward Moose Junction. (Trailers and trucks are prohibited on the route.) After about one mile you pass by a trailhead to Granite Canyon and one mile further you hit pavement again. After two more miles, you pass by a trailhead to Death Canyon. The road then leaves the forest and after passing a couple of scenic overlooks, you come to a junction at the Moose entrance to Grand Teton National Park. Here you can continue north through the park to Jenny Lake, Jackson Lake, and US-89 north of Moran. Also at this junction, you can turn east for one mile to US-89 at Moose Junction.

Trip Eleven

The Gros Ventre drive and return road off US-89

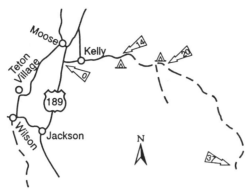

This trip begins by turning off US-89 at Gros Ventre Junction (mile #162) and going northeast toward Kelly. Here you can see East Gros Ventre Butte and Miller Butte to the south. To the west are the Tetons and to the east is Sheep Mountain in the Gros Ventre Mountains. After about four miles, you pass by the Gros Ventre Campground and the road swings east to Kelly. The road then turns north for one mile to a junction. Here you can take the Antelope Flats Road to US-89 at mile #168.

Turn east and after a half mile, you pass by Kelly Warm Springs. The road then begins to climb a bit (leaving the national park and entering the national forest) and you come to an interpretive site for the Gros Ventre Slide. You then travel along Lower Slide Lake to the Atherton Creek Campground and a boat ramp. Here the pavement ends.

The dirt road continues along the lake for about one mile. You then cross Horsetail Creek and the road climbs to an overlook high above the river. Here you can see the Red Hills to the northeast a bit. The road then drops down to the Gros Ventre River. A half mile after crossing the river are the Red Hills and Crystal Creek Campgrounds. Just after crossing Crystal Creek is a small junction. Here you can go south to the Crystal Creek trailhead. Stay to the east and the road follows along the river to Upper Slide Lake (seven miles) and the Upper Gros Ventre Trailhead (17 miles).

Scott, Kelly, and Linda (alias Jack, Janett, and Krissy) hoping to catch the next quake at the Gros Ventre Slide.

Trip Twelve

The Brooks Lake drive and return road

This little trip begins by turning off US-287 (mile #33) southeast of Togwotee Pass. As you head north on NF-515, you can see Lava Mountain to the southwest. The road travels below the Pinnacle Buttes and follows along Brooks Lake Creek. The trees is this area are lodgepole pine, spruce, and fir. (Nice little drive.) After about four miles, you pass by a road going to the Bonneville Pass Trailhead. A bit further is the Pinnacle Campground and the Brooks Lake Campground. Here the trip ends for most people. The road continuing to US-287 at mile #28 is 4WD only and travel is not recommended.

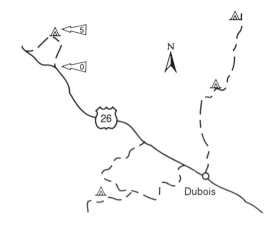

Matthew (center) came all the way from England to be in this photo at Brooks Lake with his friends Erika, Ben, and Will.

Trip Thirteen

The Buffalo Valley Road side trip to Turpin Meadows

This trip begins by turning off US-287 east of Moran Junction at mile #3. Here the Buffalo Valley Road runs northeast and then east along the Buffalo Fork River. On this stretch of the road you can see Leidy Mountain to the south, the Tetons to the west, Randolf Mountain to the northeast, and Angie Mountain above Burro Hill to the east.

After three miles the road leaves the river and passes by Taco Lake, between Burro Hill and Randolf Mountain. A bit further you begin following the river again through a beautiful mountain valley. Here you can now see Terrace Mountain just north of Angie Mountain. Three miles further you pass by the Box Creek trailhead and the pavement ends in Turpin Meadows (10 miles from the highway). Here you can go north a half mile to the Turpin Meadow Campground and a trailhead for the Teton Wilderness.

Turn south across the river and the road begins climbing up the eastern edge of Rosies Ridge. The trees through here are mainly lodgepole pine mixed with a few spruce and aspen. Watch for deer, elk, and moose near the small clearings and parks. Four miles from the meadows is US-287 (mile #13) and the Four Mile Meadow Picnic Area.

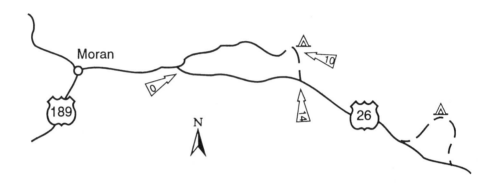

Good friends around the campfire at Turpin Meadows (Dave, Daniel, Sharon, Donna, Matthew, and Scott).

Trip Fourteen

The drive and return road from Dubois to Double Cabin

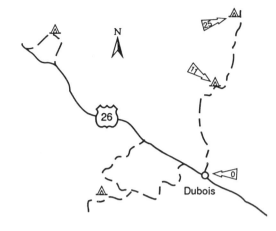

This trip begins by turning north at the Horse Creek Bridge in Dubois (US-287, mile #55). As you follow the creek out of town, you can see Whiskey Mountain to the south and to the northeast a bit is Spring Mountain and Elk Horn Ridge. After four miles, the road crosses Little Horse Creek and the pavement ends. Here you can see Ramshorn Peak to the northwest.

The road travels along the base of EM Mountain and then swings north between EM Mountain and Battrum Mountain. Five miles from the end of the pavement, you enter the national forest and come to a junction. Here you can go west to Brent Creek on NF-511.

Turn east to the next junction in a half mile. Here the Burroughs Creek Road turns north toward Amoretti Park.

Turn east past the Horse Creek Campground across Horse Creek. A bit further you can see Baedeker Butte to the northeast and part of the cliffs forming the Ramshorn along to the northeast. (Nice view.) A couple miles further is another junction. Here you can turn north on NF-504 to Parque Creek and Ramshorn Basin.

Stay east on NF-285 (Wiggins Fork, 13 miles) and the road climbs up the southern end of Elk Horn Ridge. As the road swings north along the side of the ridge, you have a good view of Indian Ridge on the east. Further north, a view opens up of the Wiggins Fork drainage and you can see Mount Ken to the northeast. After a couple more miles, the road passes through a small park and you can now see Baedeker Butte to the west. Here the road drops down and crosses Cartilage Creek below Lincoln Point (nine miles from the Horse Creek Bridge). After crossing the creek, the road climbs up again and swings around the back side of Lincoln Point. Four miles further is the end of the road at Double Cabin Campground. Here you can see Nortons Point above the confluence of Frontier Creek and Wiggins Creek. (This is a spectacular area.)

A tepee layover on Wiggins Creek before continuing to the rendezvous at Fort Bridger. Life is good!

Trip Fifteen

The Louis Lake Road from Lander southwest to Atlantic City

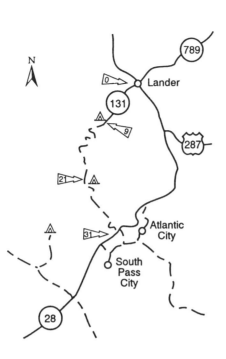

Chuck catching breakfast at Louis Lake.

This trip begins by turning off US-287 (Main Street) in Lander and taking W-131 (Fifth Street) southwest out of town. The road travels through a wide red rock canyon and follows along the Middle Popo Agie River. Near mile #6, you enter the Sinks Canyon State Park and pass by the Rise and Sinks (mile #7 and #8). The pavement ends at mile #9 at a couple of campground. (Popo Agie Falls are along the trail one and a half miles to the west.)

After crossing the river, the road climbs a series of switchbacks up the side of Fossil Hill. (If your ears don't pop on this drive they never will!) Near the top you can see the Bighorn Mountains to the far northeast. If you look up the river drainage to the west, you can see the Wind River Mountains above timberline.

One mile from Fossil Hill is Frye Lake. Here you can look due west and see Wind River Peak. To the north a bit is Big Sandy Mountain. South of Wind River Peak is Mount Nystrom and south a bit more is Roaring Fork Mountain. The forest here is composed of spruce, aspen, lodgepole and limber pine.

After leaving the lake, the road climbs up and you pass by a road going to Worthen Meadows. You then travel through Neff Park where you can see Cony Mountain and Blue Ridge to the south. To the north is Mount Arter. The road then crosses Sawmill Creek and after two miles you can see Meyer Lookout off to the east.

One mile after going over Blue Ridge is Fiddlers Lake and you have a better view of Cony Mountain. (A cony or pika is a small rabbit-like critter that prefers to live on rocky mountain slopes.) Three miles south of the lake, you cross the Little Popo Agie River. (Beautiful!) About two miles further, you go around Louis Lake (a great place for middle to late summer swimming) and past the Louis Lake Campground.

The road then climbs up for a bit and travels southeast along Rock Creek. Three miles further after crossing Rock Creek, you cross Slate Creek where you have a good view of Granite, Pabst, and Rennecker Peaks to the northwest. The road then leaves the creek and drops down to W-28 at mile #46 near Atlantic City. Along this stretch you can see Pacific Butte and Oregon Buttes to the southwest.

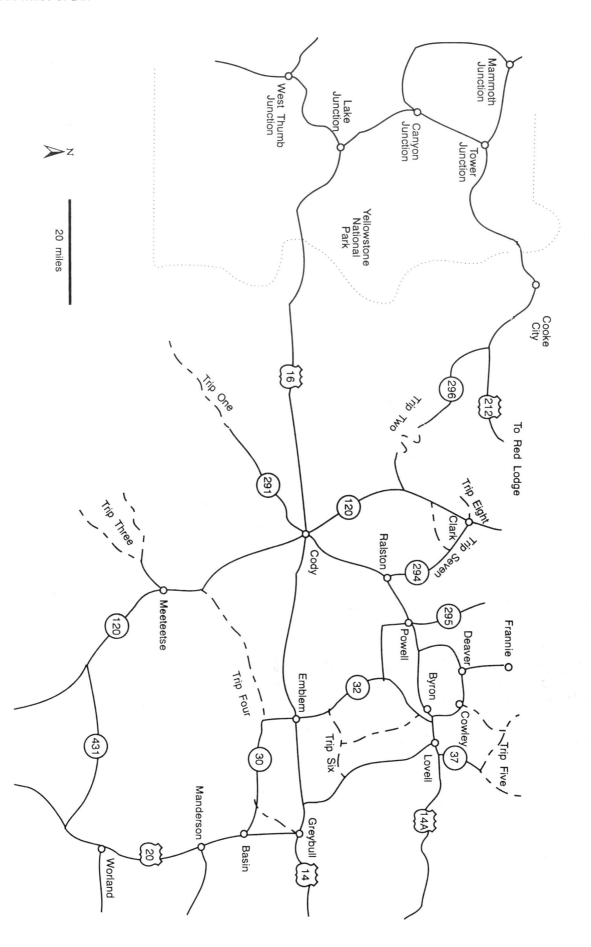

Trip One

The South Fork Shoshone River drive and return road from Cody

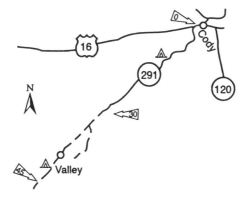

This trip begins by turning off US-14 on the west side of Cody and taking W-191 up the hill to the south. Here you can see Heart Mountain to the north, the McCullough Peaks to the east, and to the west is Shoshone Canyon (between Cedar Mountain on the south side and Rattlesnake Mountain on the north side). The road turns southwest around Cedar Mountain and toward Carter Mountain.

After four miles, you pass by a road going to Diamond Basin and you begin traveling across Irma Flats. Two miles further, Bartlett Lane turns off to the state park. Continue southwest and you begin following the South Fork Shoshone River through the valley.

At mile #9 you pass by the Lower South Fork Road and Buffalo Bill Reservoir. Here

Sheep Mountain is to the west. To the southwest is Wapiti Ridge and to the south is Carter Mountain. About five miles further, you pass by the other end of the Lower South Fork Road. Here the road begins traveling between Carter Mountain and Wapiti Ridge and you go by Castle Rock. (Nice drive.)

Two miles after passing Castle Rock, the Carter Mountain Road turns east. Here you can see Ishawooa Mesa to the southwest. As you head toward the mesa, the road crosses several small streams. After 10 miles you begin passing through part of the national forest. Here you can see the confluence of the South Fork Shoshone River and Ishawooa Creek.

The road crosses the river and goes past a trailhead into the wilderness. Two miles further, the pavement ends and the road now begins traveling between Boulder Ridge and Ishawooa Mesa. You then pass by the Hunter Creek Road (going across the river and to a trailhead further to the southwest). Also at this junction is the Ishawooa Mesa Trailhead.

Four miles from the Hunter Creek Road is the Deer Creek Campground and another trailhead. In this area you begin passing spruce, fir, cedar, and limber pine. Two miles further you pass by Hawkeye and one mile further is the end of the road and a trailhead at Cabin Creek.

The confluence of Ishawooa Creek and the South Fork Shoshone River is "plain pretty".

Trip Two

The Sunlight Basin Beartooth Road from Cody to Montana

This trip begins by turning off US-14 in Cody and going north on W-120. As you head out of town, the road crosses the Shoshone River and climbs to the top of a small bench. Here you can see Heart Mountain to the north, Pat O'Hara Mountain to the northwest, and Rattlesnake Mountain to the west. To the southwest a bit is Cedar Mountain; to the far southwest is Carter Mountain, and to the southeast are the McCullough Peaks.

At mile #104 you drop down along Cottonwood Creek and at mile #108 the Rattlesnake Mountain Road (P-7UH) turns west to the national forest (12 miles). As you continue north on W-120, you pass by Heart Mountain and begin following Skull Creek to a junction at mile #117. Here W-120 continues north to Red Lodge, Montana.

Turn west on the Sunlight Basin Road (county P-7RO and W-296, the Chief Joseph Highway) and cross O'Hara Creek. You pass by a ranch road going southwest while the main road climbs up a hill to the northwest toward the Beartooth Mountains. The road then turns southwest toward O'Hara Mountain for one mile and then swings west along Blaine Creek for about four miles. You now begin climbing up a few switchbacks and enter the national forest where the pavement ends. The trees in this area are limber pine.

After entering the forest, the road continues climbing and you begin seeing spruce and fir trees. Six miles from the boundary, you reach the top of Dead Indian Hill at Vista Point. Here you can see Heart Mountain to the southeast, Pat O'Hara Mountain to the south, and the Beartooth Mountains to the north. To the west is Sunlight Basin and the Absaroka Mountains.

As the road drops down the switchbacks (past fir and lodgepole pine), you have a great overlook of the Clarks Fork Canyon. (Note: If you adjust your descent speed to about three ear-pops per mile, you can avoid a crushed anvil and disarticulated stirrup in the inner ear.) Eight miles from the top is the Dead Indian Campground and a trailhead. The road then climbs up a bit and winds around to a junction on Sunlight Creek. Here you can turn west and follow the creek into the basin.

Stay north across Sunlight Creek on W-296 (mile #23). The road climbs past a picnic area and begins following above the Clarks Fork Canyon. At mile #19, you pass below Sugarloaf Mountain and seven miles further is the Reef Campground. You then travel past Cathedral Cliffs (above Crandel Creek) and go by the Crandel Ranger Station.

The road crosses the Clarks Fork River and travels below Hunter Peak to the Hunter Peak Campground and the Clarks Fork Trailhead (mile #5). As you continue northwest, you can see Pilot Peak and the Index to the northwest. To the west is Cache Mountain. You then pass the Lake Creek Campground and to a junction with US-212.

OPTION: To Cooke City & Yellowstone.

Turn west toward Pilot Peak. The road continues along the river and through a beautiful valley. About two miles from the junction, you pass the Crazy Creek Campground and a trailhead. Two miles further is the Pilot Creek Trailhead. You then pass by the Fox Creek Campground and the road begins to climb up a bit. Two miles from the campground is the state line. Here you begin dropping down along Cache Creek and pass by two campgrounds. Cooke City is five miles from the state line. Three miles further west, you go through Silver Gate and enter Yellowstone National Park.

OPTION: To Red Lodge.

Turn east and the road climbs up above the Clarks Fork River. After about one mile, you pass by the Lily Lake Road and cross Lake Creek below a small waterfall. As you continue to climb the mountain, you pass by the Muddy Creek Road and come to the Pilot-Index Overlook (seven miles from the junction). The road then goes by the Clay Butte Lookout Road and you pass Beartooth Falls. The road then swings

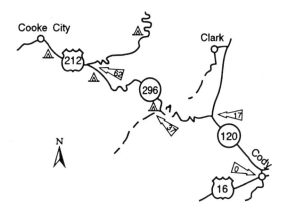

around Beartooth Lake and goes past a campground. (Just plain pretty.)

After leaving the lake, the road travels through a high mountain park and follows along Little Bear Creek. Three miles further is the Island Lake Campground and the road travels between Little Bear Lake and Chain Lake. You then go by Long Lake and a trailhead to the Clarks Fork River. Here the road climbs above timberline to the West Summit Rest Area at Beartooth Pass. (Terrific area.)

As the road drops down a bit, you can see Glacier Lake in a small pocket to the west and you have an inspirational view of Rock Creek far below. The road continues above timberline and you can see Garden Lake (below and to the south) and the Twin Lakes (below and to the north).

Twenty-six miles from the junction with US-212 is the Montana state line. Here you begin an unnerving drop to the valley below (12 miles). (On the way down, stop off at the Rock Creek Vista Point for an informative scenic overlook and to let the brakes cool down.) After reaching the bottom, you pass by three campgrounds on your way to Red Lodge (about 10 miles further).

The Sunlight Basin area is scenic to say the least. Shown here is Beartooth Falls near the Montana border on US-212 heading northeast. This is Grizzly Bear Country so keep a clean campsite!

Trip Three

The Wood River - Greybull River drive and return road from Meeteetse

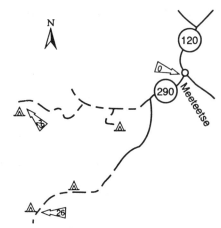

This trip begins by turning off W-120 in Meeteetse and going west on W-290. As you follow the Greybull River out of town, you can see Carter Mountain to the far west. At mile #6 you cross the Wood River to a junction. Here you can continue west along the Greybull River to a junction at the end of W-290. There you can turn south on P-5XS for three miles to Sunshine Reservoir, or you can continue west to the Timber Creek, Jack Creek, or North Fork Pickett Creek access roads to the national forest. (See option below.)

Turn south on the Wood River Road (P-4DT) and you travel through the valley for about four miles. The road then swings south-

Papyo Butte near the confluence of the Greybull river and Wood River.

west across the river where the pavement ends. Here P-4CP turns south toward Gooseberry Creek.

Continue southwest along the river and toward the Absaroka Mountains. After about two miles, the road crosses the river again and you begin traveling below some bluffs. Six miles further, you pass Noon Point (off to the south) and enter the national forest (three more miles).

After entering the forest, the road turns west and you pass a trailhead to South Fork and Brown Creek. In this area you begin seeing limber pine, aspen, cedar, and spruce trees. One mile further is the Wood River Campground and the confluence with the Middle Fork. (Nice drive.)

After leaving the campground, you pass by a trailhead to Timber Creek and come to the Brown Mountain Campground. Here a rough road continues west to The Meadows (two miles) and then enters private property.

OPTION: Greybull River Road to Jack Creek

Continue west along the Greybull River to mile #11 where the pavement ends at a junction at the base of Papyo Butte. Here you can turn southwest to Sunshine Reservoir. (Papyo means "buffalo paunch". The name comes from an indian legend about a tribe of indians seeking protection on the butte from another hostile tribe. The tribe at the base of the butte was trying to starve the tribe on top and win the battle. Sometime during the siege, a brave made a desperate run for water collected from the river in a buffalo paunch. The battle was turned around as the tribe on top rallied around this heroic event.)

Continue west around the butte and in five miles is another junction. Here the Timber Creek Ranger Station Road turns south toward Jojo Mountain. Stay west for two miles to another junction. Here the Pickett Creek Road turns northwest to the national forest.

Continue west and after crossing Frances Creek, the road leaves the river and makes a long climb up the mountain to an oil field station. Here the road drops down along the base of the mountain to the Jacks Creek Campground on the Greybull River (18 miles from the end of the pavement).

Trip Four

The Greybull River Road from Meeteetse to Basin

Although Trip Four is paved, there are other "roads" in the basin. Hoping to avoid the scene found on page 135, Black Irene waits patiently on top while Smeagle and I scout the 2-track road below.

This trip begins by taking W-120 along the Greybull River north of Meeteetse. After a couple of miles you cross Meeteetse Creek to a junction at mile #58.

Turn northeast toward Burlington and the road (P-3LE) continues along the river through a small valley. After about seven miles, you can see Tatman Mountain off to the east and you begin traveling across Sheets Flat. Two miles further, the road climbs up to a junction. Here you can take the YU Bench Road northwest to US-14.

Continue northeast along the YU Bench and then east toward the Bighorn Mountains. After about eight miles, you enter Big Horn County and begin traveling through a wetland area on Lane 40. (Nice drive.) Seven miles from the county line, you join W-30 at mile #120. Here you can go north to Burlington and US-14 near Emblem.

Continue east and you can see Table Mountain to the north and Sheep Mountain to the south. The trees in this area are mainly Russian olive. At mile #112, you pass through Otto and you can see Gould Butte to the northeast. Five miles further is a junction. Here you can continue east to US-20 at Basin (eight miles), or you can turn northeast on the Greybull River Road to US-20 on the south side of Greybull (nine miles).

Trip Five

The Bighorn Canyon drive and return road from Lovell

This trip begins by turning off US-310 on the east side of Lovell and taking US-14A east. You pass by the Bighorn National Park Information Center to a junction at mile #2. Here you can continue east on US-14A toward the Bighorn Mountains.

Turn north on W-37 and you head toward Sykes Mountain and the Pryor Mountains in Montana. Here you can see Little Sheep Mountain to the southeast. At mile #1 you cross the Shoshone River and the road swings northeast for a bit (past a couple of roads going east into the Yellowtail Wildlife Unit). The road turns back to the north after a couple of miles and you can see Little Mountain off to the east. At mile #9 the Crooked Creek Road turns west to US-310 at Cowley. (See option below.)

Continue north into the Bighorn Canyon National Recreation Area. One mile further, the road to Horseshoe Bend turns east. Stay on the main road traveling between Sykes Mountain and the Pryor Mountains.

The road now begins to climb up past cedar trees and enters the Wild Horse Range. (Very nice drive.) Five miles from the area boundary is the Montana state line. You then pass by a side road going east one mile to the Devils Canyon Overlook. (Great view of the confluence of Porcupine Creek and the Bighorn River.)

As you continue north, the road travels between the canyon and the Pryor Mountains. After about four miles, you leave the Wild Horse Range and cross Hough Creek. (Beautiful string of cottonwoods here.) Three miles further is a junction. Here the main road drops down along Trail Creek (past some campsites)

The drive through the wildhorse range and Pryor Mountains is nice. Also nice is the view of Devil Canyon and the Bighorn River.

to Barry's Landing. The pavement ends on the road going north. (This road enters the Crow Indian Reservation and I do not know the accessibility along this route.)

OPTION: The Crooked Creek Road to Cowley

The Crooked Creek Road heads west away from Sykes Mountain and follows the creek along the foothills of the Pryor Mountains, entering part of the wild horse range. After about two miles, you pass by a road going north to the fish hatchery. The main road leaves the creek and travels along some gray bluffs to another junction. Here Road-7.5 cuts south over the bluffs and rejoins the main road. (This is a short cut **IF** the road is dry!) Turn west on the Gypsum Creek Road for four miles to a third junction. Here you can take a BLM road northwest into Montana and hit US-310 north of Frannie, Wyoming.

Turn south and you pass several roads going east and west. Along this stretch you can see Carter Mountain to the south and Heart Mountain to the southwest, with Rattlesnake Mountain on the left side and Pat O'Hara Mountain on the right side. To the west are the Beartooth Mountains. Six miles south of the BLM junction you hit pavement at the airport turnoff. Continue south for three more miles to Cowley.

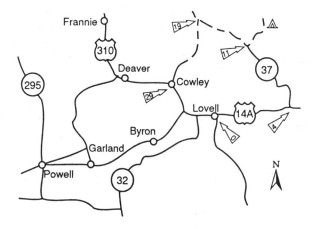

Trip Six

The Little Dry Creek Road cutoff from W-32 to W-789

This trip begins by turning off W-32 just north of Emblem. As you travel east on the Little Dry Creek Road, you can see the Bighorns to the east, McCoulgh Peaks to the southwest, Carter Mountain to the west, and Heart Mountain to the northwest. To the north are the Beartooth Mountains and to the northeast are the Prior Mountains.

The road winds around the top of a small divide and across the barren badlands. After six miles you come to a junction. Here you can take the Sand Draw Road north to Byron and Lovell. Turn southeast to the next junction in one mile. Here you can take the Foster Gulch Road north to Byron.

Continue east toward the Sheep Mountain uplift and across Little Dry Creek (four miles). A couple of mile further, you begin passing through some rocky breaks and hit W-789 at mile #220.

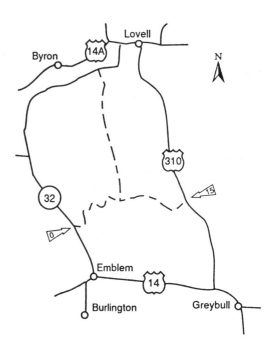

There are several 2-track roads that run across the basin. These "paths" are great places to explore but they may require a certain amount of effort and take some bridge-building abilities.

Trip Seven

The Badger Basin Cutoff from Ralston to Clark

This trip begins by turning off US-14A just west of Ralston (mile #15) and taking W-294 north. Here you can see McCullough Peaks to the south, Carter Mountain to the southwest, and Heart Mountain to the west. To the northwest are the Beartooth Mountains, to the near northeast is the Polecat Bench and above them in the distance are the Pryor Mountains.

At mile #3 is Kamms Corner and you begin travels across the Ralston Flats. Four miles further, the road drops down through some small breaks and travels across the arid badlands below. At mile #11 the Sand Coulee Road (BLM) turns southwest and hits W-120 at mile #120. Continue west on W-294 for eight more miles to W-120 at mile #130 near Clark.

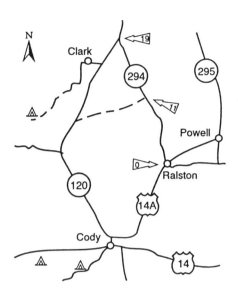

Heart Mountain is one of the dominate landmarks in this area. It is shown here in the background behind the Heart Mountain Relocation Center (off US-14A at mile #14).

Trip Eight

The drive and return road from Clark to the lower Clarks Fork Canyon

This little trip begins by turning off W-120 at mile #129 and taking county roads 1AB and 8VC to the west. As you near the mouth of the canyon, everything begins to get very impressive. The pavement ends 12 miles from the highway and you enter the national forest.

A dirt road continues up the canyon for a mile or so and then turns into a rough 2-track requiring a high clearance vehicle or 4WD. There are no maintained campgrounds here, but there are some NICE VIEW camping sites.

Two miles from the end of the pavement is a small rocky stream crossing. Here the trail north leads to Bridal Veil Falls. The 2-track continues up the canyon for four miles where it deadends (at least for all practical purposes). There you can make a steep climb up to the Clarks Fork River Trail. This trail follows along the north edge of the canyon to W-292 near the junction with US-212 (see page 131).

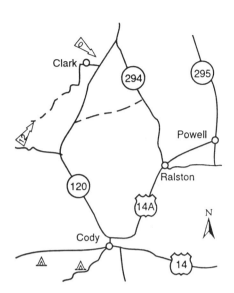

The Clarks Fork River is Wyoming's first and only Wild and Scenic River (and Boyce would probably concur that it is worthy of the classification).

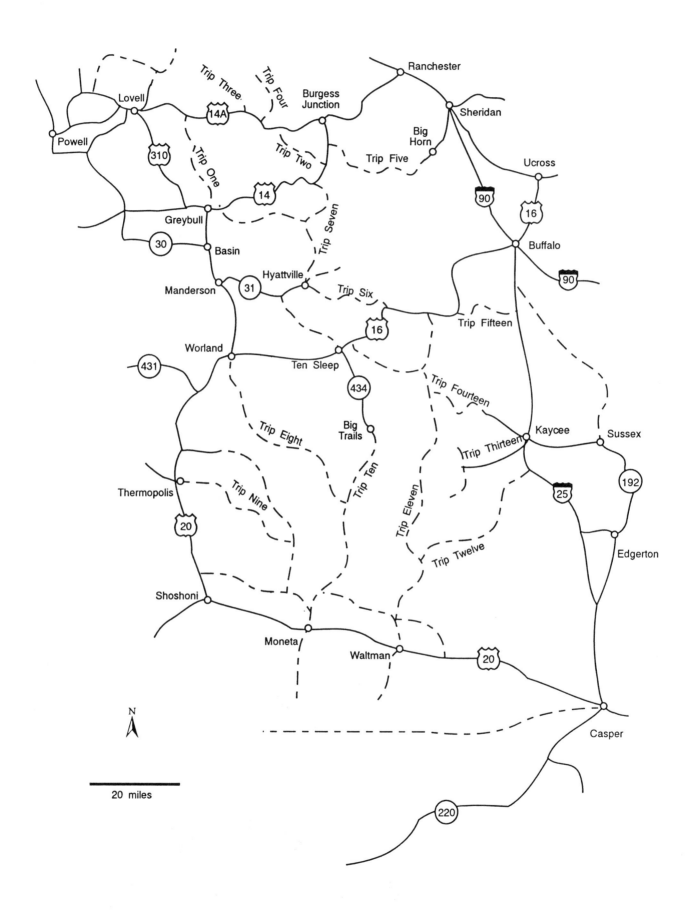

20 miles

Trip One

The Crystal Creek Road from Greybull to Lovell

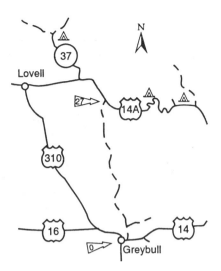

This trip begins by taking US-14 east from Greybull. Just after crossing the Bighorn River, you turn north on Division Street, west on Sandy Row, and then follow it around to Rim Rock Road. Turn north again and you follow along the river for about one mile. Here the pavement ends and as you drop down a small hill, you turn north again on Rd-27. The road crosses Shell Creek to a junction in one mile. Here a mine road turns west.

Turn east on the Crystal Creek Road (Lane-33) and head toward the Bighorn Mountains. The road follows along Shell Creek and past lavender and pink buttes. After three miles you come to a junction. Here Lane-33 continues east toward the Devils Kitchen.

Turn north toward Crystal Creek (12 miles) and you pass by a mine haul road after two miles. Stay to the north and over a small hill. You now begin traveling between Sheep Mountain on the west and a ridge on the east. To the far north you can see the Pryor Mountains. Five miles from the haul road you cross Bear Creek. (Beautiful area.)

After crossing Bear Creek the road climbs over a hill to Dry Bear Creek. The road climbs up again and you can now see the cut in Sheep Mountain where the Bighorn River flows through. To the far west are the Absaroka Mountains and to the far northwest is Heart Mountain and the Beartooth Range.

The road then drops down through some fantastic badlands to Crystal Creek. Just after crossing the creek you pass by a ranch road going east. Turn west toward the river and after three miles, you come to a "Y" in the road. Both branches connect after one mile and you begin traveling northwest again across Red Flat. After a couple of miles, the road turns back to the north and you can where see the Bighorn River cuts through Little Sheep Mountain. You pass by several small roads turning east and 14 miles from Crystal Creek you hit US-14A at mile #14.

A section of the Big Horn Basin badlands between Crystal Creek and Dry Bear Creek.

Trip Two

The Hunt Mountain Road from US-14 to US-14A

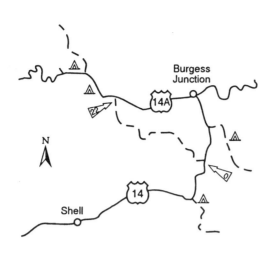

This little trip begins by turning off US-14 at mile #38. The road (NF-10) heads west along Little Prospect Creek to a saddle. Here the road turns northwest along the Continental Divide. The trees in this area are spruce and fir and the rock is Bighorn Dolomite. (I understand that some of the trees up this high make a noise when they fall - even though no one is around to hear it.)

There is nothing special about the remainder of the route (eg. there are no waterfalls, major junctions, or lakes). You just have a nice drive along the top of the world for the next 20 miles. You then drop down to US-14A at mile #43.

The Hunt Mountain Road is primarily above timberline and runs for 20 miles along the backbone of the Big Horn Mountains.

Trip Three

Medicine Wheel Drive and Return

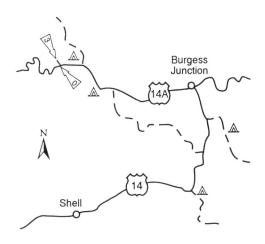

This little trip begins by turning off US-14A at mile #36. Here a dirt road turns northwest up Medicine Wheel Mountain for three miles to a parking area at the Medicine Wheel. Enough said!

NOTE: Please write to the U.S. National Forest Service to protest any future development of this site. If you think it should be developed—don't do anything!

This photo at the Medicine Wheel took no power and it holds nothing but the small amount of light needed to make it.

Trip Four

The Porcupine -Bucking Mule Falls drive and return road

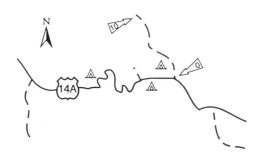

This little trip begins by turning off US-14A at mile #38. As you head north on the Sheep Mountain Road (NF-11), you can see Roster Hill to the north, northwest is Cone Mountain and Duncum Mountain, and to the west is Medicine Wheel Mountain. To the south is Bald Mountain and to the southeast is Little Bald Mountain. After about one mile, you pass by

the Littlehorn Road turning east. Stay to the northwest and you pass by the Burn Mountain Road after a half mile.

Continue northwest and after passing by the Little Bighorn Trailhead, you come to another junction. Here NF-11 climbs up Duncum Mountain to the northwest, and NF-13 turns south to the Porcupine Campground and US-14A at mile #36.

Continue west on the Devils Canyon Road (NF-14). After about four miles, you pass through part of the Duncum Mountain burn area to a parking area and a trail going down to Porcupine Falls. (It's a steep climb, but the falls are terrific.) Here the road turns back to the north for about three miles to a road closure. There you can take the trail to Bucking Mule Falls at the head of Devils Canyon. (Nice area.)

Smeagle contemplating the steep climb back from Porcupine Falls.

Trip Five

The Red Grade Road from Big Horn to Burgess Junction

This trip begins by turning off I-90 at exit #33 and heading toward Big Horn. You travel west for one mile on W-342 and then north for five miles to W-335. Here you turn west for three miles to Big Horn. As you leave town and head west toward the Bighorn Mountains, you can see Little Goose Canyon and Little Goose Peak to the southwest. To the northwest a bit is She Bear Mountain and Walker Mountain.

At mile #9 the pavement ends and you begin climbing up Red Grade on S-26. Along this stretch of the road you see limber pine, ponderosa pine, aspen, and fir trees. You also have a good view of the basin to the east. (You can almost see Dorothy and Toto from up here.) The major climb is over about three miles from the end of the pavement. Here you can see Little Goose Peak to the near south above Tepee Creek and to the far south is Black Tooth Mountain in the Cloud Peak Wilderness Area.

You then enter the national forest and begin traveling on NF-26. The road goes by a trailhead to Black Tooth Mountain and you should pass by a terrible road going south to Little Goose Campground (NF-314, 4WD).

The road continues along the top and then drops down a bit. You pass by NF-238 going north to lower Rapid Creek, and you continue to drop down Swamp Creek Hill to upper Rapid

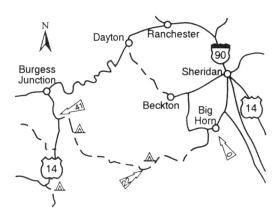

Creek. (Nice area.) The road climbs up a bit past a small cascade to a trailhead to Rapid Creek and Penrose Park. The road continues along through a small park and over a hill to a junction. Here you can take NF-293 south to Park Reservoir and a trail to Geneva Pass.

Continue west past the East Fork Campground and across East Fork Big Goose Creek. Here you can see Spear Mountain to the south and Eagle Peak to the southwest. You pass by the ranger station and the Ranger Creek Campground and begin following along Ranger Creek toward Dome Peak. After about three miles, the road begins to climb up a bit and you pass by Duck Pond. (Cute!) Just around the bend you cross West Fork Big Goose Creek to the Twin Lakes Picnic ground and a trail to Sawmill Lakes.

After leaving the picnic area, the road passes by an overlook of Sawmill Lakes and the Bighorn Mountains to the north. About five miles further you go through Sawmill Pass. Here Dome Peak is to the south and Bruce Mountain is to the west.

The road travels along the East Fork Tongue River through a long park where you pass by NF-226 going south to Woodchuck Pass. (Watch for moose in this area.) The road now meanders around to the north and along the river. (Nice drive.) After about five miles, you cross the South Tongue River (just below the confluence of the east and west forks) to the Dead Swede Campground.

After leaving the campground, the road continues north through a tornado blowdown (June 25, 1991) for two miles to the Tie Flume Campground. The road now turns west for three miles to US-14 at mile #43. Here you can go north to Burgess Junction, or southwest through Shell Canyon to Greybull.

Part of the 1991 tornado blowdown south of Burgess Junction.

Trip Six

The Hyattville Road from Manderson to Meadowlark Lake

Backcountry clothes-drier in use after a terrific hail storm.

This trip begins by turning off US-20 at mile #185 and taking W-31 east to Manderson. After passing through town, the road crosses the Nowood River and you head toward the Bighorn Mountains. At mile #5, you cross the river again and the road turns southeast. You continue along the river, past McDermotts Butte, to the next crossing at mile #14. One mile further is a junction. Here you can continue along the river to Ten Sleep.

Stay east on W-31 and you begin following Paint Rock Creek. At mile #19 the road crosses Alkali Creek and two miles further is another junction. Here the Alkali Creek Road turns north to Shell Canyon and the archeological site (see page 145). Stay on W-31 and the road turns south across Medicine Lodge Creek to Hyattville.

As you leave town, the road crosses Paint Rock Creek and the pavement ends. Continue south for a half mile to a junction. Here the road south goes to Ten Sleep.

Turn southeast and the road goes around Cedar Mountain to a small junction (six miles). Here the road through Ziesman Canyon turns southwest and joins the Nowood River Road to Ten Sleep.

Stay on the main road to the east and up the hill. Here you have a terrific view of the Paint Rock Creek drainage to the north and the Brokenback Creek drainage to the south. The road continues to climb along this overlook and you begin seeing limber pine and ponderosa pine trees. A bit further you see fir trees and then a few aspen and lodgepole pine in an old burn area. The road now travels along the top and you enter the national forest on NF-408.

Two miles inside the forest boundary, you cross South Paint Rock Creek to a junction. Here you can go northeast along Soldier Creek to Bellyache Flats.

Turn southeast on NF-24 and you wind around the side of the mountain to another junction in four miles. Here you can turn north along Bald Ridge to the Lily Lake Trailhead. Stay southeast on NF-24 and you continue to drop down (past some small ponds) to another junction in two miles. Here you can take NF-27 north to West Ten Sleep Lake. Stay southeast and you pass by the Boulder Creek Campground and hit US-16 at Deerhaven Lodge (mile #44).

Trip Seven

The Paint Rock Road from Ten Sleep to US-14

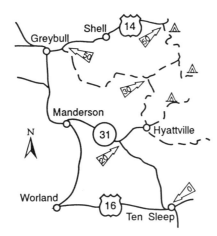

This trip begins by turning off US-16 at mile #26, just west of Ten Sleep. The Nowood River Road heads north along the river and below the Bighorn Mountains. After five miles, you cross the river and begin following Blue Ridge off to the west. Three miles further is a junction. Here you can continue along the river to W-31 and US-20 at Manderson.

Turn north up the hill toward Hyattville. The road follows along Buffalo Creek and passes through the Renner Wildlife Unit. After four miles is a junction in Buffalo Flat. Here you can turn northeast through Ziesman Canyon and join the road to Meadowlark Lake.

Continue up the hill to the north and past Cedar Mountain (off to the east). After leaving the wildlife unit, the road travels through the basin to a junction (four miles). Here you can turn southeast to Meadowlark Lake.

Damon looking for a good place to land.

Continue north and you cross Paint Rock Creek and join W-31 in Hyattville. The road crosses Medicine Lodge Creek, and after one mile you come to a junction. Here you can continue on W-31 to Manderson and US-20.

Turn north on the Alkali/Cold Springs Road to the next junction in a half mile. Here you can take the Cold Springs Road to the Medicine Lodge Archeological State Park (nice place) or the Bighorn National Forest.

Stay north on the Alkali Creek Road. Along this stretch you can see Paint Rock Canyon to the east and to the northeast is Medicine Lodge Creek Canyon (between Black Butte and Bear Mountain). The road snakes around along Alkali Creek and you pass buttes, bluffs, and painted badlands.

After about eight miles, you begin climbing up a steep hill and the road loops around some terrific canyon country. You continue to climb up a ridge for about five miles where you begin passing cedar trees. The road then travels along the top and you can see the Absaroka Mountains to the far west. Fifteen miles from W-31 is a junction. Here you can take the Red Gulch Road northwest to US-14 at mile #10.

Stay north on the Alkali Creek Road and you begin passing limber pine and a few aspen trees. Further up the mountain you begin seeing lodgepole pine. After six miles you enter the national forest to a junction. Here NF-17 turns south to Paint Rock Lake and three campgrounds.

Turn north on N-17 and you drop down past spruce and lodgepole pine to South Trapper Creek. You then cross North Trapper Creek, Johnny Creek, and Jack Creek (one more mile). The road then climbs up to a junction and trailhead on a small saddle. Here you can turn east to Shell Lake.

Continue north up Crooked Creek Hill. The road drops down a bit and after about four miles you go through Snowshoe Pass. Here a small road goes up the mountain to the northwest.

Continue north, down the mountain, to Shell Creek and the ranger station (three miles). You then pass by the Shell Creek Campground and at the Cabin Creek Campground, you hit US-14 at mile #31.

Trip Eight

Worland to Moneta on the Nowater Trail

This trip begins by turning off US-20 in Worland and taking Railway Street south to W-432. At mile #2 the highway turns west, but continue south (past the airport turn off) for one mile where the pavement ends. Cross the canal and turn southeast on the Nowater Trail. One mile further the road crosses another irrigation canal and you begin traveling across the Bighorn Basin. In this area you can see the Bighorn Mountains to the east, the Bridger Mountains to the south, the Owl Creek Mountains to the southwest, and the Absoraka Range to the west.

Four miles from the end of the pavement, you cross the East Fork Nowater Creek and the road begins following along a ridge above Nowater Creek (off to the southwest). After four more miles, you pass by a road turning east, but continue southeast down to Little Sand Draw. You then pass by the Neiber Road going west and continue on the Nowater Trail to another junction in three miles. (Nice view here.) Here the Devils Slide Road turns east along the ridge.

Stay southeast toward the Lake Creek Divide. As the road drops down to Nowater Creek (two miles), you can see Potter Butte off to the west. After crossing the creek, the road ambles along toward Black Mountain. In six miles you come to another junction. Here the Mud Creek Road turns south toward Black Mountain.

Stay east on the Nowater Trail and you cross Scorpion Draw (one mile) and Black Mountain Draw (two more miles). The road makes a loop north and back east again across Nowater Creek. The road follows along the creek for a bit and then climbs up along a ridge. Here you can see Klondike Peak to the south (on the edge of the Lake Creek Divide). To the east are the Bighorn Mountains and to the north is South Butte. Seven miles after crossing Nowater Creek is a junction. Here the Blue Bank Road turns north to US-16 (25 miles).

Stay to the east and after two miles you cross Blue Bank Draw. The road then turns southeast to the Buffalo Springs Creek crossing (two more miles). Here you can see Chalk Butte to the north. You pass by a ranch road going south and you cross Buffalo Creek. After crossing the creek, the road makes a long climb up the back side of Lightning Ridge. (Nice drive.) Along this stretch you have a terrific view to the northeast of the Nowood River drainage near Big Trails.

The road heads south along the top of a ridge between Buffalo Creek and the Nowood River. After three miles you drop down to the junction with the Nowood River Road (10 miles from Buffalo Creek). Here you can go north to Ten Sleep (see page 148).

Turn south along the Nowood River and after five miles you cross it. (This is good place to water down the dog.) The road then leaves the river and climbs up to Cottonwood Pass (seven miles). Along this stretch you can see Battle Mountain to the west.

As you drop down from the pass along Cottonwood Creek, you can see the Beaver Divide to the far south and to the west is Lysite Mountain. The road then begins traveling out into the basin and you can see Cooper Mountain to the west. Seven miles from the pass is a junction. Here the Big Horn Trail turns northeast toward Sioux Pass.

Stay to the south and after passing Snyder Creek Reservoir, you come to another junction. Here the Badwater Road turns east to Badwater and Arminto.

Continue south on the Badwater Road and along Badwater Creek to Lost Cabin (five miles). Here the Lost Cabin Road turns east to Arminto. Stay southwest on the Badwater Road, and after three miles you come to another junction in Lysite. Here the Bridger Creek Road goes west to Shoshoni or northwest to Thermopolis (see page 147). Turn south across Badwater Creek and after passing through the Moneta Hills, you hit US-20 at Moneta (eight miles).

Trip Nine

Moneta to Thermopolis on the Bridger Creek Road

This trip begins by turning off US-20 at Moneta. As you head north through the Moneta Hills, you can see the Beaver Divide to the south, Lysite Mountain to the north, and Cooper Mountain to the northwest. After eight miles, you cross Badwater Creek to a junction in Lysite. Here the Badwater Road turns east to Lost Cabin (see page 148).

Stay north and then west on the Badwater Road. After passing by the Lysite Mountain Road (going north), you follow along Badwater Creek and the pavement ends. Continue west across Bridger Creek to a junction. Here you can go west on the Badwater Road to Shoshoni.

Turn north on the Bridger Creek Road and you meander around through the badlands. You then pass several side roads the next junction in 10 miles. Here the Point of the Mountain Road turns southwest toward Shoshoni.

Stay north and you pass by Greer Peak and Fuller Peak off to the west. Two miles further, you cross South Bridger Creek to a junction with two options to Thermopolis. Here Cooper Mountain is to the west, Lysite Mountain to the east, and in the foreground to the northeast is Arapaho Butte.

OPTION: The Dry Bridger Creek Road.

Turn west on the Dry Bridger Creek Road and you begin following along the creek and a power line. Three miles further is a gate (where a 2-track road goes west) and you begin traveling on HS-5. The road swings northwest and after about seven miles you cross West Bridger Creek. Here a ranch road turns west along the creek.

Stay north and the road climbs up a bit. You then begin dropping down along Reed Creek and below Guffy Peak on the west. As the road continues down, you begin seeing cottonwood and chokecherry trees. (Nice Drive.) At the mouth of the canyon, the road swings west and crosses West Kirby Creek.

After crossing the creek, you climb up to a small pass. Here Guffy Peak is to the south, Klondike Peak is to the east, and the Bighorn Mountains are to the northeast. The road drops down a long hill to Alkali Creek and then climbs up Blue Hill. You now begin going down along the side of the hill and travel through a sagebrush canyon. A bit further the road winds around and passes through Buffalo Basin.

The road continues to drop down and after one mile you begin traveling through Red Canyon. (Nice drive.) After about two miles, the road swings west and follows along Buffalo Creek through a terrific canyon. Twelve miles further, you join W-173 at mile #2. Turn northwest across the Bighorn River and you hit US-20 at mile #130 south of Thermopolis.

OPTION: The Kirby Creek Road.

Continue north on the Bridger Creek Road, past Arapaho Butte, to a junction on Bridger Creek (two miles). Here the road continuing along the creek to the north ends on private land.

Turn up the hill to the northwest on the Kirby Creek Road and cross West Bridger Creek. The road continues to climb up to a saddle on top and you drop down the other side along Kirby Creek. Eight miles from the top, you cross the creek and leave the canyon. The road crosses the creek again and then leaves it for a bit. Along this stretch, you can see the Bighorn Mountains to the northeast. To the northwest is Zimmers Butte and to the east is Lake Creek Divide.

As you begin following along the creek again, you pass through an oil field area. About 10 miles from the canyon you hit pavement. Turn west along Kirby Creek and, as you pass Zimmers Butte, you join W-172 (three miles). Continue west on the highway and at mile #4 Cedar Mountain is on the north and you can see the Owl Creek Mountains to the far southwest. At mile #1 you cross the Bighorn River and hit US-20 (mile #139) at Lucerne, just north of Thermopolis.

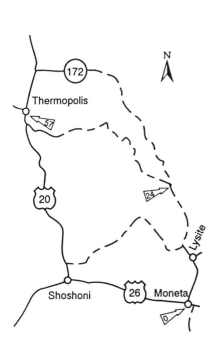

Trip Ten

Moneta to Ten Sleep on the Nowood River Road

Mahogany Butte and the Nowood River drainage as viewed from Lightning Ridge.

This trip begins by turning off US-20 mile #79 at Moneta. As you head north through the Moneta Hills, you can see the Beaver Divide to the south, Lysite Mountain to the north and Cooper Mountain to the northwest. After six miles, you cross Badwater Creek to a junction in Lysite. Here you can go west to Shoshoni on the Badwater Road or north to Thermopolis on the Bridger Road.

Turn east on the Badwater Creek Road and after three miles you come to a junction in Lost Cabin. Here the Lost Cabin Road goes east to Arminto.

Turn north on the Badwater Creek Road and after two miles the pavement ends. Continue north toward Lysite Mountain and along Badwater Creek. After about three miles is another junction. Here the Badwater Road turns east toward Cedar Ridge and Powder River.

Stay north on the Nowood Road and you begin following Snyder Creek. After two miles, you come to the next junction. Here the Big Horn Trail goes east to Sioux Pass.

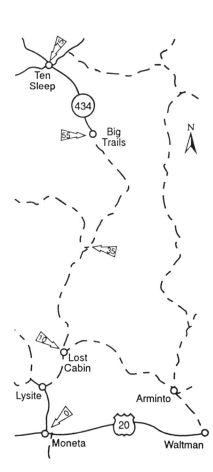

Continue north on the Nowood Road and you begin following Cottonwood Creek up a small canyon to Cottonwood Pass (seven miles). As the road drops down the other side (along Stove Creek and Lone Tree Creek), you have a good view of the Bighorn Mountains to the north and Battle Mountain to the northwest. After about six miles, you cross the Nowood River and follow it to a junction (five miles). Here you can take the Nowater Road northwest to Worland.

Continue northeast along the river and the base of Lightning Ridge. You then pass through Nowood. One mile further you go by the Split Rock Road going east to Cherry Creek Hill.

Stay on the Nowood Road and you follow the river through the gap below Mahogany Butte. (Nice drive.) Along this stretch, you see boxelder, cottonwood, willow, chokecherry, and ash trees. After going through the gap, the road travels through a beautiful valley and crosses Cherry Creek. You then follow along Redban Creek for about five miles. The road turns back to the north where you begin following Little Canyon Creek. Here you can see Horse Butte to the east. (Beautiful drive.)

After crossing the creek, you hit W-434 mile #21 at Big Trails, and you begin following along the Nowood River again. The road crosses Otter Creek at mile #12, and at mile #8 you pass by the Spring Creek Road (loops back toward Big Trails). Seven miles further, you cross Ten Sleep Creek and hit US-16 in Ten Sleep.

Trip Eleven

Waltman north to US-16 on the Buffalo Creek - Hazelton Road

This trip begins by turning off US-20 (mile #50) at Waltman. As you head north on the Buffalo Creek Road (N-104), you can see the Rattlesnake Hills to the south, Lysite Mountain to the northwest, and the Bighorn Mountains to the north. The road climbs up a bit and then gradually drops down to a junction in Arminto (eight miles). Here the Baker Cabin Road (N-108) turns east to Powder River. Continue north to another junction in one mile. Here the Lost Cabin Road (N-103) turns west to Badwater and Lost Cabin.

Continue on the Buffalo Creek Road (33 Mile/Arminto Stock Trail) and the dirt road begins following EK Creek through a flagstone lined canyon. (Nice drive.) After about eight miles, you cross the creek at the base of Deadman Butte. Here the road swings northeast a bit and then crosses Cottonwood Creek and North Fork Creek. One mile further is a junction. Here the Baker Cabin Road turns southeast to Powder River. Also at this junction, the Buffalo Creek Road turns northeast to Kaycee (see page 150).

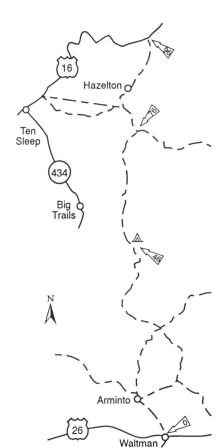

Turn north on the Big Horn Mountain Trail (N-109). The road climbs up through the foothills above First Water Creek where you have a nice view to the south.

After about seven miles, you cross South Fork Buffalo Creek and begin seeing limber pine, aspen, and spruce trees. You then pass by a couple of campgrounds at the Middle Fork Buffalo Creek crossing (two miles) and the North Fork Buffalo Creek crossing (two more miles).

After crossing the North Fork, the road drops down along Spring Creek to a junction at Kidd Flat (six miles). Here you can go southeast on the Thirty-three Mile Road to Casper.

Turn north on the Thirty-three Mile Stock Trail. After three miles, you cross Bar C Creek and the road drops down the side of the mountain to a small campground at the Middle Fork Powder River crossing. (Nice place.)

The road then climbs up the mountain above Rock Creek and travels along the open top above Sullivan Creek. You pass by a couple of roads turning east, and after 10 miles you can see Horse Butte off to the west. The road now begins to drop down a bit and you can see the South Fork Red Fork Powder River to the east. After about four miles is a junction. Here the Big Trail Stock Road turns west toward W-434.

Continue north on the Hazelton Road, and after crossing a couple of small creeks, you follow along the top of a divide at Hairgrass Springs. The road continues along the top for the next nine miles. On this stretch of the road, you can see Castle Rock, Table Top, and the North Fork Red Fork Powder River to the east. To the west is the Nowood River and to the north is Hazelton Peak.

The road drops down along Sawmill Creek and then Beartrap Creek to a junction in Beartrap Meadow. Here you can turn east on the Mayoworth Stock Trail to Mayoworth and Kaycee (see page 152).

Stay to the north and after passing through a saddle, you can see Hazelton Peak and Hazelton Pyramid. The road drops down across Pass Creek and three miles further is another junction. Here you can go west on the Rome Hill Road to US-16 near Ten Sleep (see page 152).

Continue north and the road travels past a few lodgepole pine and then goes past the Goldmine Road (turning off to the northwest). The road then swings around Dull Knife Reservoir and crosses the North Fork Powder River. You cross several small creeks and the road swings past Hazelton Pyramid and follows along Doyle Creek to a campground. You then leave the national forest and begin following Middle Fork Poison Creek. Here you can see Hesse Mountain off to the west (north of Hazelton Peak).

Three miles from the Doyle Creek Campground, you pass Hazelton and hit pavement. The road crosses Poison Creek and you enter the national forest again. One mile further, you hit US-16 at mile #63.

Trip Twelve

Kaycee to Waltman on the Willow - Buffalo Creek Road

The general area containing the Red Wall and the Island is terrific and well worth the trip.

This trip begins by turning off I-25 exit #249, and turning south across Jack Rabbit Draw to a small junction. Here you turn southwest toward the Willow Creek School (23 miles). At this junction you can see The Horn and the Bighorn Mountains to the north and to the east is Pine Ridge.

After one mile you begin winding around some breaks along Murphy Creek. Five miles further the road crosses the creek and swings south. You pass by Frewens Castle (off to the east) and the road turns southeast (toward Tisdale Mountain) and then back south again. Here you cross Posey Creek and three miles further is a junction. Here you can continue south on the Lone Bear Road (N-112) to Powder River or Casper.

Turn west on the Willow Creek Road (N-111) and follow along the creek. After two miles the road turns southwest past ponderosa pine and cedar trees on the hillsides and peachleaf willow and cottonwood trees below. Six miles from the last junction, you cross a creek at the Willow Creek School. Here a ranch road continues along the creek.

Turn west up the hill and to the top of a divide. The road winds around a bit and after three miles, you drop down through a cut in The Red Wall. Just a bit further, a road turns north along the wall, but continue west to a small junction. Here a ranch road turns south.

Stay west and you get a terrific view of The Red Wall along to the north and across to the south. The road winds around past some small buttes and then travels out across the flats. Two miles further you begin passing between The Wall on the south and The Island on the north. (Great place.) You then come to a junction. Here the Thirty-three Mile Road (N-110) turns southeast and joins the Lone Bear Road.

Turn west on the Thirty-three Mile Road and you cross Buffalo Creek in one mile. One mile further is another junction. Here N-110 continues northwest toward US-16.

Turn southwest on the Buffalo Creek Road (N-105) and you follow along Buffalo Creek and The Wall for one mile to a crossing. You now begin following Baker Creek and The Wall (now a double wall, red below and gray above). After seven miles, you come to a junction. Here the Big Horn Trail (N-109) turns northwest to US-16 and the Baker Cabin Road (N-108) turns southeast toward Powder River (see page 149).

Stay southwest on the Arminto Stock Trail/Buffalo Creek Road. The road winds around past some domed hills and along the wall (somewhat less defined now). After six miles the road swings around Deadman Butte (on the east) and you begin following EK Creek down to the flats. Seven miles further is a junction. Here the Lost Cabin Road (N-103) turns west to Badwater and Lost Cabin.

Stay south on the pavement to another junction in Arminto. Here the Bakers Cabin Road (N-108) turns east toward Powder River. Continue south for eight miles to US-20 (mile #50) at Waltman.

Trip Thirteen

Kaycee to the Outlaw Cave Trail

This trip begins by taking I-25 exit #254 to Kaycee and turning west toward the Bighorn Mountains on W-191. At mile #1 you come to a junction. Here W-191 continues west to Mayoworth and the Slope Road to Ten Sleep (see page 152).

Turn southwest on W-190 toward Barnum and you begin following the Middle Fork Powder River. At mile #104 you cross Alkali Creek and one mile further you cross Cottonwood Creek. Here you can see the White Castle Rock to the south. At mile #108 you cross the Red Fork Powder River, and after two more miles W-190 ends. (Nice drive.)

Continue west on the pavement and after crossing the Middle Fork Powder River for the second time (three miles), you follow along Beaver Creek a junction at Barnum (three more miles). Here the pavement ends and the road to the Dull Knife Battle site turns north. (See option below.)

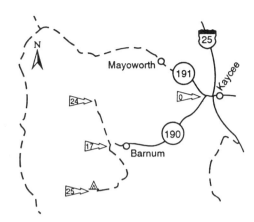

Stay to the west and the road turns south after crossing the creek (the access road west has been closed). As you travel south, the road crosses Blue Creek and two miles further you cross Sheep Creek. You then travel past Red Castle Rock. As you cross the Middle Fork Powder River, Steamboat Rock is off to the east.

You now follow Buffalo Creek for one mile to the Outlaw Cave Trail. Turn west and after two miles you pass a small road going over to the canyon (and I do mean canyon). Stay to the west and up the hill. After one more mile, you come to the Outlaw Cave Trail camping area. A 4WD road continues west.

OPTION: The Dull Knife Battle Site

Turn north at Barnum and the road travels along the base of the Red Wall above Beaver Creek. (Beautiful drive!) Six miles further you cross the creek twice and climb up through some breaks. Just before dropping down the other side is a gate. **STOP HERE!** The landowner below charges a trespass fee to let people view the monument. Just park on the south side of the gate and view the white stone monument about 200 yards to the east. Then imagine the following inscription, "Here Nov. 25, 1876 gen. R.S. Machenzie with U.S. forces composed of detachments of the 2nd, 3rd, 4th, 5th cavalry; 4th and 9th artillery; 9th, 23rd infantry defeated the Cheyennes under Dull Knife. Lieut. McKinney and six soldiers were killed in battle." The drive is certainly worth the trip, but the unfortunate surroundings on this end of the road makes me wonder which road really leads to the "Outlaw Cave".

While the trip to the historical monument IS beautiful, the 200 yard walk to the actual marker is NOT worth the trespass fee.

Trip Fourteen

Ten Sleep to Kaycee on the Rome Hill/Slope Road

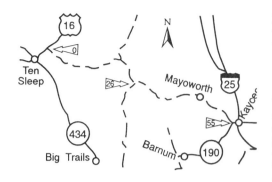

This trip begins by turning off US-16 at mile #30, three miles east of Ten Sleep. As you head southeast on W-436, the road climbs up through a cedar forest and follows along Canyon Creek. (Nice drive.) At mile #3 you pass through a small saddle, and at mile #6 the pavement ends at the Nature Concervancy Preserve (old Girl Scout Visitor Center).

Continue southeast along the edge of Cooks Canyon and after about five miles you pass by the Murphey Road going north to the old Girl Scout Camp. Continue up the hill. Along this stretch you can see the Nowood River drainage on the west. As you climb further up, the road swings east where you can see part of the Cloud Peak Wilderness to the northeast.

The road travels along the open top for seven miles to a junction at Billy Creek. Here you can take the Hazelton Road north to Dull Knife Reservoir and US-16 (see page 149).

Turn south on the Hazelton Road and you drop down past fir, spruce, and limber pine trees. After three miles, you cross Pass Creek and then drop down to a junction at Beartrap Meadows (three more miles). Here you can continue south to Casper or Waltman (see page 149).

Turn southeast on the Mayoworth Stock Trail (the Slip Road). The road follows along the creek for a bit and then climbs to the top of Red Hill Mountain. Here you drop down to Mud Springs and then begin following Arch Creek. After about three miles, you cross the creek and climb up a steep hill.

The road follows along a ridge for a bit where you have a good view of the Powder River Basin. East are the Punkin Buttes and to the southeast is Pine Ridge. To the northeast is The Horn (large protrusion of the mountain out into the valley). You then begin dropping down the mountain and after passing Government Reservoir, you start a steep descent down The Slope. (Unless the road is better than when I traveled it, you'll need a super-low gear to climb up the mountain.)

You reach the Foot of the Slope four miles from the reservoir. You then travel east to the Mayoworth Road. You pass by the Elk Mountain Road going south and just after crossing the North Fork Powder River is a junction at Mayoworth. Here the Mesa Road goes northeast toward Horn Creek Reservoir.

Stay southeast on W-191 and along the river. At mile #5 you cross the river and at mile #1 you come to a junction. Here W-190 turns southwest to Barnum and the Outlaw Cave Trail (see page 151). Continue east for one mile to I-25 at exit #254 in Kaycee.

After droping down the Slope during a torrential rainstorm, Black Irene takes a well deserved break and updates a county grader on current road conditions.

Trip Fifteen

The Crazy Woman Canyon Road from US-16 east to I-25

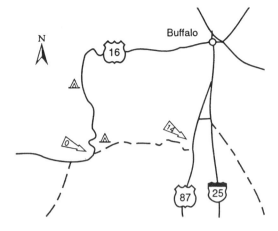

This trip begins by turning east off US-16 at mile #63. The road (NF-33) drops down through a steep canyon, past lodgepole pine, ponderosa pine, aspen, and spruce trees. (Very nice drive.) Two miles from the highway is the Canyon Campground. The road then crosses North Fork Canyon Creek and follows it down the canyon below Crazy Woman Mountain.

As you continue down this fantastic area, you begin seeing a few cottonwood and fir trees. After about five miles, you cross the creek and leave the canyon. Here you have a good look at Crazy Woman Mountain back to the west. You continue to follow the creek east for a couple of miles and then pass by the Klondike Road going north to Buffalo. Here you can see Sisters Hill to the northwest and to the north is Kingbury Ridge. Continue east for three more miles and you hit US-87 at mile #288. Here you can turn north three miles to the Trabing Road and then east one mile to I-25 at exit #291, or you can turn south to I-25 and Kaycee.

The Crazy Woman Canyon trip is a terific shortcut between I-25 and US-16. However, trailers and RV's are prohibited due to the narrow road and extremely steep grade.

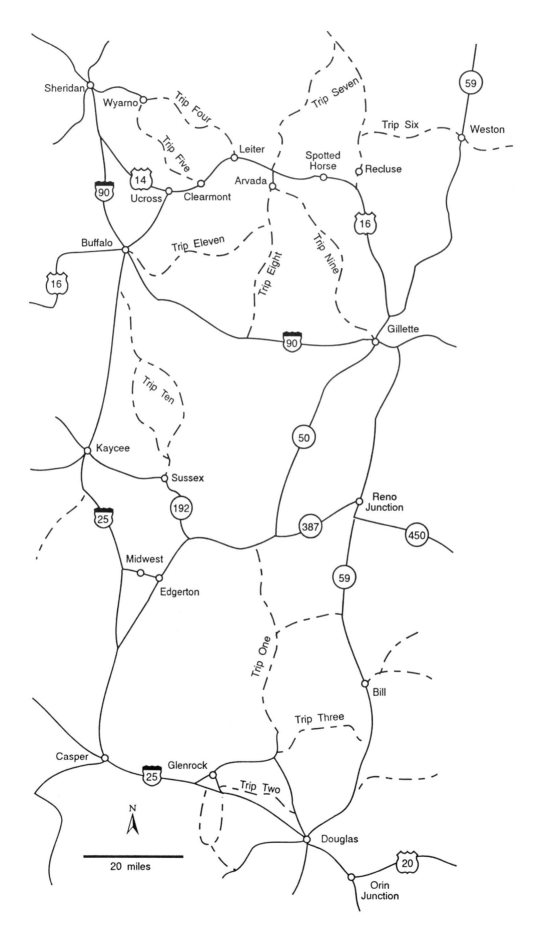

Trip One

The Ross Road from Douglas to nowhere

This trip begins by taking W-93 northwest toward Fort Fetterman (accessed from the west side of Douglas near I-25 exit #140). As you climb Water Tank Hill, you can see Chalk Buttes to the near south and to the far south is Laramie Peak. The road follows along I-25 for a bit and then along the North Platte River. At mile #7, the Inez Road (C-29) turns west across LaPrele Creek to I-25. One mile further is the Fort Fetterman turnoff and at mile #9 you cross the river to a junction. Here you can turn west on the Tank Farm Road (C-27) to Glenrock.

Pappy.

Stay north and as you pass Gilbert Lake (mile #13) you can see Casper Mountain to the west and the Laramie Mountains to the southwest. At mile #15 the road crosses Sage Creek and at mile #18 is a junction with W-95 going southwest to Glenrock. Stay north for 100 yards to the next junction. Here you can continue north and then east on W-93 to W-59 at mile #22 south of Bill (see page 157).

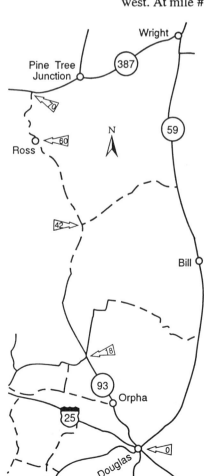

Turn northwest on the Ross Road (C-31) and you begin following Sage Creek. After crossing the creek (five miles), the road travels along Frank Draw and climbs to the top of Blizzard Heights (Sage Creek Divide). You then drop down through Holdup Hollow and begin traveling across the rolling plains.

After about five miles, the road crosses Spring Creek and you follow it through Harland Flats to the Cheyenne River. The road then climbs over the Cheyenne River Divide and drops down to a junction. Here a paved road turns east to a mine site.

Stay north on the dirt road and you cross Bear Creek to another junction. Here the Jenne Trail Road (C-34) turns northeast to W-59 at mile #49 north of Bill. (Southwest a bit is where my Grandparents homesteaded.)

Continue northwest on the Ross Road to the old Bear Creek Store (my Great Uncle ran this place years ago). One mile north of the store, the road crosses Stinking Water Gulch and Stinking Water Creek (one more mile). The road then climbs over a small divide and you can see Pine Ridge to the northwest. A bit further, you cross Sand Creek and Friday Draw.

The road passes by a Bozeman Trail marker and, as you continue northwest on C-31, you can see Pumpkin Buttes ahead in the distance. Three miles from the trail marker is Antelope Creek, and four miles further you cross Wind Creek at Ross. After leaving Ross, the road follows along a divide for five miles and enters Campbell County. **This is where the trip ends.** The road north enters private property and the gate just before reaching W-387 could be locked.

If you do choose to continue north, after two miles the road turns northeast and travels along the edge of a rim. You hit W-387 at mile #124 about six miles from the county line. There you can go east to W-59 at Reno Junction, or west to a junction on Pine Ridge. There you can go north to Linch and Kaycee, or west to Edgerton and Midwest.

Trip Two

Douglas to Glenrock on the Tank Farm Road

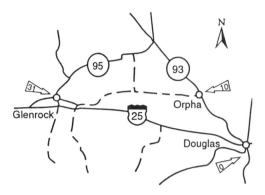

This trip begins by taking W-93 northwest toward Fort Fetterman (accessed from the west side of Douglas near I-25 exit #140). As you climb Water Tank Hill, you can see Chalk Buttes to the near south and to the far south is Laramie Peak. The road follows along I-25 for a bit and then along the North Platte River. At mile #7, the Inez Road (C-29) turns west across LaPrele Creek to I-25. You then pass by Fort Fetterman and cross the river to a junction at mile #10. Here you can continue north to Ross.

Turn west on the Tank Farm Road (C-27). After one mile you pass by the Orpha Road (C-28) going back to the river bridge. Continue west along the river and toward Casper Mountain (to the far west). After about three miles, you cross Sage Creek and the road travels along between the floodplain on the south and some small hills on the north.

Five miles after crossing Sage Creek is a junction. Here you can see Muddy Mountain to the southwest (south of Casper Mountain) and the Laramie Mountains to the south. At this junction you can take the Leuenberger Lane (C-26) north to W-95. There you can travel east to W-59, or you can go north to W-387 (see page 157).

Continue along the river and you pass by a public hunting and fishing area (one mile). Two miles further, you cross Little Sand Creek and the road winds around through an old oil field area. You then pass another public access area and cross the river.

After two more miles, you hit pavement at the turnoff to the power plant. One mile further you hit US-20, near I-25 exit #160, four miles east of Glenrock.

Holly and Sarah take a break after riding out to Fort Fetterman on their bikes.

Trip Three

Glenrock to W-59 on the Highland Loop Road

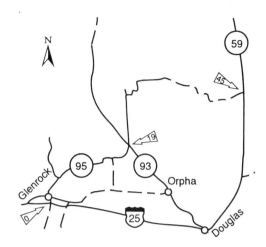

This trip begins by turning off Birch Street (US-20) in Glenrock and going north on Fourth Street. After about three blocks, you turn east on Platte Street and cross the North Platte River. As you leave town, you begin traveling on the Monkey Mountain Road (C-25). The road climbs to the top of Monkey Mountain where you can see Casper Mountain and Muddy Mountain to the southwest. To the south are the Laramie Mountains. Two miles from the river bridge is a junction. Here the 55 Ranch Road (C-23) turns north to a mine site.

Continue northeast and you begin traveling on W-95. At mile #7 you cross Sand Creek and climb to the top of a divide called "On Top Of The World". The road then swings east across Little Sand Creek to a junction at mile #16. Here you can see Laramie Peak to the south. At this junction the Leuenberger Lane (C-26) turns south and hits the Tank Farm Road (see page 156).

Continue east on W-95 for three miles to another junction. Here you can take W-93 south to Douglas, or you can take the Ross Road northwest to W-387 (see page 155).

Turn north on W-93 and at mile #20 you cross Sage Creek. A bit further, you travel across the Taylor Flats to a junction where W-93 ends. Here you can continue north for a few miles on the Willow Creek Road (C-33). Turn east on the Highland Loop Road (C-32) for two miles to another junction. Here you can continue on the pavement to a mine site.

Turn north on C-32 and after two miles the road turns east across the Highland Flats. Along this stretch, you can see the Rochelle Hills to the northeast. Seven miles after leaving the pavement, the road drops over a rim and travels through Bobbie Draw and an oil field area. Five miles further, you cross Box Creek and the road begins to zig-zag to the south and to the east. Ten miles from Box Creek, you hit W-59 at mile #22 just north of the Lightning Creek bridge.

My cousins A.W. and ManDee with their cow dog Sugar.

Trip Four

The Buffalo Creek Road from Leiter to Sheridan

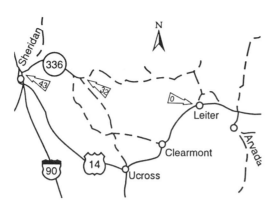

This trip begins by turning off US-14 at mile #47 at Leiter. One mile north on the Pasic Road (S-255), you cross Clear Creek to a junction. Here you can turn east on S-70 and hit US-14 at mile #51. Stay to the north and the road climbs over a ridge to another junction at Buffalo Creek (four miles). Here you can continue north on S-255 to Otter and Ashland, Montana.

Turn west on the Buffalo Creek Road (S-86). The road follows along the creek and crosses Hay Creek (three miles). You then pass the Foster Buttes (off to the south) and continue along the creek. The trees in this area are cottonwood, boxelder, and peachleaf willow. Twelve miles from Hay Creek, the road climbs to the top of a divide. (Nice little valley drive.) Here you have a good view of the Badger Hills to the north and the Bighorn Mountains to the west.

The road drops down along SR Creek to a junction in seven miles. Here S-183 turns north for a few miles. Stay west for four more miles to the next junction. Here you can turn south on S-42 to Ulm and then US-14 at Clearmont.

Continue west on S-42 and after passing by S-157 going north, you join W-336 at a junction. Here you can go south on S-161 to Clearmont (see page 159). Stay west on W-336 and you pass Wyarno after one mile. The road travels past Hazel Peak off to the south and at mile #8 you cross Dutch Creek. Three miles further is Wildcat Creek and you come to a junction at mile #4. Here the Lower Prairie Dog Creek Road (S-1211) turns north to Decker, Montana. Stay west across Prairie Dog Creek to I-90 exit #23 at Sheridan.

Many a pheasant like this was an evening meal for me while I was attending the junior college at Sheridan.

Trip Five

Sheridan to Clearmont on the Dutch Creek Road

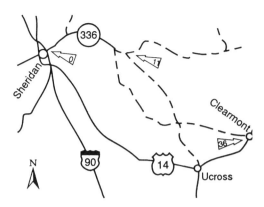

This trip begins by taking I-90 exit #23 and going east from Sheridan on W-336. At mile #3 you cross Prairie Dog Creek and pass by the Lower Prairie Dog Creek Road going north to Decker, Montana. At mile #5 you cross Wildcat Creek and three miles further you cross Dutch Creek. Here you can see Hazel Peak to the south and the Bighorn Mountains to the west. You pass Wyarno and the pavement ends at mile #11. Here you can continue east on S-42 to US-14 at Leiter (see page 158).

Turn southeast on the Dutch Creek Road (S-161) and you follow the creek through a small valley. Along this stretch, you pass by plum, boxelder, cottonwood, and peachleaf willow trees on the bottom land. On the hillsides are ponderosa pine and cedar. Five miles from W-336 is a junction. Here S-151 turns south along Dow Prong Creek to US-14 between Sheridan and Ucross.

Stay southeast on S-161 and you begin following East Middle Prong Creek. The road continues through the valley for about nine miles and then climbs over a ridge to a junction at Ulm. Here S-195 goes south to US-14 at Ucross. Turn north, across the railroad tracks, to a junction with the Ulm Road. Here you can take S-42 northwest back to Wyarno.

Turn east on S-42 and the road follows along Lone Tree Creek. After five miles you cross Ash Draw and then Pinhead Creek (three more miles). One mile further you hit US-14 at mile #36 just west of Clearmont.

This old jail in Clearmont is some sort of historical site, but I couldn't find any information about it. I checked with the Post Office and a couple of people on the streets, but they didn't seem to know much about it (and mayor seemed to be missing). I did run across one old guy who was confined in the jail many years ago, but he didn't want his picture taken because he didn't want to be recognized.

Trip Six

Spotted Horse to W-59 north of Weston

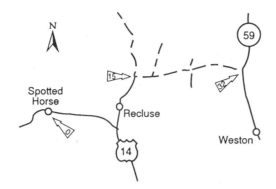

This trip begins at Spotted Horse on US-14 at mile #70. As you head east on US-14, the road travels through Chicken Creek Draw. At mile #74 you drop over the Chicken Creek Divide to a junction. Here you can continue southeast on US-14 to Gillette.

Turn north on the Recluse Road and, as you travel across the rolling hills, you can see Horse Creek Butte to the south. You pass through Recluse after five miles and three miles further is a junction at the end of the pavement. Here you can continue north on the Bitter Creek Road to Broadus, Montana (see page 161).

Turn east on the Woods Road. After two miles the road swings north past an OFR going east. A bit further is another junction. Here the Bay Horse Road continues north toward Broadus.

Turn east on the Elk Creek Road and you travel along a divide between Elk Creek on the north and White Tail Creek on the south. You travel past the base White Tail Butte after about four miles and two miles further is another junction. Here the Hart Road turns northeast to W-59 near the state line, and the Collins Road turns south to US-14 north of Gillette.

Continue east and the road drops down along Corral Creek, and past ponderosa pine, boxelder, cottonwood, and peachleaf willow trees. You follow along the creek for seven miles and hit W-59 at mile #156, across from the Little Powder River and 12 miles north of Weston.

To some, eastern Wyoming is plain and dull. If you get OUT of your cars and look around for a bit, your view may change.

Trip Seven

Arvada to Recluse on the Powder River - Bitter Creek Road

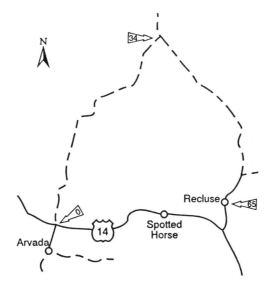

This trip begins by turning off US-14 at mile #55 north of Arvada. (Here you can turn south on W-341 to Arvada and I-90. See page 162.) Take the Lower Powder River Road (S-269) north along the river and through a small valley. (Nice drive.) After about five miles you begin traveling between the L-Quarter Circle Hills on the west and the Powder River Breaks on the east. Eight miles further north the road follows along Clear Creek for a bit and then crosses the river above the confluence.

The road then loops around through some breaks (past ponderosa pine and cedar trees) and four miles from the river crossing is the county line. Here you can see part of Hells Half Acre Canyon to the north. Three miles from the county line, you cross Bar Creek to a junction (two more miles). Here the SA Road turns south to US-14 near Spotted Horse.

Continue north across SA Creek and after five miles you enter Montana. Three miles from the state line, you cross Bitter Creek to a junction. Here you can continue north across Dry Creek and travel along the Powder River to Broadus, Montana.

Turn south on the Bitter Creek Road and you enter a small canyon. This is a nice area with cedar and ponderosa pine trees on the hillsides and cottonwood, peachleaf willow, and boxelder along the creek. After three miles you enter Wyoming and four miles further you cross Rosie Draw.

The valley now begins to widen a bit. After about three miles you cross Bitter Creek and four miles further you cross Armstrong Prong. During the next six miles, you pass by several roads going east, but continue southeast across the rolling hills to a junction. Here the Beason Road turns north to Montana.

Turn south on the Recluse Road and cross the East Fork Bitter Creek. Four miles further, you cross the head of Bitter Creek to another junction. Here you can take the Woods Road east to W-59 (see page 160). Stay south on the pavement and toward Horse Creek Butte. After four miles you enter Recluse and five miles further south you hit US-14 at mile #76.

Please remember that range fires are destructive too.

Trip Eight

Arvada to I-90 on the Powder River Road

This trip begins by turning off US-14 at mile #55 and taking W-341 south to Arvada (four miles). Here you can go southeast to Gillette on the Echeta Road (see page 163).

Continue south on the Upper Powder River Road (S-273). The road crosses Coal Draw after one mile and you begin following along a ridge above the Powder River. Here you can see Tincom Butte off to the southeast. This is a nice drive along the meandering river below and the eroded hills to the east.

Six miles from Arvada is the Cottonwood Creek crossing and one mile further you enter Johnson County. Along here the valley becomes more pronounced and you begin crossing several small draws. Seven miles after crossing Cottonwood Creek is a junction at the Crazy Woman Creek confluence. Here you can turn southwest along Crazy Woman Creek to Buffalo (see page 165).

Stay to the south and across the creek. As you follow the meandering river through the valley to Kinney Draw (seven miles), the road crosses broad floodplain loops with pretty stands of cottonwood trees. Five miles south of Kinney Draw is Coal Gulch. In this area you

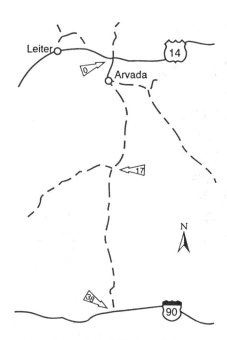

have a nice view of the Bighorn Mountains to the west.

The road then travels through some small breaks and crosses Flying E Creek (four miles) and Dry Creek (two more miles). Four miles south of the Dry Creek crossing, you hit I-90 at exit #88 between Buffalo and Gillette.

Almost the entire length of this trip follows along the crumbling banks of the Powder River. The floodplain is wide with stands of cottonwood on every loop and bend.

Trip Nine

Gillette to Arvada on the Echeta Road

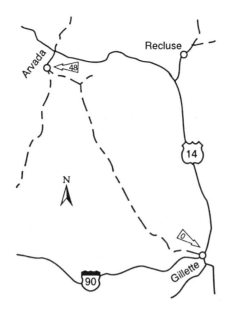

This trip begins by turning off US-14/W-59 on the west side of Gillette, between I-90 exit #124 and the railroad tracks. Here the Echeta Road travels west along I-90 for a bit and six miles from Gillette is a junction. Here the Montgomery Road turns southwest.

Stay on the Echeta Road and you begin following along the tracks to the northwest.

After two miles the road crosses Rawhide Creek and the pavement ends. You travel past some domed hills and then along a ridge between Hay Creek on the north and Wild Horse Creek on the south.

Eight miles from the end of the pavement the road crosses Hay Creek and you begin following Wild Horse Creek. (Nice drive.) After about five miles the road crosses the creek and you can see Twenty-mile Butte to the northeast a bit. You continue along the creek for 10 miles to another crossing and six miles further is the county line (S-293, South Prong Road). Three miles further is a junction. Here the Wild Horse Road (S-38) goes east to US-14 near Spotted Horse.

Turn west on S-38 and cross Wild Horse Creek. You follow along the tracks (past Tincom Butte off to the south) for five miles to the next junction. Here S-40 turns north to US-14.

Continue west across the Powder River and to a junction in Arvada. Here you can turn south along the river on the Powder River Road to Buffalo (see pages 162 and 165). Continue north on W-341 for four miles to US-14 at mile #55.

Avoid being gored when photographing wildlife such as this "bull pumping unit". Either use a telephoto lens or include background scenery to keep your distance.

Trip Ten

Sussex to Buffalo on the Sussex - Trabing Road

A "string" of tethered range bikes graze while the young wranglers learn the 3-R's.

This trip begins at W-192 mile marker #18, just north of Sussex and the Powder River Bridge. As you head north on the Lower Sussex Road, you cross Four-mile Creek where you can see Pine Ridge to the south, Pumpkin Buttes to the east, and the Bighorn Mountains to the west. The road follows along the Powder River and after five miles you cross Soldier Creek to a junction at the end of the pavement. Here you can take the Nine Mile Road (Bozeman Trail) northwest to Buffalo.

Stay north along the river for two miles to the Fort Reno Site Monument. Here you can see Table Mountain off to the east. The road continues along the river and after about five miles you cross Ninemile Creek. The road then climbs up a bit and travels along a ridge and through the Powder River Breaks.

Three miles from Ninemile Creek is School Section Draw and two miles further is

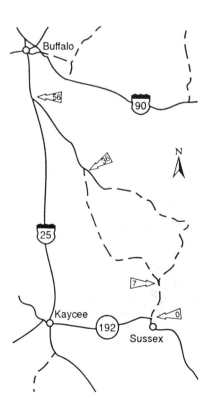

a junction. Here the Irigaray Road turns east across the river.

Turn northwest and you follow along a divide toward the Bighorn Mountains. After seven miles, you pass by a road turning north and one mile further you hit pavement. The road then crosses Goble Draw and, after three more miles, you cross South Fork Four-mile Creek. The road then swings west to a junction (five miles). Here you can turn south on the Bozeman Trail back to Sussex.

Turn northwest and you can see Robinson Canyon (Middle Fork Crazy Woman Creek) to the west. After five miles, you cross Trabing Dry Creek to the next junction. Here you can go south seven miles to another junction. There you can continue south to W-192 west of Sussex, or you can turn southwest to I-25 north of Kaycee.

Stay to the northwest where you cross Crazy Woman Creek and pass by Trabing Reservoir. Seven miles further, you begin following Wallows Creek and pass by a stock trail road going east. After four more miles, you hit I-25 at exit #291, seven miles south of Buffalo. Here you can see Kingsbury Ridge to the northwest, Sisters Hill to the west, and Crazy Woman Canyon to the southwest.

Trip Eleven

Buffalo to Arvada on the Crazy Woman Creek Road

This trip begins by taking I-90 exit #58 and turning southwest on US-16 toward Buffalo. After a half mile (and before crossing Clear Creek), you turn off US-16 and head southeast, back along the interstate on the TW Road. (You can also access this route by taking I-25 exit #299 and going northeast on US-16. Just after crossing Clear Creek, you turn southeast along I-90.) As you follow along the south side of the interstate, you can see Kingsbury Ridge and Bald Ridge to the near west and to the far west are the Bighorn Mountains. To the southwest a bit is Sisters Hill.

After two miles, you pass by the Green Trees Road going south. A bit further east, you go under I-90 where the pavement ends. The road follows along a small creek and travels past some knobby hills to a junction (four miles). Here you can go south to I-90.

Turn northeast toward the Dry Creek Petrified Tree Area on the Tipperary Road and you begin following Dry Creek. After three miles, you pass by the turn off to Petrified Tree (nice side trip and short hike). The road crosses several draws as it continues along the creek and after nine miles you come to the confluence with Crazy Woman Creek. (Nice drive.) You follow along Crazy Woman Creek for seven miles to a small junction. Here you can turn northwest on the Thompson Ck Road to US-14 at Clearmont.

Stay northeast along the creek and through a shallow, arid valley. After nine miles, you come to a junction at the confluence with the Powder River. Here you can turn south along the river to I-90 at exit #88.

Turn north along the Powder River and the road travels through a much larger valley. After six miles, you enter Sheridan County and cross Cottonwood Creek. Three miles further, you cross OK Creek and you can see Tincom Butte off to the east. The road follows along a ridge above the river, and after three miles you cross Coal Draw and enter Arvada. Here you can turn southeast on the Wild Horse Road (S-38) to Gillette (see page 163). Stay to the north on W-341 and after four miles you hit US-14 at mile #55.

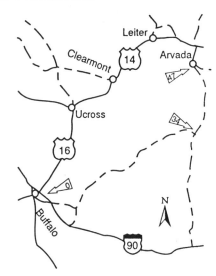

The BLM Petrified Tree Site is a nice side trip with a short hike.

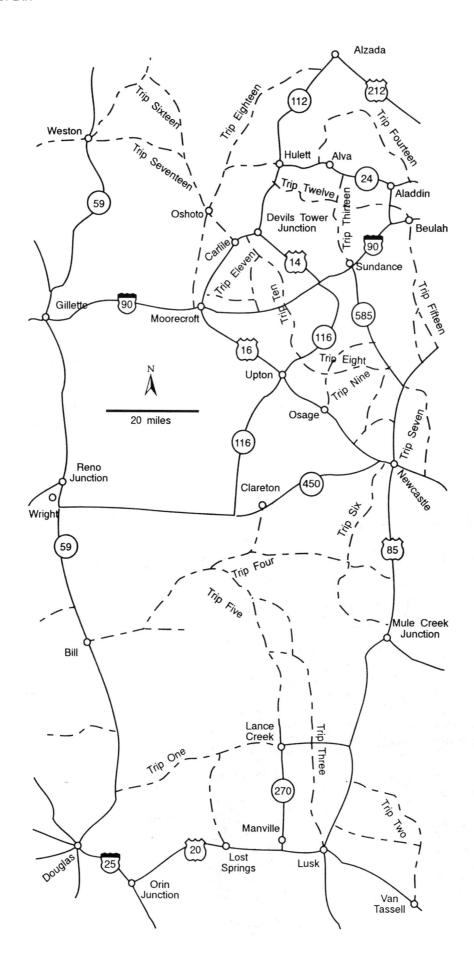

Trip One

The Walker Creek - Manning Road from Douglas to Lance Creek

My cousin Ammie and her 4-H winning pony Dutch.

This trip begins by going north from Douglas on W-59. As you follow along Antelope Creek (off to the east), you can see Laramie Peak to the far south and to the southwest is Sheep Mountain. At mile #6, you pass the Bill Hall Road (C-63, going east and then south to US-20 at Shawnee) and cross Antelope Creek. At mile #9, you pass by the Flat Top Road (C-48, going east to the Bill Hall Road) and you can see Casper Mountain to the far west. At mile #11 you come to a junction. Here you can continue north on W-59 to Bill and Gillette.

Turn east on the Walker Creek Road (C-43) and after two miles the road swings northeast along Walker Creek. Here you can see Flat Top to the southeast and to the east are the Cedar Breaks. A few miles further, you cross the creek and come to a junction where the pavement ends (10 miles from the highway).

Here you can continue northeast on the Walker Creek Road toward Cow Creek.

Turn east on the Manning Road (C-53) and you cross Walker Creek again. Three miles is the next junction. Here you can take the Dickau Road (C-47) south to the Bill Hall Road or US-20 at Shawnee.

Continue east on the Manning Road. The road crosses Piney Creek and drops over a small cedar ridge to a junction on Twenty-mile Creek (five miles). Here you can take the Twenty-mile Creek Road (C-46) south to US-20 at Lost Springs.

Continue east along the cottonwood lined Twenty-mile Creek. (Nice drive.) After about four miles, you enter Niobrara County and after four more miles, you pass by the Lightning Creek Road going north (unmarked).

Stay northeast and you cross Twenty-mile Creek after one mile. The road then climbs up along a ridge and swings back to the east. Along this stretch you begin seeing ponderosa pine and cedar trees. To the northwest are the Cow Creek Buttes and to the northeast are the Elk Mountains (Black Hills) in South Dakota. To the southeast a bit is Flat Top. Five miles further, you join W-271 and cross Little Lightning Creek at West Lance Creek (city). Three miles further, you cross Lance Creek and hit W-270 in Lance Creek (city). Here you can go south to US-20 at Manville, or you can travel east to US-85, 20 miles north of Lusk.

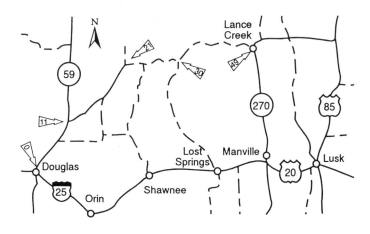

Trip Two

The Hat Creek Breaks Road from Van Tassell northwest to Hat Creek

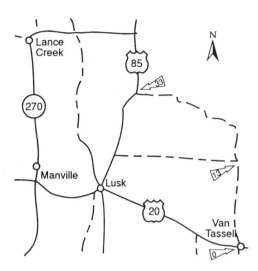

This trip begins by turning north off US-20 (mile #61) at Van Tassell. Here you can see Rawhide Butte to the west. The road travels by some small buttes and bluffs and after about five miles you pass Steamboat Rock (off to the west a bit). You then follow above Van Tassell Creek and travels across the rolling prairie for six miles to a creek crossing. The road turns west for one mile and then north one mile to Kirtley Junction. Here you can turn west for 15 miles to US-85 mile #155 north of Lusk.

Continue north and after about two miles, you drop down through the Hat Creek Breaks. (Nice drive.) As you pass through this beautiful

area of ponderosa pine trees and ravines, you can see the Sherrill Hills to the northeast, Table Mountain to the north, and Swanski Rock to the west. About one mile north of the breaks is S Bar Junction. Here you can take the Colosseum Road northeast across S Bar Creek, and then turn east below the rim. On this road you can go to Harrison, Nebraska, or you can loop back to the Indian Creek Road and the Hat Creek Road.

Turn northwest across Fitzsimmons Creek and the road swings west past Swanski Rock (off to the south). After about four miles, you cross Plum Creek and the road turns north. One mile further, you come to a junction. Here the Indian Creek Road continues north (toward Shepherds Point and Table Mountain) and then southeast to Harrison, Nebraska.

Turn west and you cross Indian Creek after about three miles. Three miles further is another junction. Here the Thompson Road turns northeast to the Indian Creek Road.

Stay west for two more miles and you hit pavement. After two miles you come to the last junction. Here the Stage Road turns south for one mile to the Old Fort Hat Creek Site (a private ranch now) and then continues south to the Kirtley Road. Stay to the west and in two miles you hit US-85 at mile #163.

One of the many advantages to traveling backroads is the opportunity to meet interesting people. Here Raymond, Lynard, Floyd, and Fred take a break after running me through the small town gambit.

Trip Three

The Twentyeight -mile/Cow Creek Road from Lusk to Bill

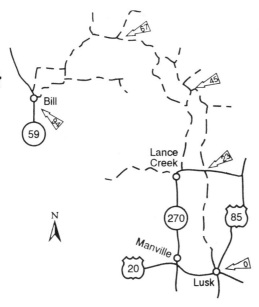

This trip begins by turning off US-85 on the north side of Lusk. You go by the highway department and then head north past the cemetery on an old paved road. After about eight miles, the road drops down through the western edge of the Hat Creek Breaks. The broken pavement ends 12 miles north of Lusk.

As you continue north, the road begins following Young Woman Creek and at the creek crossing you can see Tim Butte off to the east. The road then climbs up a small bench and you can see the Seaman Hills off to the far east.

A little reminder to respect private property.

Five miles from the crossing, you hit W-270 at mile #125. Here you can turn west to Lance Creek and then west to Douglas or south to Manville, or you can travel east to US-85 (20 miles north of Lusk).

Stay north on the Ridge Road. After one mile, you cross Buck Creek. Here you can see the Old Woman Creek Hills to the east. The road climbs up a bit and follows a divide to the north. Along this stretch, you pass by a couple of ranch roads going east, but stay on top and above the Lance Creek drainage off to the west. Here you can see the Buck Hills to the east, Cow Creek Buttes to the northwest, and to the northeast are the Elk Mountains (Black Hills) in South Dakota. The road then drops down to a junction on Lance Creek, 14 miles from W-270. Here you can take the Wasslrburger Road east to US-85.

Turn west along Lance Creek. After three miles you cross Lance Creek and follow Dogie Creek to a junction. Here you can go north across the creek to another junction. There you can go east on the Redbird Road to US-85, or continue north to W-450 at Clareton (see page 171).

Turn south over the hill and in two miles is a junction at Cow Creek. Here you can continue south to W-270 at Lance Creek.

Turn northwest and you begin following Cow Creek. After five miles, you pass a small reservoir and the road climbs up a ridge and turns away from the creek for a couple of miles. You then drop down across a draw and pass by a small road going south. Stay to the northwest for two more miles to another junction. Here a cutoff road continues west to C-45 and Bill. This road runs across private land so you will need to ask for permission to trespass.

Turn north for about seven miles to a junction with the North Lance Creek Road (going back to Dogie Creek). Turn west and after 10 miles you enter Converse County (C-38) and come to a junction with C-39. Here you can head north to Clareton (see page 170).

Continue west for about six miles and then southwest for 10 miles to a junction with C-40. Here you can either continue south and then west to Bill (about 12 miles) on the Dull Center Road (C-38), or you can turn west and then south to Bill (also about 12 miles) on the Steinly Road (C-40).

Trip Four

The Cheyenne River Road from Bill to Clareton

This trip begins by turning off W-59 at mile #36, a half mile north of Bill. As you head north on the Steinle Road (C-40), you can see the Red Hills to the north. After six miles the road turns east and after three miles you pass by the Woody Creek Road (going north). Stay east for three more miles to a junction. Here you can take the Dull Center Road south to Bill or US-20 at Lance Creek.

Turn northeast on the Dull Center Road (C-38) and you pass several OFR's. Along this stretch, you can see the Rochelle Hills to the north and the Miller Hills to the east. After traveling through the badlands for six miles, you cross Lake Creek and follow the Cheyenne River to a junction. Here you can go north across the river and into the Rochelle Hills.

Continue east along the river. The road crosses Meadow Creek (one mile) and passes north of the Miller Hills. After four miles, you come to a junction on Sheep Creek. Here you can continue east and then south toward W-270 and Lance Creek.

Turn north on the Clareton Road (C-39) and after three miles, you cross Wagonhound Creek. Three miles further, you enter Weston County and cross the Cheyenne River. The road then climbs a ridge to the north and you can see the Elk Mountains (Black Hills) in South Dakota to the northeast. Five miles from the river crossing is a junction. Here the Keyton Road turns west toward the Rochelle Hills. Stay northeast for a half mile to another junc-

tion. Here you can continue north on the Lynch Road to W-450 at mile #37 (seven miles).

Turn east along the top on the Cheyenne River Road. Here you can see the Cow Creek Buttes to the south (and east a bit of the Miller Hills). You travel along the top and above the river for about nine miles and then drop down to an unmarked junction. Here you can turn south to Lance Creek (see page 171). Stay to the northeast and across Thunder Creek to the next junction (two more miles). Here you can take the Cheyenne River Road east to US-85 (see option below).

Turn north on the Bruce Road. The road climbs over a divide and after about four miles you cross Wildcat Creek. Six miles further north, you hit W-450 (mile #25) at Clareton.

OPTION: The Cheyenne River Road to US-85.

Going east on the Cheyenne River Road, you follow along Thunder Creek for about two miles and then along a ridge above the river. Five miles from the junction, you pass by The Nose (a bend in the river). Here the road leaves the river and after four miles you cross Lodgepole Creek to a junction. Here you can go north on the Grieves Road to W-450.

Continue east and during the next few miles you pass by several small buttes. The road then travels across the broken short-grass prairie and you come to a junction at Morrisey. Here you can turn south (and then east) on the Roxson Road to US-85 near Mule Creek Junction (see page 172).

Turn northeast across Alkali Creek to another junction in three miles. Here you can go north on the Morrisey Road to Newcastle.

Continue east on the Cheyenne River Road. After five miles, you pass by the Hunt Road (going northwest to the Morrisey Road) and cross Robbers Roost Creek. Three miles further east, you hit US-85 (mile #207) between Mule Creek Junction and Newcastle.

Trip Five

Clareton to Lance Creek on the Bruce - North Lance Creek Road

This trip begins by turning off W-450 (mile #25) between Newcastle and Reno Junction. As you head south on the Bruce Road, you

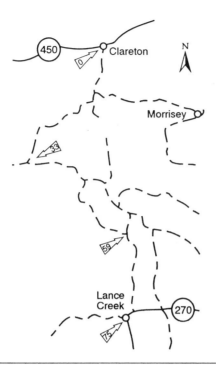

go by Clareton (just off to the west) and pass by the Darlington Road going east. As you continue south (past numerous OFR's), the road crosses Wildcat Creek after five miles. You then climb over a small divide and drop down to a junction at Thunder Creek. Here you can go east on the Cheyenne River Road to US-85 (see page 170).

Stay south and after crossing the creek, you come to an unmarked junction (one half mile). Here the road south crosses the Cheyenne River (no bridge though) and travels across private land to the Dixon Road in Niobrara County.

Turn west on the main road and you pass by the Sears Road (dead end) and follow along a divide above the Cheyenne River. Nine miles from the Sears Road is a junction. Here you can head north to W-450 on the Lynch Road, or northwest to the Rochelle Hills on the Keyton Road.

Turn south toward the Miller Hills. After five miles you cross the Cheyenne River and enter Converse County to another junction (five more miles). Here you can head southwest to Dull Center and Bill (see page 169).

Turn east on C-38 and you enter Niobrara County on the North Lance Creek Road. Eight miles from the county line is a junction with the Cow Creek Road. Here you can turn south and rejoin the Lance Creek Road.

Turn east and after three miles you pass by the Dixon Road going back north to the river. Stay south and you follow along a ridge between Dogie Creek on the west and Spring Creek on the east. After six miles, the road crosses Spring Creek and you follow along Dogie Creek to a junction. Here the Redbird Road turns east to US-85. Stay south and after crossing Dogie Creek is a junction where the Wasslrbruger Road turns east to US-85.

Continue south and over the ridge to another junction at Cow Creek (two miles). Here the Cow Creek Road turns back to the northwest. Continue south across the creek. After two miles you cross Lightning Creek and begin following Lance Creek. (Nice drive.) Ten miles south, you hit W-272. The road crosses Lance Creek and in two miles, you hit W-270 at mile #121. Here you can go east to US-85 north of Lusk, or you can travel west to Lance Creek and then south to US-20 at Manville.

As with most creeks in eastern Wyoming, the riparian habitat bordering Lighting Creek offers a striking contrast as it travels through the breaks and across the rolling plains.

Trip Six

The Morrisey Road from Newcastle south to Mule Creek Junction

Although the Cheyenne River is usually only a trickle, it does add a bit of fringe and lace to the land.

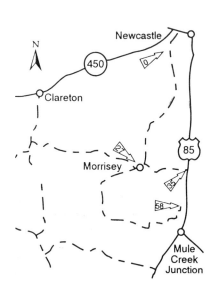

This trip begins by turning off US-16 at mile #246, between Newcastle and W-450. The Morrisey Road follows Oil Creek south across the grasslands. About eight miles of town, you can look back to the north and see Jumbo Table, Sweetwater Mountain and Mount Pisgah. To the northeast is Summit Ridge and to the east is Elk Mountain and Wildcat Peak. Six miles further south is the Beaver Creek crossing, and as you cross South Beaver Creek (two more miles), you can see Rattlesnake Ridge to the far southeast.

After climbing to the top of a small bench, you can now see Alkali Butte to the west. The road turns south again and after four more miles you drop down a bit to a junction on Robbers Roost Creek. Here the Hunt Road turns east to the Cheyenne River Road and US-85. Stay south for three miles to the next junction. Here the Cheyenne River Road turns east to US-85 at mile #207 (see page 170).

Continue south for two miles to a junction near Morrisey. Here the Cheyenne River Road turns west toward US-59. On this route you can go north to Clareton, west to Bill, or south Lance Creek (see pages 170 and 171).

Stay south across Alkali Creek on the Roxson Road and then west toward the Cheyenne River. The road then travels through some breaks and past table rock, draws, and buttes for about the next five miles to the county line. The road swings south again and follows along the cottonwood lined Cheyenne River for six miles, to the top of Sheldon Hill.

From Sheldon Hill, the road turns east across Seven-mile Creek and climbs up through some more breaks. After traveling east for nine miles, you "zig-zag-zig" to the northeast for about 10 miles to US-85 at mile #200, just north of Mule Creek Junction and the Cheyenne River Bridge.

Trip Seven

Newcastle to Four Corners and back on the Beaver - Oil Creek Road

Mamie, John, and Wes ice fishing and throwing washers at LAK reservoir.

This trip begins by turning off US-16 at mile #254, five miles east of Newcastle. As you head north on the Stockade Beaver Creek Road, you follow along the creek and pass LAK Reservoir after one mile. This beautiful drive travels through a canyon lined with pine, cedar, cottonwood, and boxelder trees. Three miles from US-16, you come to a junction. Here you can take the Beaver Creek Cutoff west and join the Salt Creek Road from Newcastle to Cambria.

Continue north along the creek and during the next seven miles, you cross numerous small canyons that come in from the east. The main canyon then widens to a small valley and swings northeast for a bit. The road climbs up to Canyon Springs Prairie where you can see Mount Pisgah to the west. After traveling on top for one mile, you come to a junction. Here the road east drops down a steep hill to the Mallo Camp. There you can travel through a terrific canyon into the Black Hills of South Dakota.

Turn west for two miles and you hit US-85 at mile #247 at Four Corners. At this junction, you can see Red Butte to the south (and west a bit from Mount Pisgah), Sweetwater Mountain and Northwestern Table are to the southwest, and to the west is Mount Tom. To the northwest, rising above Strawberry Hill, is Inyan Kara. Here you can take US-85 south to Newcastle or north to Buckhorn.

Turn northwest on W-585 to a junction at mile #4. Here you can continue north on W-585 to Sundance. Turn west on the Skull Creek Road and after two miles you come to another junction. Here you can continue west on the Skull Creek Road to Osage or Upton (see page 175).

Turn south on the Oil Creek Road and you travel along Oil Creek through a wide canyon, toward the edge of Northwestern Table. After about four miles, you pass by the Ertman Road east to US-85 and the road then crosses Red Creek. You now have a nice drive through some breaks, and travel past several small buttes and draws. Twelve miles from the Red Creek crossing is a junction. Here the Plumb Creek Road turns northeast and joins US-85 at mile #239 (10 miles). Continue south on the Oil Creek Road and after three miles you hit US-16 at mile #242, five miles west of Newcastle.

Trip Eight

The Green Mountain - Dry Creek cutoff from W-585 to W-116

This trip begins by turning off W-585 at mile #8, northwest of Four Corners. Here you can see Sweetwater Mountain and Northwestern Table to the south and Iron Mountain to the north. Rising above the hill to the northwest is Inyan Kara.

The Green Mountain Road heads west toward Mount Tom and goes around the base of Strawberry Hill. After passing by the base Strawberry Hill, you climb up to a good view of Mount Tom to the southwest and Inyan Kara to the northwest. The road passes between these two mountains and then swings south along West Fork Skull Creek to a junction. Here you can continue south on the Green Mountain Road and hit the Skull Creek Road (one mile). There you can either loop back to W-585 or continue south to US-16 at Osage (see page 175).

Turn west on the Dry Creek Road and you cross West Fork Skull Creek and climb over a small divide. The road then swings north and drops down along Dry Creek. After seven miles you hit W-116 at mile #17.

Two of my favorite little people, Zachary and Lauren, feeding the chickens. Life is good.

Trip Nine

The Skull Creek Road from Osage northeast to Four Corners

This trip begins by turning off US-16 at mile #234 and going into Osage. After heading north into town, you turn east just before climbing a small hill. Here the Skull Creek Road crosses the tracks and turns northeast. Along this stretch you can see Inyan Kara to the north and Northwestern Table to the east. The road follows along a ridge above Skull Creek and you pass by the Seeley Road (going east) and the East Upton Road (going west).

The road then drops down into a small valley for about five miles to a junction. Here you can take the Green Mountain Road north and then west to either W-585 at mile #8 north of Four Corners, or north and then northeast to W-116 at mile #17 north off Upton (see page 174).

Turn east on the Skull Creek Road and you pass Mount Tom (off to the north) after three miles. The road crosses the creek a couple of times and climbs past the base of Star Butte to a junction. Here you can take the Oil Creek Road south to Newcastle (see page 173).

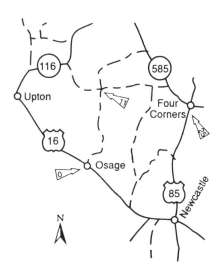

Continue east for two more miles and you hit W-585 at mile #4, four miles northwest of US-85 at Four Corners. Here you can see Sweetwater Mountain and Northwestern Table to the south and to the southeast is Mount Pisgah.

Star Butte near the junction with the Oil Creek Road.

Trip Ten

The Arch Creek - Inyan Kara Creek Road from Upton to Devils Tower

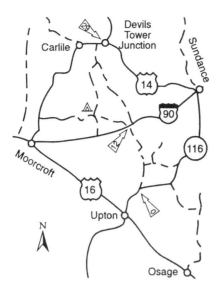

This trip begins by taking W-116 northeast from Upton. At mile #23 you come to a junction. Here you can continue on W-116 to Sundance. Turn north on the Arch Creek Road for four miles to a junction at Arrowhead Lake. Here you can see the top of Missouri Buttes to the north, the Bear Lodge Mountains to the northeast, and Inyan Kara to the east. At this junction, the road east crosses Mason Creek after two miles and then turns northeast for five more miles to a junction on Inyan Kara Creek. There you can go south to W-116 (mile #14), or north to I-90 (exit #178).

Continue north along Arch Creek and after two miles you pass by Hageman Reservoir. You now follow along above Inyan Kara Creek on the Norris Divide to a junction in five miles. Here you can go north across I-90 and then northwest to Keyhole Reservoir (see page 177).

Turn east down to the creek and I-90 at exit #172. To continue on the road to Devils Tower, you go under I-90 and follow along the creek to the north. After seven miles, you cross Inyan Kara Creek to a junction. Here you can go south for five miles and then west to Keyhole Reservoir.

Stay to the north and you cross the creek again in one mile. The road follows along the creek for about five more miles to a junction at the confluence with the Belle Fourche River. Here you can go south to Keyhole Reservoir and then to either I-90 at exit #165, or US-14 north of Moorcroft (see page 177).

Continue north and you begin following the Belle Fourche River. To the northwest you can see Missouri Buttes and to the north is Devils Tower. Four miles further, you hit US-14 at mile #179, just west of Devils Tower Junction (W-24 and US-14).

Liza and Jim—good friends and good people—playing cow pasture croquet.

Trip Eleven

The Keyhole Reservoir Road from Devils Tower to Moorcroft

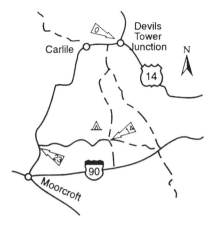

This trip begins by turning off US-14 at mile #179, just west of Devils Tower Junction (W-24 and US-14). As you head south on the Kara Creek Road, you can see Missouri Buttes to the northwest and Devils Tower to the north. The trees on the hillsides are cedar and pine, and along the bottoms are cottonwood, boxelder, and a few oaks. After four miles you come to a junction. Here the Kara Creek Road continues southeast to I-90 at exit #172 (see page 176).

Turn southwest and after crossing Inyan Kara Creek, you begin following the Belle Fourche River. (Nice drive.) After four more miles, you cross Arch Creek where the road climbs up a bit and travels along the top to a junction. Here you can turn west to Keyhole Reservoir.

Continue south on the pavement and you pass several more access roads to the reservoir. After traveling on the pavement for four miles, you come to a junction. Here you can see Inyan Kara to the east and the Bear Lodge Mountains to the northeast. At this junction you can turn east to the Inyan Kara Road and I-90 at exit #172, or you can continue south over Iron Mountain to I-90 at exit #165.

Turn west and you continue to pass by access roads going north to the reservoir (and one road going south to I-90). Nine miles from the junction at Iron Mountain, you hit US-14 at mile #160, five miles north of Moorcroft.

Too many people look for and find only the grand views in Wyoming. As a result, they are often rushing from one place to another with little time to enjoy the more subtle things in life. Take some "real time off" and look for the uniqueness in all that is around you. (Photo courtesy of a House Mouse hitchhiker I had the pleasure of riding and camping with for awhile.)

Trip Twelve

The Farrall - Blacktail Road from Beulah west to Hulett

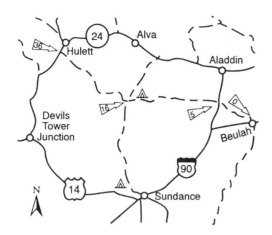

This trip begins by taking the Redwater Creek Road west from Beulah (I-90, exit #205). The road follows along Redwater Creek for about five miles to a junction with W-111 at mile #5. Here you can go north to W-24 at Aladdin, or south to I-90 at exit #199.

Continue west on NF-843 and after passing by Schoolmarm Butte (on the north), you come to a junction at Farrall. Here you can take the road south to the Government Valley Road (six miles). From there you can either turn east to I-90 at exit #199, or west to Sundance.

Continue west and you follow along North Redwater Creek to the forest boundary (three miles). Stay on NF-843 and you pass by NF-833 (a loop road going south toward Warren Peak) after three miles. Two miles further is a junction with the Cook Lake Road. Here you can take NF-830 north to W-24 at mile #30 (eight miles, see page 179), or you can take NF-842 down to the Cook Lake Campground.

Continue west on NF-843 for one mile and then south for three miles to another junction. Here NF-841 follows along Beaver Creek to the south.

Stay on NF-843 and take the sharp turn to the west. After two more miles, you come to the next junction. Here you can take NF-838 south to Sundance, or you can go north across the Taylor Divide toward Alva and W-24.

Turn northwest on NF-849 (Hulett, 17 miles) and you pass by the Winchester and Hershey Creek Roads. The road then follows along Blacktail Creek past stands of Paper Birch, Aspen, Ponderosa Pine, and Bur Oak, and you leave the national forest (five miles from the junction with NF-843). The road continues to follow the creek through a shallow redrock canyon lined with pine and oak. Ten miles further you hit W-24 at mile #14, just south of Hulett.

While the Black Hills are not noted for backpacking trails, my nephew and nieces (Barbie, Ashley, and Zac) report the dayhikes to be of exceptional quality.

Trip Thirteen

The Cook Lake Road from Alva south to Sundance

This trip begins by turning south off W-24 at mile #30, five miles east of Alva. After about one mile, you enter the national forest and come to a junction. Here the road south (NF-838) follows along Beaver Creek and then crosses the Taylor Divide. Along that route, you can take NF-859 back to Alva (this road was closed when I was here), or you can continue south for seven miles to another junction. There you can either go west to Hulett on the Blacktail Road, or south to Sundance on the Cook Lake Road (see page 178).

Turn southeast on NF-832 and you cross Beaver Creek and climb up past oak, pine, boxelder, aspen, and birch. (Pretty!) After about five miles you come to another junction. Here NF-830 and NF-832 turn east for a couple of miles. Turn southwest on NF-830 and the road swings over to a junction with the Farrall/Blacktail Road (NF-843). Here you can

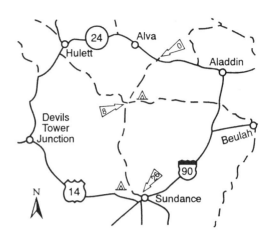

turn east and follow North Redwater Creek to Farrall (eight miles) and W-111 (three more miles, see page 178). Also at this junction, you can take the road northwest (NF-842) down to the Cook Lake Campground.

Turn west on NF-843 for one mile and then south along Beaver Creek for about three miles to a junction. Here NF-841 continues along the creek for a few miles.

Stay on NF-843 and take the sharp turn to the west. After two more miles, you come to the next junction. Here the Blacktail Road (NF-849) turns northwest to W-24 south of Hulett. The road going up the hill to the north (NF-838) follows the Taylor Divide back toward Alva.

Turn south on NF-838 toward Sundance and you climb up along Deckelman Ridge and pass through a nice stand of aspen trees. After about three miles is a junction. Here you can take the Lytle Creek Road (NF-847) west to Devils Tower, or you can take NF-851 and loop back to NF-841 and Beaver Creek.

Continue south for two miles to the pavement near the Warren Peak Fire Lookout. Here you can see Inyan Kara and Sweetwater Mountain to the far south. As you drop down the mountain, you pass by the Reuter Campground (five miles) and travel along the base of the mountain to US-14 at mile #199. Here you can go west to Devils Tower, or east to Sundance and I-90 at exit #185.

The Black Hills offers a blend of eastern and rocky mountain flora. Pictured here is the Paper Birch.

Trip
Fourteen

The Mona Road from The Forks west to Ava

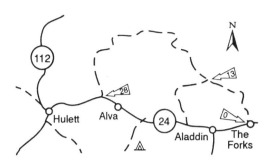

This trip begins by turning off US-24 at mile #45 (The Forks), two miles west of the state line. After traveling northwest for five miles, you come to a junction on the top of Norgrain Hill. Here you can turn east to Belle Fourche, South Dakota. At this junction, you can see Schoolmarm Butte, Table Mountain, and Little Table to the southwest.

Continue west and after crossing Oak Creek (well named) a couple of times, the road swings northwest to a junction at Four Corners (10 miles from US-24). Here you can take the road south to W-24 at mile #42. The road west goes to The Notch and then south to W-24 at mile #36.

Stay to the northwest and after one mile you cross Alum Creek. One mile further, you cross Pine Creek to a junction. Here a road turns west and then south, joining the road going by The Notch to W-24.

Continue northwest for two miles and you cross Deep Creek and a nice little canyon. From this area you can see the tree lined Belle Fourche River to the north. After crossing Deep Creek, the road makes a large zig-zag and crosses Horse Creek. Here the road turns back to the west and travels across the rolling hills, past stands of pine and oak trees.

Six miles after crossing Horse Creek, the road turns south to Mona and away from Windy Point (a rock outcropping to the north). From here you can see Branaman Mountain to the northwest. To the near south is Blue Ridge and to the far south are the Bear Lodge Mountains.

After leaving Mona, the road drops down into part of Buffalo Basin and crosses Beaver Creek (seven miles). (On a hot day, Beaver Creek is a great place to let the dog cool off and lap up some water.) The road then follows along above the Belle Fourche River for a bit, and you can see Missouri Buttes and Devils Tower off to the southwest. Six miles south of Beaver Creek, you hit US-24 Trip #23, just west of Alva.

Besides the Paper Birch (page 179), Bur Oak is another species of tree found only in northeastern Wyoming.

Trip Fifteen

The Sand Creek Road from Beulah through the Grand Canyon to US-85 at the State Line

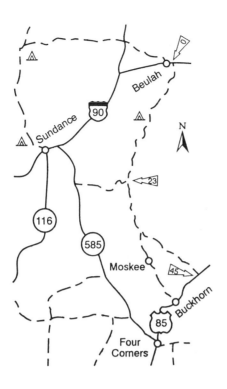

True to his nature as a water-dog connoisseur, Smeagle inspects the clarity and savors the bouquet at O'Brian Springs

This trip begins by turning off I-90 at the Beulah Exit (#205). As you head south, you can see The Brakes to the north, Sugarloaf and Table Mountain to the northwest, and the Bear Lodge Mountains to the west. After one mile a side road goes east to Shepherd Draw, but continue south below the rimrock and past some public fishing areas. The road travels through a canyon and past beautiful stands of boxelder, ponderosa pine, bur oak, and American elm trees. Further up the road are also hawthorn, paper birch, and aspen trees.

Five miles from the highway is the Ranch "A" Fish Hatchery and the Black Hills National Forest boundary. For the next 17 miles you pass by several side roads (4WD) and gulches (Thompson, Idol, Manhattan, Surprise, Williams, and Plato). Several of these roads connect in South Dakota, where you can go to US-14A, south of Spearfish, but I have not traveled these routes. This entire route is just "plain pretty" and well worth the trip.

Twenty-three miles south of I-90, you come to a couple of junctions. At the first, you can turn north on the Moskee Road (NF-807) to I-90 exit #191 at Sundance. Stay south for a half mile to the next junction. Here you can take the Moskee Road south along Cold Creek, to US-85 at mile #254 at Buckhorn.

Turn east on the Grand Canyon Road (NF-875). During the next six miles, you pass several side roads going to such places as Calvert Sacket Draw, Deer Lick, Schoolhouse Gulch, and Wagon Canyon. (Some of these roads also hit US-14A near Savory.)

Stay south on NF-875 and after 10 miles you pass O'Brian Springs. The road then begins to climb up the side of Bald Mountain. As you travel along the mountain, the road winds around and goes up and down for the next nine miles to the state line (where NF-875 changes to NF-175). You also pass by a few logging roads, but stay on the main road southeast and above some mountain meadows. Three miles from the state line, you hit US-85 in South Dakota, three miles from the state line.

Trip Sixteen

Weston to Carlile the hard way: via Rockypoint

This trip begins by turning off W-59 at Weston (mile #144). As you head east on the Rockypoint Road, you can see the Mitchell Creek Breaks to the south and to the west is the "Ridge west of the Store". After two miles, you cross the Little Powder River and come to a junction at Soda Wells. Here the Soda Wells Road turns southeast toward Adon and The Breaks. A bit further to the north, you pass by the Heald-Bergreen Road going east to Oshoto (the easy way, see page 183).

Continue north along the river, and after a couple of miles the road swings northeast. Three miles further, the road crosses ZV Creek and climbs up a divide where you can see Rocky Butte to the northwest. As the road continues northeast, you cross Duck Creek (five miles) and you begin to climb up a bit. You then cross over part of the Duck Creek Breaks and drop down Bowman Hill to a junction on Dry Creek. Here the Jenkins Road turns south and the Parks Road turns north.

Continue northeast across the creek. After two more miles, you cross the North Fork Little Missouri River to a junction (25 miles from Weston). Here you can turn north to Rockypoint (three miles) and another junction. There you can turn west to W-59 near the state line, or you can continue north to Broadus, Montana.

Smeagle demonstrating the phenomena that the sun can make and take heat.

Turn east and then south on the D Road. Along here you can see the Missouri Buttes and the top of Devils Tower to the southeast. After three miles, you enter Crook County. You then pass by a couple of roads going west and after about five miles you begin following Cracker Creek. Here you can see Monument Hill just off to the east a bit. Two miles after crossing Cracker Creek, you cross Prairie Creek and begin following Short Prong Prairie Creek. Four miles further is a junction. Here you can take the road west to the Heald-Bergreen Road and go back to Weston.

Continue south and you cross Good Lad Creek to a junction (11 miles from the Prairie Creek crossing). Here you can go south to I-90 at Moorcroft. Turn east along Deadman Creek to Oshoto (two miles). Here you can go north along the Little Missouri River to New Haven or Alzada, Montana, or you can turn south to Moorcroft (see page 184).

Continue east and cross the river on the Cabin Creek Road. The road swings southeast and then zig-zags across the flats. About eight miles from Oshoto, you begin following Cabin Creek (peachleaf willow, boxelder, and cottonwood trees along the bottom and ponderosa pine on the hillsides). Four miles further, you hit US-14 at mile #176, just north of Carlile.

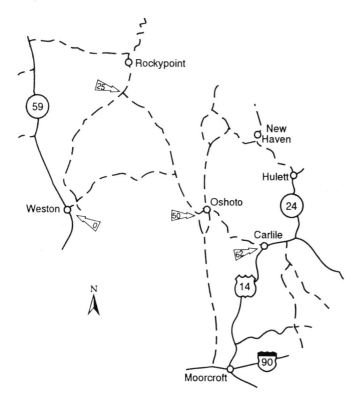

Trip Seventeen

New Haven Road from Hulett west to Weston

This trip begins by turning west off W-112 at mile #1, just north of Hulett. The road travels past pine, oak, cottonwood, aspen, and boxelder, and follows the creek through Moore Canyon to a junction at the top of Moore Hill. Here you can turn north to the Little Missouri River Road at Bush Creek Reservoir (six miles to Elkhorn Creek and five more miles to the Little Missouri River, see page 184).

Continue west for three miles and then south for two miles to another junction. Here a small road crosses Barnard Creek and heads southeast along the ridges for about four miles. That road then drops down to Barlow Creek and turns southeast to W-24 at mile #9, north of Devils Tower.

Turn west and then northwest (past the cemetery) for seven miles to another junction. Here the road north goes past New Haven (one mile) and on over to the Little Missouri River Road (five more miles).

Continue west through a burn area and the road drops down a steep hill to Hulett Creek. Along here you can see Missouri Buttes and Devils Tower to the south. You continue to drop down to a junction with the Little Missouri River Road near Poison Creek. Here you can turn north to Alzada, Montana.

Turn south and after one mile you cross the river. Here you can see the Missouri Buttes to the southeast. As you continue south, the road enters an oil field area, so stay on the main road along the river. After seven miles, you come to a junction at Oshoto. Devils Tower now is off to the east. Here you can turn east on the Cabin Creek Road to US-14 at **Carlile**, or continue south on the D Road to I-90 at **Moorcroft** (see pages 182 and 184).

Turn west along **Deadman Creek** for two miles to another junction. Here you can turn south and join the D Road going to Moorcroft. Turn northwest and after three miles, you cross Good Lad Creek. Four miles further, you come to a junction on Short Prong Prairie Creek. Here you can continue north to Rockypoint (see page 182).

Turn west across the creek. After three miles you cross Prairie Creek and enter Campbell County on the Heald-Bergreen Road. You follow along Prairie Creek to the southwest for a bit and then west along Flat Creek. The road drops over a small divide and travels past ponderosa pine and cedar trees. Here the road follows **Dry Fork Creek** to the next junction (16 miles from Oshoto). Here you can turn north to Rockypoint. At this junction you can see the Mitchell Creek Breaks to the south and to the west is the "Ridge west of the Store" (local name).

Turn south and then west past the Soda Wells Road. The road then crosses the Little Powder River and you hit W-59 (mile #144) at Weston.

Soda Well near the junction with the Rockpoint Road.

Trip Eighteen

The Little Missouri Road from Moorcroft to Alzada, Montana

Although Devils Tower is more well known (eg. "Close Encounters of the Third Kind"), the Missouri Buttes are also a prominent feature to this area.

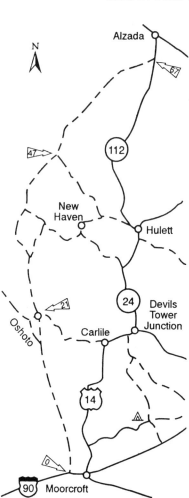

This trip begins by taking W-51 west from Moorcroft and turning north on the D Road (one mile from I-90, exit #153). You go under I-90 and begin following along the west side of the Belle Fourche River. After about four miles, you leave the river and climb up a bit. Here you can see Inyan Kara to the southeast, Keyhole Reservoir to the east, and the Bear Lodge Mountains to the northeast. Further to the northeast you get occasional glimpses of the Missouri Buttes.

The pavement ends about 10 miles from I-90. A few miles further north, you can see Pine Ridge to the east and Devils Tower to the northeast. (There are several OFR's in this area so stay on the main road heading north.) Six miles from the end of the pavement, you cross Cabin Creek to a junction. Here you can turn northwest to Weston (31 miles) and Rocky Point.

Continue north for four miles to a junction on the Little Missouri River at Oshoto. Here you can turn east to US-14 at Carlile, or west to Weston and Rocky Point (see pages 182 and 183).

Continue north along the Little Missouri and after seven miles you cross the river. One and a half miles further is a junction. Here you can turn northeast to New Haven and Hulett (see page 183).

Stay to the north. After crossing the river two more times, you pass by another road going southeast to New Haven and Hulett. Continue north for three more miles and you once again cross the river. (If it's 7:41 pm on the seventh of June, you then head right into the blinding sun for about 100 yards.)

Just after passing by a small lake, you begin traveling past burr oak, ponderosa pine, and cedar trees. With the rolling hills and tree lined river, it makes for a "plain pretty" drive. About eight miles from the last river crossing, you come to a junction at Bush Creek Reservoir. The road to the southeast goes past Strawberry Hill and joins the New Haven Road (12 miles) about seven miles north of Hulett.

The road to Alzada (25 miles) continues northeast and travels through a mine reclamation area (stay on main road). After 16 miles you cross the Little Missouri River again, and four miles further you come to a junction with W-212 at mile #28. Here you can take the road east and hit US-212 at mile #18 (five miles). You can also take W-112 south to Hulett (29 miles). The road north goes to US-212 at Alzada, Montana (three miles).

8000.0

The End.

INDEX